You're Making a Scene

Scenes from Canadian Plays

Playwrights Canada Press
Toronto

You're Making a Scene - Scenes from Canadian Plays
© Copyright 1993 Tony Hamill - editor

Playwrights Canada Press is the publishing imprint of
the Playwrights Union of Canada: 54 Wolseley St., 2nd fl.,
Toronto, Ontario CANADA M5T 1A5
Tel. (416) 703-0201 Fax. (416) 703-0059

Playwrights Canada Press operates with the generous assistance of The
Canada Council - Writing and Publishing Section, and the Ontario Arts Council.

*Front cover : "Evening Lake Temagami " by George Agnew Reid.
Reproduced with the kind permission of the Government of Ontario
Art Collection. Colour photo - Tom Moore Photography, Toronto.
Edited and designed by Tony Hamill.*

Canadian Cataloguing in Publication Data
Main entry under title:
        You're making a scene - scenes from Canadian plays
Includes index.
ISBN 0-88754-489-4
1. Canadian drama (English) - 20th century.*
I. Hamill, Tony

PS8307.Y68 1993   C812.5408   C93-093265-X
PR9196.3.Y68 1993

First edition: April, 1993. Second printing: October 1996.
Printed and bound in Toronto, Canada by Coach House Printing Co.

Table of Contents

Introduction

Playwrights Canada Press, the publishing imprint of the Playwrights Union of Canada, is pleased, gentle reader, to present this book of scenes from Canadian plays. It serves many purposes. Primarily it is a guide for actors and student actors, at all levels: high school, university, or acting studio — a guide in their search for material to hone their acting craft. Much like *The Perfect Piece - Monologues from Canadian Plays*, this collection is also a living catalogue highlighting some of the thrilling writing of Canadian playwrights today.

The book also serves as an exciting entrée for anyone interested in Canadian drama. While it is difficult, not to mention expensive, to see as many plays as one would like, *You're Making a Scene* is an introduction to plays from all over the country. There are many more scenes in the particular plays these pieces came from, and there are many more plays from these same authors, and there are more than 300 professional playwrights in the Playwrights Union of Canada. That's a lot of plays.

It was simply impossible to include scenes from every playwright who submitted to this book, much less include scenes from all those who didn't, but with three dedicated and insightful co-editors — Marion Gilsenan and David Ferry, master artists on and off the stage both, and Ann Jansen, an accomplished dramaturge and editor — we strove to be as inclusive and representative of the many different voices and styles in this country as we possibly could be. Marion, Ann and David explain the pain and pleasure of the selection process eloquently in their Forewords.·

A glance at the index in the back of the book will illustrate that this is not a collection of just the better-known playwrights in Canada, (we could have filled a book with them alone) though a good many of them are represented here. It also presents many new, young writers from all regions of the country, from different theatrical techniques, traditions, and forums — mainstage, backstage, and fringe festival. These are just some of the plays that are being produced and seen across Canada This is surely a fascinating, vibrant country as shown us by our playwrights.

As well as being of different styles, and wide age ranges, the scenes are of different lengths. The long scenes do not have to be tackled by actors in their entirety. Jeeps!, to borrow an apt phrase from Judith Thompson, you can spend days working on the opening beats of a scene, then discovering the *through line* of the scene after determining how it fits in with the whole play. We have provided a set-up 'blurb' to briefly describe the scene and its relationship to the play to make it accessible to the reader, but only a reading of the entire play will provide a complete sense of the scene and the playwright's intentions.

We do not presume to tell you how to act these scenes, but trust that you will discover those truths yourself through your reading and investigation of what is happening in the scene, as any intelligent actor, with the aid of insightful instructors, will naturally do.

For the advanced and the adventurous student, we have included a considerable selection of three-person scenes in many different styles and gender configurations — life doesn't only happen in pairs. At the back of the book is a small section of Fourth-wall Exercises to aid the actor in constructing that fourth side of his reality between him and the audience.

If you are interested in reading any of the plays from which these scenes were taken from, or other plays by these playwrights, or almost any Canadian play written in the last 20 years, simply call the Playwrights Union of Canada (*see copyright page*). While not all plays are published as trade paperback books, there are more than 1000 professionally-produced plays, available as cerlox-bound manuscripts, in the PUC catalogue. Call us and ask for this catalogue or the Playwrights Canada Press catalogue listing more than 80 Canadian plays and collections in trade paperback format. If you would like to buy the published plays represented in this book you can call the PUC office, or the distributors and publishers listed on the Publishers Page at the back of the book, or — better yet — call Theatrebooks in Toronto, or ask your own bookseller to order the books by calling his regional representative from the Literary Press Group (*see Publishers Page*).

We trust you will enjoy reading these selections by our talented playwrights.

Tony Hamill
Managing Editor

About the Editors

Tony Hamill

Tony has been the Managing Editor at Playwrights Canada Press since 1988, and is one of the luckiest actors he knows — when he is not on stage (or looking for work on stage), he is reading, editing and seeing plays through to publication. After graduating from Carleton University clutching a degree in Journalism and Political Science, and spending a few years in the newspaper biz, his true love for the theatre drew him to New York City where he studied for four years at the Herbert Berghof Studio, including one year with Uta Hagen, and worked with the Manhattan Rep. Co. In between auditioning and the occasional show, Tony is seeing plays as a member of the jury for the Chalmers Award, or finishing his short play on Beatrice Lillie's early life in Canada, for The Smile Theatre Company in Toronto.

Marion Gilsenan

As both an actor and a teacher, Marion has been part of Canadian theatre for a couple of decades. On stage, she has run around in a gorilla suit in a piece of craziness by John Palmer and covered herself in mud for George F. Walker. She's been uptight in Montreal with Michel Tremblay, schizophrenic in Vancouver with Margaret Hollingsworth, bald and dying in 1483 with Normand Chaurette. She has done Shaw, Shakespeare, and Stoppard — Tchekov, Tilly and 'Tennessee'. Off-stage, she is based in Southern Ontario, is a member of the Talent Bank of Theatre Ontario, and serves on the Board of Directors of The Actors' Fund of Canada.

About the Editors

Ann Jansen

Ann has been working as a dramaturge at CBC Radio Drama for the past four years. She is now the series script editor for *Studio'93* and previously worked with the program *Vanishing Point.* She is the editor of two anthologies of radio plays, *Airborne: Radio Plays by Women* (Blizzard Publishing), and *Adventures for (Big) Girls* (Blizzard Publishing). Her twelve years of criticism and editing of Canadian drama includes working as editor for Playwrights Canada Press in the early 1980s. She is now completing her Ph. D. at the Graduate Centre for Study of Drama, at the University of Toronto, specializing in Canadian and Australian drama.

David Ferry

David has been active as an actor in Canadian theatre, film, television and radio for more than 20 years. A graduate of the National Theatre School in 1973, he earned his first professional spurs workshopping Canadian plays at Tarragon and other companies. He has worked across the country, the U.S., on and off-Broadway, was nominated for a Genie Award for the film *The Hounds of Notre Dame*, by Ken Mitchell, and won a best actor award for his radio work in James Nichol's *John*. He has recently released *Canajun, eh?* — an audio cassette collection of Canadian dialects intended as a resource tool for actors. David now also teaches, and directs and writes for film and the stage.

Foreword by Marion Gilsenan

After the enormous success of Tony Hamill's *The Perfect Piece,* a collection of monologues from Canadian plays, I guess it was only to be expected that this enterprising staff member of The Playwrights Union of Canada would go on to bigger things. And 'bigger' than 'The Monologue' is 'The Scene'!

I was delighted to be asked to help edit the new book, not realizing the time, how difficult and challenging a task it would prove to be. There are just so many great playwrights in Canada. Each editor having been given a stack of photo-copied scenes to read — and some playwrights had submitted two or three alternatives to the one requested — we staggered off and, over Christmas and New Year's 92/93, we read and read and read.

For me, the most extraordinarily exciting thing about these scenes I was reading was their diversity. There were scenes about love and hate; scenes from the cities and scenes from the farm; from the East, West, the North, and the South; funny scenes, sad scenes, and all-out bizarre scenes; stylistic scenes and naturalistic scenes; WASP-y scenes and Native Canadian scenes; gay-sexy, lesbian-sexy ,and 'straight'-sexy scenes; scenes with mothers and fathers, daughters and sons, sisters and brothers, and total strangers; drunken and sober scenes; old and young scenes; ancient and modern. We, as editors, were privileged to be looking at the vast richness of the Canadian Mosaic. And how brightly it sparkled.

Individual decisions were made and our separate 'Yes' stacks grew. Later, when the editors re-convened, a remarkable near-unanimity emerged. So, now, for you the scene-players, this book contains as many of our 'Yes' scenes as we could squeeze in. Use them, enjoy them, play with them. We are fortunate, indeed, to have them.

Foreword by Ann Jansen

The task of reading scenes from many Canadian plays to contribute to this collection was both pleasant and frustrating. The pleasure came from the variety and intensity of all the scenes, drawn from the ever-swelling ranks of Canadian plays available. The frustration came from my longing to immediately return to favourite plays or search out as yet unread ones, to fill in all the scenes leading up to and stemming from the ones in front of me. Of course, the enjoyment won out, and I was delighted by the fact that there were so many strong plays in recent Canadian theatre from which to choose.

Now that *You're Making a Scene* is published, it's your turn to make choices. This is a book of charged moments, a smorgasbord of scenes inviting you to select the ones you want to enter and explore. But then drama is about choices, about reacting and interacting — and about what happens next.

There are scenes of tensions and truths. Characters must respond to each other *now*. Scenes of revelations — oops! or aha! — mingle with scenes of confrontation and reconciliation. Something happens. The character configurations are equally varied. What these scenes have in common is that none of the characters is indifferent to what is going on or to the person sharing the stage. Death and life and everything between — yours for the shaping.

I was pleased to be asked to participate in selecting this compilation of scenes from recent Canadian plays. When I worked at the Playwrights Union of Canada in the early '80s, editing plays for publication, there was already a striking body of plays by Canadians, about Canadians, and for Canadians and others. It's delightful to have been reminded so concretely of the rich and ongoing development of Canadian theatre in the past ten years, and to have that wealth of drama tapped and made accessible in this collection.

The process of choosing scenes, in conjunction with Tony Hamill, David Ferry, and Marion Gilsenan, was a great deal of fun. It was splendid to talk about Canadian plays with three people who love them so. We each went to bat for scenes we cared for, while looking for variety and balance in characters and situations. And we took time for a few jokes about life in general and that odd variation, life in the theatre in particular. Throughout, there was a surprising unanimity about what makes a scene, despite the differences in taste and perception.

A few interesting patterns emerged. It's not surprising that so many of the scenes focus on people intensely connected, couples and family members included. I was surprised, however, at just how many mother-daughter scenes there were to be considered. There were certainly more marriage proposals than I expected. Overall, the scenes are hard to categorize, though, with perhaps one exception. Most of the scenes we looked at (from submissions) and hence the bulk of this book were 'realistic', to use a troubled term — everyday talk, though 'everyday' is an elastic word, depending on the day and the characters' usual means of expression. Perhaps the paucity of scenes relying on stylized or poetic language or on an externalized theatrical presentation (self-conscious staging) isn't surprising after all. These scenes have to do with people evading or embracing communication, with the possibility or denial of connection between character, rather than with the motion on stage and accompanying props, costumes and sets. Two characters communicate well or poorly for a brief space of time: distilled moments, summations and striking interactions.

I came to this selection of key characters and moments as a dramaturge, and was, as always, fascinated by the interpretations of actors, though we all looked at the scenes from a number of different angles, our shared conclusions had a common basis in concern for language at play and characters in moments that matter.

Audiences are meant to react, just as characters and actors are. Theatre is about those moments that call for decision, actions, change — and a response from the viewer. I hope these scenes make you and others take notice.

These scenes are moments, powerful though they are. To engage with them fully may mean finding out the beginnings and endings, the surrounds of those chosen scenes. Each scene is part of a whole, but they also stand alone, inviting your exploration here and now.

The choices are all yours.

Foreword by David Ferry

When I graduated from Theatre School, I, like most actors starting out, had struggled to choose, learn and rehearse a handful of audition pieces to take on the road with me — (I think the term 'party pieces' is still current) — hours of pacing my room figuring out how to impress with 'To be, or not to be...' and other 'bits'.

French Canadian friends of mine were astonished that we Anglos were expected to audition alone with well-worn soliloquies. They auditioned partners...doing scenes. Surely, they argued, acting (and showcasing to a director what skill one might have) was better demonstrated by doing something that required listening, reacting, pursuing an objective, dealing with conflict than by doing something practiced to a mirror.

I was envious. Those Quebecois — not only did they have Michel Tremblay, they had a great way to audition.

It took a couple of years for me to get the courage but, eventually, I started to bring a partner to my auditions and saying, 'Would you mind if I did a scene instead of a speech?'

Directors were so tired of having tense young actors making heavy eyeball contact during hunchbacked 'Now is the winter of our discontent...' passages that they were relieved to be able to sit back and watch how someone connected with another living and breathing actor.

For the last two years, I have spent some of my time directing and teaching at a theatre school. Whether addressing the technical problems presented to young actors by the film or video camera, or by the thrust, proscenium, or 'in the round' theatre, my various, well-thumbed copies of 'Scenes for the Actor' have been invaluable as workshop tools. They provide an instant survey of the dramatic canon of a country. Alas, the best such compilations all seem to be American. There are a few Canadian scene books out there but, as the energetic Playwrights Canada Press editor, Tony Hamill, points out, they contain less recent material that is mostly 'hit' oriented. This not only limits the actor's and student's choice, it proves tedious for the auditor. Whether in a scene study class or in the audition process, the Canadian 'classic', excellent pieces that they are, start to tire with constant repetition.

When I was preparing to collect regional dialects for my *Canajun, eh?* tape collection, I spent about a month at the Playwrights Union of Canada (PUC) library searching for scenes from scripts that actors could refer to when practicing a dialect for a role. Not only was I knocked out by the number of scripts available, but also by the variety and quality of the writing. So many of these scripts have, unfortunately, been produced once or twice and then left behind in the search for next year's hit. Now, again, I have had a chance to read through a wonderful selection of material in order to find scenes which presented basic challenges to the actor in their 'search of a character'.

What I've looked for in my reading is basic conflict, emotional range, an array of writing styles which provide various language and imaging challenges, humour, and silences. When these various elements are present in a scene, from my experience, the actor is stretched and exercised to the greatest advantage.

A reminder to all who work with this scene book — read the whole play. These plays are available. 'I didn't have time', or 'I couldn't afford it', or 'The library was closed', don't wash. Go the extra mile. These scenes don't exist in isolation from their original context. As every true lover of drama will tell you, every character comes from a unique universe and lives and breathes before coming on the stage and after leaving it. If you have to 'exit, chased by a bear' you'd better be ready to run.

female ∞ female

Flowers

Deborah Porter

Based on the lives of the Dionne quintuplets, five sisters strive to find their own identities and purpose in a world of containment, rules, expectations of who and what they should be and, above all, the mystery of love. Sylvie, the "eldest" and the leader, has entered a convent. Josee, who is now married and pregnant, comes to visit.

> SYLVIE, *in nun's habit, carries a tea tray.*

SYLVIE   Shiny, shiny white and silver. Surfaces streamlined. Starched collars, freshly laundered nightgowns and the scent of lysol on a chilling breeze.

These are the clear, unsullied memories of my childhood and the life that I have regained. I am at home in the Convent, I understand the familiarity of order and the sane regime of schedule. This is sweet. The bell ringing for Lauds is the same cooling breeze that disinfects my existence every morning.

Don't think that I have fled the world. Don't belittle me by placing my decision in the context of your own life. I do that which makes sense to me, what makes me content. Happiness does not exist for such as we. I know that I, we, I am different. I have a different path to tread, and this path leads not to refuge or escape, but to a place of understanding and clarity, a crystalline plateau between heaven and earth.

> SYLVIE *carries the tea over to* JOSEE *who is visibly pregnant.*

JOSEE   Sylvie, Sylvie, do you want to feel my belly?

SYLVIE   What?

JOSEE   I said, do you want to feel my belly?

SYLVIE   No! That is, it's hardly the place. I mean, I would feel too strange...do you think it would be alright?

JOSEE	Of course. No one's here to see...go ahead.

SYLVIE touches JOSEE's belly.

SYLVIE	Oh! *(pulling back)*
JOSEE	What is it?
SYLVIE	It's so hard. Not what I thought it would be.
JOSEE	What were you expecting?
SYLVIE	I don't know. Something softer, I guess.
JOSEE	Like maman.
SYLVIE	No. Not like her.
JOSEE	Well, it certainly isn't soft.
SYLVIE	*(touching her again)* It's so round. So perfect.
JOSEE	Robert says I'm glowing like a Madonna.
SYLVIE	Does he.
JOSEE	But I just feel fat, like a pig. It's a little piglet. Oink!

They laugh.

SYLVIE	That's not a very nice thing to say about your baby.

Pause. SYLVIE pours the tea.

JOSEE	Sylvie, the doctor says I'm going to have twins.
SYLVIE	Twins?
JOSEE	Yes. Twins. I don't know if I can care for one baby let alone two. What if they're carbon copies of each other? I couldn't bear that. I just don't know if I'm capable of being a mother.
SYLVIE	You can always put them in a nursery.
JOSEE	Don't say that.
SYLVIE	I'm just kidding.

JOSEE	You probably think this shouldn't have happened.
SYLVIE	Did I say that?
JOSEE	You probably think we all should have taken vows.
SYLVIE	That's not true.
JOSEE	It's what maman said. That we mustn't take on this part of life. But it's what I wanted. Sylvie, it's what I want. Can you understand that?
SYLVIE	I think you must seek what you need. And you have. You've got it.
JOSEE	That doesn't mean I'm not afraid. God! How am I supposed to raise these children? I don't know anything. All those things that mothers help their daughters with — I haven't been given anything. I have no experience. Can't you help me?
SYLVIE	How am I supposed to help you. I don't know anything either.
JOSEE	But you always have words, good words.
SYLVIE	All I can tell you is, wait and see. God, Josee, I don't know. What am I supposed to say? That everything will be alright? Perfect? Yes. No. Maybe. Wait and see.
JOSEE	That's not much, coming from you.
SYLVIE	Whatever happens, I'm sure you'll deal with it.
JOSEE	You're my sister! Sylvie!
SYLVIE	What!
JOSEE	Just give me your support. Let me know you'll be there. How difficult can that be?

* * *

Available from Playwrights Union of Canada - copyscript

Dreamgirls

Janis Rapoport

Linda is a social worker at a half-way house for battered and homeless women and their children. In this scene she tries to confront Hazel with the responsibilities that she is shirking. As usual, Hazel manages to turn the situation around.

	N.B. HAZEL's children are offstage in the adjoining living-room but visible to HAZEL and LINDA.
HAZEL	*(crossing to kitchen)* Hi, Linda, something wrong with your back?
LINDA	Hazel, there are a few things I would like to talk to you about.
HAZEL	Yeah, okay. *(making sandwiches)*
LINDA	Now, have you looked at the duty sheet for this week?
HAZEL	No I haven't. Why?
LINDA	Why? Do you care, Hazel?
HAZEL	Hold on. One second. *(crossing to living-room)* Adam, will your mother let you eat whole wheat bread? Rye? Bernie, whole wheat? Okay, coming up. *(back to kitchen)* Huh? Sorry.
LINDA	Hazel, on the duty sheet, under 'clean the stove' and 'defrost the refrigerator', we have Hazel's name.
HAZEL	Oh no, I'm woman of the day. I don't have to do anything today.
LINDA	No, no, no. Hazel, there's your name in black and white, *(spelling)* H-a-z-e-l, Hazel,
HAZEL	That should read V-e-r-a. Vera and I switched.

LINDA	Just because Vera's sharing your room, it doesn't mean you have to treat her like your maid.
HAZEL	Hey, c'mon, she was going to do the fridge and stove and I was going to do the dishes.
LINDA	Yeah?
HAZEL	Shit. I forgot them. I had to go to the dentist. I couldn't help it.
LINDA	That brings up another point.
HAZEL	*(to living-room)* Hold it, will you calm down. This is not a hotel. I'm sorry. *(back to kitchen)*
LINDA	Who was supposed to mind your kids while you were at the dentist? Listen, Mary-Margaret tried to shave Adam.
HAZEL	Where?
LINDA	Hazel, that's not funny. Ruth has been on my back about this all day.
HAZEL	*(taking sandwiches to living-room)* Like your haircut, Adam. *(back to kitchen)*
LINDA	Ruth has been on my back about this all day.
HAZEL	She's on my back all the time.
LINDA	Wait a minute, wait a minute. We're not talking about Ruth here.
HAZEL	Hey, I smell something weird.
LINDA	We're talking about you, Hazel. You can talk about Ruth at the meeting.
HAZEL	Oh shit, the garbage.
LINDA	We need your co-operation in this house...
HAZEL	Who forgot to take the garbage out?
LINDA	...if we're going to get anything done.
HAZEL	*(spraying garbage, then to living-room)* Wait a minute, Bernie. It's okay.

LINDA   Hazel, Hazel, Hazel.

HAZEL   Hey, Linda, get up.

LINDA   I give up. I give up.

HAZEL   I'll give you a massage. Listen, *(to living-room)* Bernie.
                     Sit up. Hey, I gave a guy one of these the other night and
                     it really relaxed him. It'll do wonders for you. Relax. Let
                     all the tensions out. You're working too hard. You should
                     get out of this joint. Why don't you go and find yourself a
                     husband, relax? They really take you social workers for a
                     lot, don't they? You've got to relax. There. Feel better?

LINDA   Hazel, you're so hopeless. I don't know what I'd do
                     without you around to cheer me up every day.

HAZEL   Listen, you want me to do the dishes? I'll do the dishes,
                     no big deal. Just let me have a cigarette. Come here, Bern.
                     Then I'll get right on with the dishes, even though I'm
                     woman of the day. I don't mind doing them for you.

LINDA   Hazel, I have something else I need to talk to you about. I
                     found Bernie playing with these this morning. *(showing
                     pills)*

HAZEL   *(to living-room)* Bernie, that is not funny. A little boy
                     should not be playing with pills.

LINDA   That's exactly the point. He's only four years old. He
                     doesn't know the difference between his pills and your
                     pills.

HAZEL   Oh yes, he does. Where did you find those, Bernie?

LINDA   He's just a kid, Hazel.

HAZEL   Where did you find them?

LINDA   Don't make Bernie cry. It's not his fault.

HAZEL   I'm not.

LINDA   I know you have these stashed somewhere, don't you?

HAZEL   I don't.

LINDA	You didn't give me all the pills you had when you got here.
HAZEL	I did. Bernie knows the difference between our pills.
LINDA	Hazel...
HAZEL	*(to living-room)* What colour are yours? That's right, they're blue.
LINDA	Let's go over this again.
HAZEL	C'mon, Bern.
LINDA	These pills can seriously damage a kid's brain. You know, brains. It's what if you had any, you'd give me the pills.
HAZEL	Cute, cute. I gave you all my pills when I got in here. Honest.
LINDA	Okay, I'm going to have to treat you like a child, Hazel. I'm going to have to search this house from the bottom to the top. *(exiting to basement)*
HAZEL	Be my guest. *(crossing to living-room door)* Oh forget her. Dumb social worker. Let's watch some telly. It's the Muppets, Bern. Look there's Animal. Hey, Adam, what do you mean you don't like the Muppets? What kind of kid are you? Adam, look, be quiet. Alright, Adam, if you don't shut up I'm going to put you in a coin-operated clothes dryer and set it at hot.

* * *

Available from Playwrights Union of Canada - copyscript

Karla and Grif

Vivienne Laxdal

Karla is holding Grif, an estranged, intimate friend, hostage, in an attempt to alleviate her own emotional turmoil. After an extremely tense scene where Karla has learned that Grif purposely avoided informing Karla that her lover was a woman, Karla must determine how to resolve the situation.

A mutual friend has just left.

KARLA   So...Crazy Eights? Scrabble? *(beat)* Spin the Bottle?

GRIF   Karla, listen...

KARLA   Hey, I know...How about a rousing game of Truth or Dare?

GRIF   No, Karla...

KARLA   Oh? Come on, Grif. It was your favourite. Truth. Dare. Double Dare. Challenge or repeat?

GRIF   Stop it.

KARLA   Didn't you hear the bitch? We've got a lot of catching up to do. I dare you to tell me the truth.

GRIF   Not like this.

KARLA   TRUTH!

GRIF   *(calculated)* What do you want to know?

KARLA   Kathy!

GRIF   She's my friend.

KARLA   She was your DATE!

GRIF   She's a good friend.

KARLA   She has a key to your door!

GRIF	She's a very good friend.
KARLA	*(picking up a listing)* And what's this? A 'co-operative investment'?
GRIF	Yes.
KARLA	You're moving in together!
GRIF	Yes. We are.

Pause.

KARLA	Repeat.
GRIF	You don't need to do this.
KARLA	Repeat!
GRIF	Get the hell out of my house! NOW!

KARLA *grabs her knife off of the counter and holds it threateningly at* GRIF.

KARLA	REPEAT AFTER ME!
GRIF	*(tentatively)* Karla, think about what you're doing.
KARLA	Shut up! Repeat! Kathy is my lover.
GRIF	Put the knife down, Karla!
KARLA	KATHY IS MY LOVER!

Pause.

GRIF	Yes.
KARLA	SAY IT!
GRIF	Kathy is my lover.
KARLA	Very good. Now. 'Karla did not rape me.'
GRIF	Let's...just talk...we can talk...
KARLA	*(grabbing* GRIF's *top and pulling her close)* Karla did not rape me!

GRIF	Karla did not...
KARLA	Look at me!
GRIF	Karla did not rape me.
KARLA	We loved each other.
GRIF	We loved each other.
KARLA	I hurt Karla's feelings very much.
GRIF	I hurt Karla's feelings very much.
KARLA	I am very sorry.
GRIF	I am VERY...!
KARLA	*(pressing the knife to her throat)* Don't yell.
GRIF	I am very sorry.
KARLA	*(releasing and straightening* GRIF's *top)* There now. Don't you feel better? Now that the truth is out? *(pause)* Well. What do we do now?
GRIF	You leave.
KARLA	Kiss and make up?
GRIF	I'm going to call the police if you don't go now.
KARLA	Oh, don't do that. I'll get a record.

> GRIF *goes for the door.* KARLA *is faster. She holds the knife out.*

KARLA	It's time to kiss and make up. *(moving close to* GRIF *and stroking her face)* You are so beautiful.
GRIF	Please...
KARLA	I don't want to hurt you, Grif. I didn't come to hurt you. I only wanted to see you. To ask you. Three years, I've been wondering, Grif. If I got it wrong. If it was me who started it. If it was the truth. Or if it was the dare. What was it Grif?

Pause.

GRIF   It was both.

KARLA   *(wound up)* You USED me! Used me for the attraction. Like a tattoo. The mark on your skin. And then you just peeled me off, and I shrivelled away. Why'd you do that? Why did you leave me?

GRIF   I was afraid!

KARLA   Of me?

GRIF   I didn't want you to need me.

Pause.

KARLA   Well, I don't NEED you, Grif. I just want you. I want you back.

GRIF   No.

KARLA   I was here first!

GRIF   I'm happy with her!

KARLA   You mean you're loyal? You have an on-going relationship? You've slept with her more than once? How long, Grif? How long have you been happy? How long?

GRIF   Eight months.

KARLA   Eight months. Eight months. I ought to take out an ad. 'Grif Remains a One-Woman Girl for More Than A Week.' This is big news.

GRIF   It's called commitment!

KARLA   So, when did you make the big switch? Eh? After me? Or, maybe you lied. Maybe even before me.

GRIF   No. After.

KARLA   You could have called. You could have told me. 'I'm out of the closet.' Or maybe you're not...are you?

GRIF   It depends.

KARLA   On what?

GRIF	On where we are.
KARLA	So, what's she like?
GRIF	What does it matter?
KARLA	'Cause I wanna know why she gets you and I don't. Eh?
GRIF	It's different...she's more...she's...we're...
KARLA	WHAT?
GRIF	Gentle...
KARLA	*(pausing, taking a deep breath)* Gentle? *(beginning to cry)* I can be gentle...
GRIF	It's taken me a long time, Karla. To figure things out. What I want. What I need. I was afraid. I'm still afraid. That I'm going to blow it. Or I'm making a mistake...
KARLA	*(interrupting)* I can't get rid of you. Of remembering you. I remember what if felt like to be around you. To be with you. And that night. What it felt like to be touched by you. Your smell. Your skin. Warm. So...soft. Melting... Take me back. Please, take me back.
GRIF	No, Karla.
KARLA	You can break up with Kathy. You want a house? I have a house. We could have fun. Endless fun Grif. We know how to have fun!
GRIF	I love Kathy. *(pausing)* I love her.
KARLA	Well. She doesn t love you. She told me. She said to tell you it was over. Get lost. Fuck off. You're ugly.
GRIF	Come on Karla.
KARLA	You're fat. Fat and ugly.
GRIF	Stop it.
KARLA	Fat and ugly and gay. A fat, ugly, gay slut! But, I still love you anyway.

KARLA *passionately kisses* GRIF.

KARLA   *(sexual)* Now what are we going to do? What do you want? Hm?

GRIF   *(gently pushing* KARLA *away)* I want my ring back.

KARLA   No.

GRIF   My ring, Karla. Now.

KARLA   Finders keepers.

GRIF   You promised to give it back at the end of the summer.

KARLA   Where's my wrist band?

GRIF   I threw it out.

KARLA   Then fuck you!

GRIF   I want my ring.

KARLA   It's stuck.

GRIF   Take it off.

KARLA   You try.

                   GRIF *tries but can't loosen it.*

GRIF   Take it off!

KARLA   You'll have to cut it off.

KARLA   Come on...*(offering the knife)* Cut me.

                   GRIF *takes it.*

KARLA   Cut me.

                   GRIF *slowly cuts into* KARLAs *hand.*

KARLA   Deeper.

                   The blood starts to drip off KARLA's *hand onto the floor.* GRIF *drops the knife. She is shaking.*

GRIF   I'm sorry.

KARLA   What?

GRIF   You're bleeding.

KARLA   So?

GRIF   Well, stop it! Put some pressure on it!

KARLA   No.

GRIF   Clench your fist!

KARLA   No

GRIF   Jesus Christ!

> GRIF *runs into the kitchen and grabs the tea*
> *towel, she runs back and hands it to* KARLA.

GRIF   Here, wrap it.

KARLA   That one's dirty. *(throwing it on the floor)*

> GRIF *runs into the bathroom.* KARLA *walks*
> *slowly around the couch dripping her blood*
> *purposely on the floor and over the couch; her*
> *hand in a claw-like position.* GRIF *emerges with*
> *a handful of first aid supplies.*

GRIF   *(shocked)* Karla...?

KARLA   *(deliberate)* I am a wolf. This is my territory. *(slowly*
                 wiping her hand across GRIF's *breast as she stands*
                 motionless) Mine. *(making her handprint on* GRIF's
                 crotch or leg)

KARLA   Mine. *(slowly wiping her hand across* GRIF's *face)* Mine.

> GRIF *collapses, crying.* KARLA *takes off the*
> *ring and places it back on* GRIF's *finger then*
> *picks up her knife.*

KARLA   I'm not going to hurt you.

> KARLA *holds a lock of* GRIF's *hair and studies*
> *it. She holds the knife to it. Pause. She throws*
> *the knife aside, and stands.*

KARLA   I love you. *(moving to the door, putting on her jacket and standing in the doorway)* But, I liked you better...as a dirty blonde.

KARLA *walks out, leaving the door open.*

* * *

Available from Playwrights Union of Canada - copyscript.

Claposis

Audrey Butler

Three lesbians in a love triangle, a mannequin named Betty, and a soon-to-be-demolished vintage clothing store, Claposis, all going backwards in time.

KATE *is in the back of the store when* JUDY *enters.*

JUDY	Jeezus! It's freezing out there!
KATE	You should've just called me.
JUDY	I was in the neighbourhood. I'm meeting Beth at the Wheat. She quit her job today.
KATE	Is she all right?
JUDY	I don't know. Probably not.
KATE	Oh —
JUDY	I know I said I'd come over later.
KATE	Don't you think you better check with her first?
JUDY	Kate —
KATE	Better not keep her waiting —
JUDY	We could see each other later —
KATE	Beth is more important right now —
JUDY	Oh, god. Listen, she quit her job. What do you want me to do?
KATE	Beth has been talking about quitting her job for months.
JUDY	Doesn't mean she's not upset, Kate.
KATE	Oh, I know. Better not keep her waiting.

JUDY	You're not jealous, are you?
KATE	No, no. I've got a lot of things on my mind —
JUDY	Like what? Kate, what's wrong?
KATE	Nothing. You've got Beth's problems to deal with. You don't need to hear about mine —
JUDY	What problems? Kate. Tell me.
KATE	Problems with the store —
JUDY	What kinda problems? Money problems?
KATE	Not really.
JUDY	What then?
KATE	The landlord's selling the building.

Pause.

JUDY	Oh. When did he tell you that?
KATE	He didn't.
JUDY	So how'd you find out?
KATE	The psychic upstairs has heard rumours —
JUDY	You sure she hasn't been staring into her crystal ball too long?
KATE	Judy!
JUDY	Okay, okay. Did she happen to catch on to who was buying it?
KATE	The condo vultures. They're buying up the whole block—
JUDY	Every building on this street has heard that rumour —
KATE	I know, but —
JUDY	But what?
KATE	I have this awful premonition that I'm going to lose *Claposis*.

JUDY	Just don't think about it right now, okay? Nothing you can do till you know for sure, is there?
	Pause.
	Listen, I'll call you later. Beth's waiting...
KATE	Oh, Beth, right.
JUDY	Kate —
KATE	Mustn't keep Beth waiting —
JUDY	Don't start —
KATE	Beth's quit her job —
JUDY	Come on —
KATE	That's more important.
JUDY	You know that's not true.
KATE	How do I know it's not true?
JUDY	Kate! She needs me!
KATE	Well, maybe, just once, I need you too!
JUDY	I can't be two fucking places at once, can I?
KATE	Exactly.
JUDY	So whadda ya want me to do, Kate? Just leave her there in some bar 'cause some batty psychic told you a fucking rumour? She quit her job, Kate because she couldn't take the baiting anymore. You ever heard of gay baiting? How would you like it if some numbskull breeder stuck his face in your face every day. 'Are you a dyke, honey? Boy, I'd really like to see you and your girlfriend making out sometime!'
KATE	I didn't know —
JUDY	Well, now you know.
KATE	Why didn't you tell me?

JUDY	Christ, she could hardly tell me. She made me promise not to tell anyone. Especially you.
KATE	Me? We've never even met.
JUDY	Well, she knows how close you and I are now.
KATE	Oh, I see.
JUDY	Oh, Kate, I wish you could meet her.
KATE	I want to. Someday.
JUDY	You two have a lot in common, y'know. Besides me, I mean.
KATE	How so?
JUDY	You'll find out when you meet. I could invite her over for dinner.
KATE	Oh, sure.
JUDY	It wouldn't be too awkward?
KATE	No.
JUDY	*(putting her coat on)* Good. I'll talk to her about it when I see her.
KATE	Okay.
JUDY	Bye.
KATE	Bye.

JUDY *stomps her foot at the door.* KATE *turns back.*

KATE	What?
JUDY	You didn't hug me yet.

***

Published in "Radical Perversions" by The Women's Press - trade paperback

Still Life With Genius

Jennifer Martin

*The characters are Dora Maar and Fernande Olivier, two of Picasso's mistresses.
The set: A cafe table and two chairs, wine bottle and two wine glasses. A knife.*

	In the original production the first line was spoken in blackout. In a studio situation, the actor playing DORA *can have her back to the audience for the first line and the knife game. When the characters speak simultaneously, it can be as an aside, stepping into their private thoughts.*
DORA	You can't imagine how it feels when you see in a painting that you're on the way out. *(sound of the knife hitting the table)*
FERNANDE	I don't understand your game. *(reaching over and picking up the knife)* How do you know if you've won?
DORA	The game is to throw the knife between my fingers, into the table. I have to be very sure of the throw, because the knife must land upright into the table. I can't be afraid of hurting myself because if I hesitate, the knife will fall and make a racket. And I'll know I've been a coward.
	DORA *pours* FERNANDE *a glass of wine.*
FERNANDE	I would say that you never get used to the ordinariness of other men. You just start getting used to it, and then it hits you in the face, 'This is an ordinary man.' But then, I'm not that extraordinary myself.
DORA	You're extraordinarly beautiful. The first painting that I saw of his was of you and I thought, 'That woman is Picasso's muse.'
FERNANDE	Well, that was before he began splaying faces all over the canvas.
DORA	You made him famous.

FERNANDE	He made himself famous. I'm quite good at inventing, but he invented himself without my help.
DORA	What did you love most about him?
FERNANDE	I loved many things about him, but he never believed it.
DORA	No, he said that Braque was the only woman who truly loved him.
FERNANDE	An odd thing to say.
DORA	Not really. But you loved him and you left him anyway.
FERNANDE	He thought I was too old for him. I was older, but only by four months.

FERNANDE *pours* DORA *a glass of wine.*

DORA	This is how it all began. I was sitting alone in a cafe and I was wearing black lace gloves, with roses embroidered on them. As I took them off, I could see a man watching me, watching my hands.
FERNANDE	So you took your gloves off slowly, like a striptease?
DORA	Exactly, yes. I took them off slowly. And then I reached out for the knife and took it out of the table, also slowly. I was sitting alone at a cafe table, playing with my knife. This man was watching me throw. We didn't know each other, although I knew who he was, and he just watched for a long time. I knew he wanted me to miss, to see what I would do. To tell the truth, I wanted to miss. A gift in a way because he wanted to see my blood. And I wanted to see what he would do. So eventually I did miss. Blood was spurting out of my hand and I picked the knife out of the table and started to play again, between the next two fingers. He didn't want to wipe the blood away at all. He just poured me a glass of red wine and said, 'My name is Pablo Picasso. I like your game.'
DORA & FERNANDE	*(together)* How do you know if you've won?
DORA	You've won if you have the stomach to play again when your hand is covered in blood. Then you can have a glass of wine and go home a hero.
FERNANDE	It's like a bullfight.

DORA	But when you do go home, if you are alone, and sometimes even if you aren't, your hand hurts unbearably. It throbs and the next day you have to play the game again because everyone will be watching. So I didn't want to be alone. I went to Pablo's studio and he painted me right away. It was maybe the first night that I didn't mind the hurt at all.
FERNANDE	Dora With Throbbing Palm?
DORA	No, of course not. He'd sketch me a little, kiss my palm and that would be the end of it.
FERNANDE	Let me try.
DORA	No, you don't have the stomach for it.
FERNANDE	For the knife?
DORA	For the knife. Or the game.
FERNANDE	You're right. It's too dangerous for me.

DORA *pours* FERNANDE *a glass of wine.*

FERNANDE	It began like this. I was generally disillusioned about my life, you know, just separated from my husband and it was August in Paris. You know what it's like, hot and miserable and nobody around. I was walking alone and suddenly the skies opened up, drenching me to the skin. It was an incredible downpour, unexpected and exhilarating, and I dashed into the apartment on Bateau-Lavoir for cover and inside the front door was a man with a kitten in his hand. He handed it over to me and said, 'My name is Picasso. Would you like to see my studio?' He had rescued the kitten from the storm, you see, and he just gave it to me. He dried my hair, and the kitten's fur and it was all very cosy. Officially I didn't move in with him for a few months, but once I walked into that studio I never really left. It was a terrible place, in a way. The studio was filthy, cigarette butts on the floor, the smell of paint. And he was nothing special to look at, nothing especially attractive about him...but he pulled me into his life somehow. Like a magnet. I didn't want to resist.
DORA	Would you, if you could have?

FERNANDE	I don't know, I really don't. First there was a storm that made me feel clean again and then there was Picasso, thrusting a kitten into my arms. It seemed to be the natural course of events. I don't like to think about things too much. But I like to remember that he made a sort of shrine for me in the studio. I like to think that once in my life a man loved me enough to do that.
DORA	A shrine?
FERNANDE	Well, there was a cloth that separated where we slept from where Pablo worked. Beside the bed was a box with a red cloth on it and on top of the box he put a small drawing of me and a vase of flowers. And beside it all was the white blouse I had been wearing the day we met. He pinned a red rose on it.
DORA	He was so different with you.
FERNANDE	Do you think so? I have a map of my life, you know, the map that his paintings have made. There is the drawing he made after the first time we made love.
DORA	Fernande After The Shower?
FERNANDE	Then there was a drawing of me sleeping like a baby while he sits by the side of the bed, wondering and worrying. He had never lived with a woman before me and he liked to visit prostitutes and sleep with the lovers of his friends. So he always said of me, 'Yes, she is beautiful, but she is old.' I don't know why he said that, to make me feel worse or to make himself feel better. He liked me to read to him while he painted, stories. So I would read a tale to him while he was painting, perhaps me, perhaps another mistress. He wasn't that different with us, you see, not that different at all. There were paintings of him with other women, always other women. Then and now. I look at a Picasso and I see only the women. And I'm jealous of them all, in a slight way. You get on with your life, you know, but in a way I still live in that studio on Bateau-Lavoir. I was never really happy again after we left it and I never pass by without a pang.

FERNANDE *pours* DORA *a glass of wine.*

DORA	The first time I saw myself in a painting, it was a shock. There was another woman in that picture, a sad woman. And there was me, looking beautiful and serene, so I felt beautiful and serene. He and the other woman had a child I

knew that, and I knew that there would always be a bond between them. In truth, I wouldn't want it to be any other way. Not for the child, anyway. So I knew that the child would be in the picture, but I wanted something for us, something new. A studio where we could work together. And Pablo said, 'Every time I change wives I should burn the last one. That way, I'd be rid of them. You kill the woman and you wipe out the past she represents.' I never imagined that he would say the same thing about me.

FERNANDE   You imagined that somehow it would be different with you? That the past would be wiped out, that his habits would change?

DORA   It wasn't the same for you. You were the first.

FERNANDE   I don't like to think of myself as dead to Picasso.

DORA *pours* FERNANDE *a glass of wine.*

DORA   Did he want you to look after him?

FERNANDE   No, never that. Even when he was poor, he never asked me to cook or take care of him or the house. I sat and read and drank tea and made love and posed for him. It was a nice life, but it couldn't have lasted. I sometimes thought, 'He doesn't want me to leave because he's afraid, afraid I'll meet someone outside the studio.' He wanted me to live my entire life inside with him. In some ways that suited me very well, because I'm quite lazy, you know. I liked to spend an afternoon dressing just for our stroll to the cafe. I don't think I was ever happier or more content in my life. I don't know if I could have found that contentment and that excitement with anyone else. Or on my own. I like to draw and paint a little, but I was happiest reading to Pablo when he worked.

DORA   I don't know if I could have found that contentment and excitement with anyone else. Or on my own. I painted and I photographed, but somehow my work got less and less important.

FERNANDE *pours* DORA *a glass of wine.*

DORA   It didn't end right away, of course, years later. He didn't want to keep me and he didn't want to let me go. He told everyone, 'I'd rather see her dead than happy with another man'. By that he meant happy, period, because I certainly was not happy with him. Or without him. What could I do but throw myself in the river? At first I had Picasso. Then I had God. Each one created me in his own way. Picasso would paint me and I would follow the woman I was in his paintings like a map. Then I saw myself looking on while he made love to another woman...You can't imagine how it feels to see in a painting that you're on the way out.

FERNANDE   Who was it?

DORA   Well, I didn't find out for a while, because we all look alike, don't you think? So I would walk into a cafe and wonder who it was.

FERNANDE   That's the trouble with cubism. It's so hard to tell what people really look like.

DORA   And I'd think, 'Well, you should be able to tell because the soul will come through'.

FERNANDE   Picasso was never interested in anybody's soul.

DORA   And then he invited me to a gallery opening. I was seeing him less and less and I knew for sure that there was somebody else, that she was dark and that she was his official mistress. So I was surprised when he invited me to this opening. Then I saw his last portrait of me; my face was ravaged, I was screaming and laughing and crying, all at the same time. So I was screaming and laughing and then...because I was following myself in his paintings...

FERNANDE   Like a map.

DORA   I was screaming and crying myself. I ran out of the gallery and walked for a while. And God came to me. A voice that said, 'He can't treat you so badly, he's just a man like any other.'

FERNANDE   I went to a cafe, I walked into a crowded room and everything stopped, dead.

DORA   I don't flatter myself that le tout Paris was talking about me, but I will admit that I felt self-conscious. I would definitely admit that. And Pablo was in the corner with her, with another woman. The dark woman. So I left.

FERNANDE   But you never really leave, you know. He'd rather see you dead than happy with another man.

DORA

And a couple of days later, I threw myself into the river.
A conscientious young man fished me out and took me to
Picasso's studio. He was enraged because I was never to
go there without being invited, but what could he do. The
young man was very nice and I thought, very briefly,
'Why couldn't I fall in love with someone like that?'

FERNANDE

Someone who would fish you out of the river?

DORA

Someone like that. And I was thinking that thought and
then a voice came to me, again.

FERNANDE

Dora Maar, he should thank you for being his mistress.

DORA

I pushed Pablo to the floor and I wanted him on his knees.
I wanted him to say, 'Dora Maar, I have much to thank
you for'. That was all I wanted. But he wouldn't, of
course, not even to humour me.

FERNANDE

His paintings are brilliant, but morally speaking...

DORA

He was reprehensible, yes. He called in his nerve doctor,
said I was getting on his nerves. The doctor took me to a
clinic for three weeks, shock therapy, solutions to make
me sleepy, solutions to make me forget. Solutions to my
problems.

FERNANDE

But the problem was always Picasso.

DORA

First there was Picasso. Then there was a painting of me
with my life falling apart, then there was the river. Then
there was God. I don't paint any more. I don't take pictures
and I don't play my game. I'm afraid that if the knife cut
my skin, there wouldn't be any blood. It's all gone.

DORA pours FERNANDE a glass of wine.

DORA

You left Pablo for that Italian painter.

FERNANDE

He was insane with jealousy. He told everyone,

DORA
& FERNANDE

I'd rather see her dead than happy with another man.

DORA

By that, he meant happy, period.

FERNANDE

Because I certainly wasn't happy with him. I left him,
yes. But he had already left me. He just hadn't said
goodbye.

DORA   What was it like?

FERNANDE   What?

DORA   Leaving him?

FERNANDE   At first I was excited, exhilarated. It was like your game. I
                  thought that jealousy would make Pablo love me again.
                  So I played a dangerous game. I thought I was winning.
                  Then I awoke one afternoon and looked at my new painter
                  for a long time while he was sleeping. Exhausted from
                  making love. I looked at his thin, young body, his white
                  skin, his eyelashes. He was beautiful, naked in the bed
                  beside me. And I thought, 'This is an ordinary man.'

DORA   Why couldn't I fall in love with somebody like that?

FERNANDE   So I went back to Paris, but by then, Pablo had found
                  somebody else. He wouldn't tell me, of course. But I saw
                  it in his paintings. A blonde. I was too old for him and
                  he'd found somebody else. And the map of my life ended
                  there.

DORA   You can't

**DORA
& FERNANDE**   Imagine what it's like to see in a painting what your life
                  will become.

* * *

Available from Playwrights Union of Canada - copyscript

Papers

Allan Stratton

Two lonely and articulate academics struggle with their inability to communicate with each other. In this scene, Myra, one of the academics clashes with a young student about T.S. Eliot and a mutual love - the other professor.

BOBBI	*(awkward beat)* May I come in?
MYRA	I suppose.
BOBBI	*(entering)* This sure is a nice office. I mean I just love those books. They make this place look like one of those family rooms in *Better Homes and Gardens.*
MYRA	*(very dry)* I've always maintained books are a safe way to do a wall if you can't pick art.
BOBBI	So, like, have you actually read the whole wall?
MYRA	Of course.
BOBBI	That's pretty serious reading.
MYRA	They're pretty serious books.
BOBBI	I'd go blind.
MYRA	You might. But now, if you don't mind, I'm in the middle of a major discovery, so let's cut the small talk, shall we? What do you want?
BOBBI	My Eliot essay.
MYRA	Ah yes. *(glancing through her 'Out' tray)* You were gone so long I'd almost forgotten about it. *(giving it to her)*
BOBBI	Thanks.
MYRA	Don't mention it.
BOBBI	*(seeing mark)* F?

MYRA	F.
BOBBI	So what's that supposed to mean?
MYRA	*(sweet, patient smile)* You fail.
BOBBI	That's not fair.
MYRA	Welcome to life.
BOBBI	You didn't give this essay any thought.
MYRA	Neither did you.
BOBBI	I did too. It says exactly what I think.
MYRA	How frightening.
BOBBI	And it's good — it really is — and you gotta pass me. If you don't I'll die. I'll just die.
MYRA	Miss Roy, it's too early in the day for the last act of Camille.
BOBBI	But you don't understand. Without a pass my scholarship is doomed.
MYRA	That's a shame. But hardly relevant.
BOBBI	Yeah. The only thing that's relevant is you wanted to fail me so you failed me.
MYRA	There are good, solid reasons to fail that essay.
BOBBI	Name one.
MYRA	I'll name you a dozen. Give it here. *(taking essay)* Let's start with the title: 'Ingersoll and the Objective Corelative'. Two 'R's in 'correlative'. You should invest in a dictionary.
BOBBI	What for? I mean why look up words you think you spell right?
MYRA	Don't be smart.
BOBBI	I'm just stating an opinion.

MYRA	You don't have opinions. You have notions. Such as: *(reading from the essay with vague distaste)* 'One can't read T.S. Eliot. One has to decode him. He's the original game of Trivial Pursuit. And that's not art. It's pretension.' *(to* BOBBI*)* And that's not an essay. It's a diatribe.
BOBBI	But it's true. He's a tight-ass.
MYRA	He's profound.
BOBBI	He sucks. 'This is the way the world ends / Not with a bang but a whimper.' You call that deep? It's just the same old song and dance about how the world is a sterile dust heap and everything's pointless so why not just die because what does it matter anyway. Like I mean I just want to say, 'Lighten up, eh?
MYRA	'LIGHTEN UP'?
BOBBI	Sure. He acts like it's the world's fault he's a boring old prude with a bad sex life.
MYRA	You offend me. Deeply. To trash the most important force in modern poetry without so much as a footnote!
BOBBI	You mean if I quoted academics you wouldn't mind?
MYRA	Those who have devoted their lives to literature deserve serious attention. Not some teenager who can't even spell.
BOBBI	Well somebody who's devoted his life to literature takes me very seriously.
MYRA	Who?
BOBBI	Mr. Martin.
MYRA	Mister. Aren't we formal.
BOBBI	He likes my instincts.
MYRA	I'm sure he does.
BOBBI	And he liked this essay.
MYRA	He can like what he wants. He doesn't teach this class.
BOBBI	So what? He knows books. And those are his ideas.

MYRA	They are?
BOBBI	Yeah.
MYRA	Then you get zero. For plagiarism.
BOBBI	You're just jealous.
MYRA	What?
BOBBI	Lonely and jealous. Well, I'm sorry. But it's not my fault you love Mr. Martin.
MYRA	*(stunned)* That is the most bizarre collection of sentences I've heard in my life.
BOBBI	It's the truth and you know it.
MYRA	What I know is that you have a gift for fantasy.
BOBBI	Be smug as you like. I was in the hall. I heard all about you and Mr. Martin and your lover.
MYRA	You filthy little sneak.
BOBBI	I didn't mean to. But it got so interesting.
MYRA	My conversations are private.
BOBBI	And that's how I was going to leave them. Until this.
MYRA	What do you mean 'until this'?
BOBBI	Well it's pretty obvious.
MYRA	Are you suggesting I failed you for personal reasons?
BOBBI	You got it.
MYRA	I am a professional. I don't descend to personalities, no matter how distasteful.
BOBBI	Bullshit.
MYRA	Don't bullshit me, young lady.
BOBBI	Then don't bullshit me. You're no more objective than that prissy old T.S. Eliot. You just have a lot of fancy words to cover up how mean and nasty you really are.

MYRA	Get out of my office.
BOBBI	Don't worry. I'm going. I'm going straight to the Dean.
MYRA	I beg your pardon?
BOBBI	If you don't pass this essay, your life will be hell.
MYRA	Are you threatening me?
BOBBI	Standing up for my rights.
MYRA	Three cheers for 'Bimbo Liberation'.
BOBBI	Very funny. Let's see if the Dean laughs when he hears about your ethics.

BOBBI *runs out.*

MYRA	*(calling after her)* 'Ethics Ethics' *(to herself)* That's rich. Blackmailed by a little bitch who talks about ethics.

* * *

Published by Playwrights Canada Press - trade paperback

Moon People

Aviva Ravel

This is a tense encounter between between a troubled teen and the mother who gave her up for adoption at birth. Harriet has tracked down the unwitting Marilyn, her birth mother, and is now forcibly holding her in a park.

MARILYN   May I go now?

HARRIET   Nope.

MARILYN   How long is this going to take?

HARRIET   Depends. Sing me a lullaby.

MARILYN   Sing? Here?

HARRIET   You're not shy, are you? You're an actress.

MARILYN   Very well... "Hush little baby don't say a word,
                Mama's gonna buy you a mockingbird."

HARRIET   *(pulling her to the bench)* Wait wait, first I gotta lie in your lap.

                    HARRIET *lies on bench, puts her head on*
                    MARILYN's *lap.*

HARRIET   Now sing, like you mean it, like I was your baby.

MARILYN   "Hush little baby don't say a word,
                Mama's gonna buy you a mockingbird.
                If that mockingbird don't sing,
                Mama's gonna buy you a diamond ring..."

HARRIET   Stroke my hair, go on, you see it's nice and soft. You sing nice. My Mom sings like that to keep the nightmares away. About weird men with claws burning me all over. When she sings the Moon People come out and the nightmares go away. The Moon People are good. We play games and talk about beautiful birds and tall mountains.

                    HARRIET *sits up.*

HARRIET	You ever think of going to the moon?
MARILYN	No.
HARRIET	You got no imagination.
MARILYN	Please let me go now. I have to get into my costume.

> MARILYN *tries to retrieve her keys which are in* HARRIET's *possession, but* HARRIET *holds on to them.*

HARRIET	You nervous about the play?
MARILYN	A little.
HARRIET	Suppose you forget your lines and the play don't turn out like it's supposed to.
MARILYN	That doesn't happen.
HARRIET	In real life things don't turn out like they're supposed to.
MARILYN	In a play, everything is planned.
HARRIET	If you know what's gonna happen there's no excitement.
MARILYN	The audience doesn't know.
HARRIET	If they read the play, they do.
MARILYN	Then they enjoy the acting.
HARRIET	I'd like to be an actress, but I'm too shy.
MARILYN	I never would've known. *(appealing to her)* I really have to go now. Maybe I can see you later. I'll get you a ticket for the show.
HARRIET	Never mind the show. Real life is more exciting. *(returning keys to her pocket)*
MARILYN	Please, Harriet...
HARRIET	I like when you say my name. It wasn't always Harriet. It used to be Janice, but my Mom changed it.
MARILYN	*(taken aback)* Janice?

HARRIET	Yeah, you know somebody called Janice?
MARILYN	*(uneasy)* No.
HARRIET	I know somethin' about you practically nobody else does.
MARILYN	What's that?
HARRIET	A big secret.
MARILYN	Is that so?
HARRIET	You look scared again. Don't worry, I don't do blackmail.
MARILYN	What's the big secret?
HARRIET	Guess.
MARILYN	I can't.
HARRIET	Sure you can. Everybody's got somethin' to hide.
MARILYN	I don't know what you're talking about.
HARRIET	Liar! Your name used to be Marilyn Evans. On August 13, 1972, you were at the Hillside General Hospital. You gave birth to a baby girl. She weighed eight pounds, nine ounces. That's the secret.
MARILYN	Oh, my God!
HARRIET	I told you real life is more exciting than your play.
MARILYN	Who are you...
HARRIET	Tell me about the baby. Was she pretty? Did it take long to give birth? Did it hurt a lot?
MARILYN	Are you...
HARRIET	Did you nurse her a little, did you hold her? Did you cry when you gave her away?
MARILYN	It can't be...
HARRIET	Don't you recognize me?
MARILYN	You are...

HARRIET	Maybe yes, maybe no. What do you think?
MARILYN	I...I don't know.
HARRIET	I thought after I found you, you'd grab me and hug me. 'My child! My long lost child.' Like in the fairy tales. But all you can say is 'I don't know.' Well, you do know.
MARILYN	*(pause)* How did you find me?
HARRIET	Then it is you! I knew it! I could tell! I'm glad you're so pretty.

MARILYN *stares at her, still shocked.*

HARRIET	You're sorry it's me. You wished if I turned up I'd be polite and brainy, never in trouble, you're disappointed, eh?
MARILYN	No...
HARRIET	You are sorry.
MARILYN	No. I'm just...surprised.
HARRIET	You never expected me to turn up, uh?

HARRIET *sits on the bench.*

MARILYN	No.
HARRIET	So how come I was born? Bet I wasn't planned or anything.
MARILYN	No.
HARRIET	Who was the father? Were you raped or what?
MARILYN	Oh my God...
HARRIET	Well?
MARILYN	*(shaken)* I...I was away at college. I was in love with a student. When I told him I was pregnant, he left me.
HARRIET	That's it?

MARILYN *nods.*

HARRIET	You sure it was him? Maybe you slept around.
MARILYN	I didn't.
HARRIET	I don't neither. So, why didn't you have an abortion?
MARILYN	By the time I told him, it was too late.
HARRIET	You thought he'd stick by you, so you didn't tell.
MARILYN	Yes.
HARRIET	What was he studying?
MARILYN	Medicine.
HARRIET	Oh, a doctor! So he's very smart. What's his name?
MARILYN	What difference does it make?
HARRIET	It won't do you no good to be stubborn. You better tell me.
MARILYN	*(upset, as the memories are revived)* Howard.
HARRIET	Where's he from?
MARILYN	Boston.
HARRIET	You were sorry he left you?
MARILYN	Yes.
HARRIET	You're still sorry?
MARILYN	No.
HARRIET	Sure you are. I could tell by the way you said his name.
MARILYN	Sometimes.
HARRIET	So how come you abandoned me?
MARILYN	You weren't abandoned. The Agency told me you were adopted by a good family.

HARRRIET laughs.

MARILYN	What's so funny?

HARRIET	*(rising from bench)* You wanna know what really happened? The woman that took me died when I was eighteen months. Her husband didn't wanna keep me, so he gave me back. Like you buy somethin' in the store and you change your mind, so you give it back, if you got a receipt.
MARILYN	Oh no!
HARRIET	*(mimicking her)* Oh yes.
MARILYN	So, what happened?
HARRIET	You really wanna know.
MARILYN	Yes.
HARRIET	You don't wanna go to your play now, uh?
MARILYN	No.
HARRIET	I told you real life is more exciting.
MARILYN	So what happened?
HARRIET	I screamed everywhere they put me. Like fourteen places or so. Nobody would keep me. Would you've taken me back if you knew?
MARILYN	I couldn't. I was very young. My mother said she'd throw me out. I had nowhere to go...
HARRIET	She was ashamed for the neighbours and relatives. My Dad does what he thinks is right and he don't care about the neighbours.
MARILYN	I wanted to keep you, but I couldn't.
HARRIET	Wrong. You didn't want to hard enough. Maybe you were busy becomin' an actress. Too busy to look after me.
MARILYN	I thought you were all right, I tried to forget.
HARRIET	Did you?
MARILYN	I tried not to think about it.
HARRIET	So you liked me a little, you felt sorry.

MARILYN	Yes. I cried for months. You were a beautiful baby.
HARRIET	I was?! You got a picture?
MARILYN	No.
HARRIET	Shit! Nobody took pictures when I was a baby. But you got lots'f pictures of your boys. *(picking up scraps of the photos she had torn up prior to this)*
MARILYN	Yes.
HARRIET	Everytime they did somethin' cute you took a picture, uh?
MARILYN	Yes.
HARRIET	It would be nice to have one when I was a baby, so when I got my own kids I could say: "You see, you look just like me." That's why I wanted to find you. Every person knows where his grandparents come from, I don't know nothing. Like if there's asthma in your family. Maybe my great-grandfather invented toasters...Did you ever walk down the street and wonder if any of the kids was yours?

> HARRIET *has dropped the photo scraps on the ground.*

MARILYN	Yes I did.
HARRIET	I used to do that a lot. I'd see a nice woman and ask: "Are you my mother?" Like that kids' book my Mom used to read to me. "The bird asked the horse: 'Are you my mother?' And the horse said: 'No'. The bird asked the cow: 'Are you my mother?' And the cow said: 'No'. The bird asked the bulldozer: 'Are you my mother?' And the bulldozer said: 'No.' At last he came to a big bird and he asked, 'Are you my mother?' And the bird said: 'Yes'." Only that never happened to me.
MARILYN	*(moving toward her)* I'm sorry. I'm so sorry.
HARRIET	That's the easy part.

* * *

Published in "Six Canadian Plays" by Playwrights Canada Press - trade paperback

White Weddings

Marie-Lynn Hammond

The story of three sisters, their mother, and the hidden truth. Del, the middle daughter has been away for four years and returns because her mother is dying of cancer.

N.B. A slash / indicates overlapping of dialogue with the next line.

VERA	*(waking)* Hmm...Del?
DEL	Mama —
VERA	You look real pretty today. Got a date or something?
DEL	No. I Just came from work that's all.
VERA	Bookstore, huh? You happy with your life?
DEL	Happy enough. Why?
VERA	Coulda done more, with your looks.
DEL	Mum, I've told you, I don't care about my looks.
VERA	That's the problem, if you fixed yourself up a bit more — you won the Miss Teen Timmins contest!
DEL	That was your idea.
VERA	Was not.
DEL	I didn't want to enter, but you wouldn't listen.
VERA	Tiara on your head, pink chiffon dress I made you, you looked like a fairy princess. That was a happy time...
DEL	For you, maybe.
VERA	The cabin up at the lake, your dad home more, took us flying one day, sorta flipped the plane sideways, so the lake seemd to be standing up on end — remember?

DEL	But after that summer — mama, how come you never listened to me? Like when I came to you and — when I —
VERA	That day — our wedding anniversary! Just like the day we got married — not a cloud in the sky, the lake as blue as a sapphire
DEL	Mama, we were talking about when I was fifteen / and —
VERA	Gus so proud of me — made my own dress, my going-away outfit too — navy linen, very smart. New York honeymoon, Park Plaza, seventeenth / floor...
DEL	Mama, please listen to me now.
VERA	Wait, in the room next to us...never told you this before — just like in the movies — Ginger Rogers...
DEL	Ma, remember when I tried to tell you / about —
VERA	*(sitting up)* At least she looked like Ginger Rogers...
DEL	You know what I'm talking about, even though you won't admit it. And / the truth is —
VERA	Then the strangest thing —
DEL	Doesn't matter anymore what he did to me —
VERA	*(turning away)* Next day, couldn't find Gus. I looked everywhere / and —
DEL	I mean, it's the past, he's dead now, but what still hurts / is
VERA	I was getting worried! And finally I went to the ballroom, / and there —
DEL	When I tried to tell you and you wouldn't listen —
VERA	There they were, your dad and Ginger —
DEL	You've never listened to me —
VERA	*(singing)* Heaven, I'm in heaven, and my heart beats so that / I can hardly speak...

DEL	And I know you don't want to hear this / either but —
VERA	'When we're out together dancing' — they were dancing, and / they —
DEL	...what hurts the most / now is...
VERA	They didn't notice me at all —
DEL	...is the fact you wouldn't believe me —
VERA	Didn't hear me either, thought I called and called, / and I —
DEL	...and there wasn't anyone else to go to, Alex wasn't / there —
VERA	And I just felt like crying because / it was —
DEL	And I finally couldn't stand it anymore and I tried to tell you and you slapped me across the face —
VERA	It was so beautiful, them dancing, and dancing and...*(starting to cry)*
DEL	You said I lied and I didn't, you took his side, Mama, that's why I left as soon as I could, that's why I stayed away, because you hurt me and it still hurts so you gotta tell me you believe me before it's too late...
VERA	Oh Del...*(moaning)*
DEL	Mama, I'm sorry, but — Ma, what's happening?
VERA	Pain, so much pain!
DEL	Do you want me to get someone?
VERA	No use, they can't help.
DEL	Where's the pain, Mama? Where does it hurt?
VERA	It's my heart, Del, my heart! My poor, old useless goddamn busted heart! *(collapsing into tears)*

* * *

Available from Playwrights Union of Canada - copyscript

Wintersong

Carol Libman

This scene is between Clara Nathanson, a woman still dreaming about her life in the old country, and Anna, her 39 year-old daughter, struggling to create a life for herself and her mother in Canada.

	ANNA *is at the window.* MAMA, *leaning over the checkers board, jumps three men, and looks at* ANNA *in triumph.* ANNA *doesn't notice.*
MAMA	Anna! You're not paying attention.
ANNA	*(startled)* Yes, I am.
MAMA	You can't see the board from there. I have just jumped three of your men, including two kings.
ANNA	Oh.
MAMA	What's wrong, Anna.
ANNA	Nothing.
MAMA	Why are you watching at the window?
ANNA	No reason. *(moving to the table)*
MAMA	This Henry. You're watching for him. You are worried he will not come back.
ANNA	I am not worried. *(moving a checker)*
MAMA	*(knowingly)* Aha!
ANNA	What do you mean 'Aha'?
MAMA	You had an argument.
ANNA	What are you talking about?

MAMA	I remember other occasions. The same thing...He comes, a young man. You get high and mighty, and that's the end. He leaves.
ANNA	You're talking nonsense.
MAMA	It is not nonsense. *(after a moment)* Anna, I do not mean to criticize...but sometimes...in your manner...you are...I don't know how to say it...You can be charming...After all you are my daughter...But, sometimes...sometimes you are not charming. That's not good.
ANNA	Please, Mama, not now.
MAMA	With you it is always not now! You'll never get a husband if you continue to act in this fashion.
ANNA	In the first place, I do not want a husband, and if I did...where would I find one who could measure up to your standards?
MAMA	I know what you need better than you do.
ANNA	Oh, do you!
MAMA	Oh, yes. I have made arrangements I have called even those no-good relatives...I have tried to teach you...
ANNA	Mama, everything you are about to say I have heard a million times, and I am so sick of it!
MAMA	What about this Louis Miller?
ANNA	What about him?
MAMA	You could...work on him —
ANNA	Mama I do not work on people particularly a friend like Louis. And I will thank you to stay out of my affairs.
MAMA	If only you would listen —
ANNA	*(interrupting)* I have been listening to you all my life...My God! You, with your delusions...your demands..What do you know about what is really going on? Nothing!

MAMA	You think I don't know what makes a life? Back home...here...about this there is no difference. The most important thing is to make a good marriage. After this, everything is possible. You find a good man with money, position, then you have a good life.
ANNA	And where am I supposed to find this Messiah? And these arrangements? What do you think we are offering...with these arrangements? The beautiful, talented, rich Nathansons of Warsaw? No...we're D.P.'s with nothing!
MAMA	We are not D.P.'s!
ANNA	We were. And you're going to be one forever if you don't try to forget —
MAMA	I will never forget!
ANNA	Well, I have to! And stop interfering in my life!
MAMA	It is my life, too! Because of you I am stuck in this...in this...this...*(making a gesture of disgust)*
ANNA	This is our home! And I am out there every goddamn day trying to make enough money to feed us and pay the bills.
MAMA	So do as I say. Make a good marriage then you can stop worrying about the house, the job, the money...We will live the way we were meant to live...like civilizd people...in a civilized world.
ANNA	And look what your civilized world did to you and to Papa...and to me? It's finished, that world, Mama...that beautiful, phony world you lived in...and good riddance!
MAMA	Good riddance? You mean good riddance to me, too!
ANNA	I didn't say that.
MAMA	But this is what you mean, isn't it? I am part of that world. I should have been destroyed with it...I am a burden to you...a stone around your neck. This is what you are saying.
ANNA	No, that's not true.
MAMA	Soon I will be dead. Then you'll be free. This is what you are waiting for --

ANNA   Don't put words in my mouth!

MAMA   I don't have to put them. They are alive in you, these
            words...I can see in your face...If only —

ANNA   *(flaring at her)* If only what? If only Halina were alive? If
            only she had been saved instead of me? Would that make
            you happy? You think she could do better...the wonderful
            Halina?

MAMA   Don't you talk of her like that!

ANNA   I'm talking about you! I wish she were here as much as
            you do. I wish she were here so I wouldn't be alone...I
            wish she were here so I wouldn't have to spend my life
            fighting her ghost. She is dead, and I'm alive, and when,
            Mama...when are you going to stop punishing me for
            that?

            *They stand staring at each other. Finally, the
            silence is broken by MAMA.*

MAMA   You are unjust, Anna. This accusation is unjust. I will
            not listen.

ANNA   You have never listened. You have never understood
            anything about my life.

MAMA   Nor you, mine.

            MAMA *turns and walks off.* ANNA, *stunned,
            watches her, then speaks to the absent* MAMA.

ANNA   Mama, listen to me. It has no meaning for me this life
            you keep talking about. It's gone...finished. We can't go
            back. We're nothing special, nothing important. We're no
            different from anybody else.We're like...when you read in
            the paper...the people on a bus when the terrorist's bomb
            goes off. We can't change what happened...and we don't
            know who to fight...so we tear at each other...and we only
            make it worse...

                            * * *

Available from Playwrights Union of Canada - copyscript

Gone to Glory

Suzanne Finlay

In this, the penultimate scene of the play, Lulu has just experienced the death of her beloved older sister, Winnie. After a fitful sleep, Lulu wakes to the groggy and incredulous realization that Winnie, or her spirit, is back, large as life and twice as lively.

LULU	Winnie, is it really you?
WINNIE	It's not the ghost of Jacob Marley.
LULU	Great Balls of Fire! I'll never again doubt the power of prayer! Give me a hug!
WINNIE	*(dodging)* No! Touch me and I'm gone.
LULU	Gone where?
WINNIE	Heaven, if I can get in.
LULU	Winnie, you can't go to Heaven. You're not dead.
WINNIE	Yes I am, but they won't let me in.
LULU	Are you serious?
WINNIE	I'm dead serious. Momma's having the dickens of a time up there with St. Peter —
LULU	Momma? You saw Momma?
WINNIE	She's with the Welcome Wagon up there.
LULU	Didn't give you much of a welcome. Now listen, if they're going to be uppity about it, you stay right here with me.
WINNIE	Honestly, some of your notions are harder to swallow than castor oil. You don't want to saddle yourself with a spook.

LULU	I do! You'd be somebody to talk to. And you wouldn't cost a thing to feed.
WINNIE	Lulu, I've no intention of being one of The Unquiet Dead. I'm going to get into Heaven if it's the last thing I do! Will you help me?
LULU	Of course I will. *(marching to* WINNIE's *coffin)*
WINNIE	What are you doing?
LULU	I'm coming with you. We'll lick this thing together.
WINNIE	You can't come with me. You're not dead.
LULU	I'm working on it. *(starting to climb into the coffin)* Aah! That's you in there!
WINNIE	Don't be such a ninny. This is me. That in there is just my husk.
LULU	*(climbing in)* In that case, you won't mind sharing.
WINNIE	I certainly do mind. It'd be the same old story as that bed of ours. Night after night, you kicked me out on the floor.
LULU	You fell out.
WINNIE	So would you with two knobby knees jabbing the small of your back. You've got another thing coming if you suppose I'm spending Eternity like that.
LULU	Lord, take me too —
WINNIE	Now stop quibbling.
LULU	— I've got nothing to live for —
WINNIE	If God saw fit to raise me from the dead, He must have had a larger purpose in mind than rousing you to a fit of self-pity. Do you think it's my quilt?
LULU	Winnie, God wouldn't raise you from the dead to fetch a quilt.
WINNIE	No, no, to tell you about my quilt. I know you grudged my putting so much by in the Glory Fund, but —

LULU	I don't, I don't! The minute I saw that cobbled-up coffin, I knew why you put by all that money. What would people think of me if I buried you in that? The Glory Fund's to buy us some dignity! Lilies, bronze casket, marble headstone! Would you like a marching band? I'm gonna blow every nickel in that bank account —
WINNIE	There is no bank account.
LULU	But — the Glory Fund!? Every time Mister Pete took you to town —
WINNIE	I gave you my share of the housekeeping and I stitched the rest into my quilt.
LULU	Where is your quilt?
WINNIE	Bakpak mailed it this very day.
LULU	Mailed it? Where?
WINNIE	Now listen to me, Lulu. You've been as crabby as a sore tooth about going to live with Sally —
LULU	Winnie, you didn't send that money to Sally? Tell me you didn't do that!
WINNIE	You bet I did.
LULU	All these years...these years and years of lies...
WINNIE	They were loving lies, Lulu. I put a letter with the quilt explaining that I saved that money for you. That money will be waiting when you get there.
LULU	I'm not going to Sally's.
WINNIE	But you told me that —
LULU	You're not the only liar in the family. Last time we saw Sally, she made me feel about as welcome as a case of warts. Sally shamed me, Winnie, Sally stole my pride.
WINNIE	Lulu, compared to the love of a child, pride's a piffling thing.

LULU	Pride's not piffling when it's all you've got. It's bad enough when I go to town and strangers look at me like I'm a crazy old trash picker. I'll not give Sally a chance to treat me that way again.
WINNIE	Lulu, if you deny your own child, you'll weep for the rest of your life. Give her a second chance!
LULU	Who gave us a second chance, Winnie?
WINNIE	God gave me one — and now I understand what He meant me to do with it! Lulu, Poppa wasn't your Poppa. Michael was.
LULU	Michael? That boy in the Great War? I don't believe it, a boy that age and Momma?!
WINNIE	Sometimes, Lulu, you can be duller than a poor sermon. Me, I'm your Momma.
LULU	You? Ooooh...Winnie ...
WINNIE	You're all of Michael that was ever mine. I wanted you so bad.
LULU	If you wanted me, why did you never own up to me?
WINNIE	Michael and I wanted to marry before they shipped him over. But Poppa wouldn't hear of it. He said that I was too young and that to marry in haste wasn't seemly. You coming along was a lot less seemly, but by that time Michael was dead and buried in the poppy fields...
LULU	I'm your child...?
WINNIE	I didn't want you branded a bastard. So Momma and I went away for me to have you, and when we came home we pretended you were hers. It was wrong. Just as wrong as you denying Sally. Oh Lulu, I beg you to believe me, nothing hurts worse than denying your own child.
LULU	Yes it does: your child denying you.
WINNIE	You're my child. Don't deny me.
LULU	Of what?
WINNIE	The Glory Fund was my way of asking your forgiveness.

LULU   Forgive you for what?

WINNIE   For having you.

LULU   Having me?! You must have got that notion from Poppa.
You couldn't have thought of something that dumb
yourself. Now listen, you old Whited Sepulchre —

WINNIE   Lulu! Watch your language! He'll send me to Hell! *(hiding
from God's wrath)*

LULU   I'm not talking to God. It's Poppa I want a word with.
Poppa, your notions are as out of date as button hooks.
Even if you think Winnie committed a sin by having me,
just remember that she's suffered enough afflictions sitting
on that toilet to atone for a host of sins. Forgive Winnie
for having me? I'd never forgive her if she hadn't. Being
alive is the best thing that ever happened to me! Now
Lord, it's Your turn. What Winnie did wasn't a sin. It was
just a little mistake of love. We all make those all the
time, so if it's true that You guide every step of our lives,
You've already got a bushel of mistakes to answer for.
Don't make another one by telling my Momma she can't
come into Heaven! If You do, I'll cancel my subscription.
Amen.

* * *

Available from Playwrights Union of Canada - copyscript

To Grandmother's House We Go

Joanna McClelland Glass

Three generations of family gather at Grandie's house in Connecticut. The tradition of the young taking care of the old is reversed as the marital and emotional anarchy of the youngest generation lays its angst and requests at the old woman's feet.

> MUFFY, *the granddaughter, is sitting quietly sniffling.* GRANDIE *picks up a catalogue.*

GRANDIE What *is* it, Muffy? You know I can't stand quiet weeping. It's the very worst kind. What *is* it?

> MUFFY *gazes off, making no reply.*

Ah, me. *(digging into the catalogue, impatiently)*

MUFFY *(after a moment, to herself)* I suppose, in a nutshell, it's a sex problem. I wanted it to be wild and spontaneous. When I wanted it, I really wanted it. But I didn't want it often enough. *(beat)* It's the damn regularity of the thing that kills you.

GRANDIE *(to herself)* Oh, my God, look at this! What a tacky catalogue. You can buy an ashtray shaped like a woman's breast. Wait — yes, of course, they come by the pair. Imagine. Somewhere out there people buy these things. Imagine running into people like that. Having to talk to them. Imagine being on a mailing list with people like that!

MUFFY I knew we were in trouble on our wedding night. I fell onto the bed and kicked my slippers into the air. The slippers flew, helter-skelter, and I giggled. Julian frowned. He went around and gathered up the slippers and set them together, neatly, by the bed. I thought, 'Oh, my God.' *(brief pause)* Grandie, may I talk to you?

GRANDIE Of course, darling, of course.

MUFFY Would you mind putting the catalogues aside? It's quite serious.

GRANDIE   It's the *quiet* weeping, Muff. It calls for private rooms.
            East wings, or attics. I don't mind screams, you know.
            There's something very complete about a scream. But
            moans are a different matter. True anguish is best kept
            upstairs.

MUFFY   Gran, I'm really on the ropes in Baltimore right now. I
            have a small apartment — it's so dreary it actually has a
            flashing neon sign across the street. My friends, and
            Julian's, too, are holding us at arm's length until the dust
            settles and the lawyers get done with the haggling. It's so
            demeaning, Grandie. We've had to put a value on
            everything in the house — the furniture, the wastebaskets,
            the hose in the garden, the ladder in the garage. 'How
            much will you need', they ask, 'for your new life?' How
            can I put a figure on it when I don't even believe in the
            possibility of a new life? *(pause)* I need to come home.
            Gran. May I come and live with you for awhile?

GRANDIE   Oh, my. Oh, dear. I don't know. You see, four years ago,
            when your Grandfather died, Clemmie and I and your
            mother decided a small bungalow would be quite adequate.
            This place is hell to clean, hell to heat, and the repairs
            never stop. It seemed a proper time to condense. We
            actually had fun, searching real estate ads in the Classified.
            And Muffy, I was surprised. There was no tinge of sadness
            at giving up all the old things. We thought we'd have a
            rather elegant auction, and Clem would serve her lemon
            tea. Well, then my brother Jared arrived. After his
            retirement he'd tried it with both children — disastrous
            results in each case. They live in the south, you know,
            and he wrote me such a touching letter. He said, 'The
            South is one long season, monotonous, like sleep or
            death. And always there is, hanging over me, the sick
            smell of slavery.' New Orleans is no place for an old
            Yankee, certainly no place for someone who taught art
            history for forty years in the Ivy League. *(an annoyed
            pause)* I've lost my train.

MUFFY   Gran, I'm in very serious mental trouble, and I need to
            come home.

GRANDIE   Ah. It's just, you see, when Jared came we couldn't
            condense. We're forced to live so carefully, Muffy, always
            observing each other's boundaries. And we all try to keep
            our weeping upstairs. Except Clementine, of course.
            Clem has wept profusely since the day she came to tend
            your mother. She was nineteen and I was twenty-three.
            How old are you now?

your mother. She was nineteen and I was twenty-three.
How old are you now?

MUFFY   Twenty-eight.

GRANDIE   You see, we're all so old now, darling. Heavens, I'll be
eighty-two next year! I'm afraid another presence, now,
would be jarring.

MUFFY   Please, Grandie, I so desperately need six months here, in
your routine. A little healing period. Please consider it.

GRANDIE   Let me think on it, Muff. Let me think on it.

* * *

Published by Samuel French, Inc. - playscript

For amateur performance rights please contact Samuel French, Inc., at 45 West
45th St., New York, N.Y. 10010; or 7623 Sunset Blvd., Hollywood CA 90046;
or 80 Richmond Street East, Toronto, Ontario, Canada M5C 1P1

For professional performance rights please contact the Lucy Kroll Agency, 390
West End Avenue, New York, N.Y. 10024 U.S.A.

male ∞ male

Stephen Markel *(left)* and David Bolt *(right)* in the Toronto
Free Theatre production of *Zastrozzi*.
Photo by Robert Ragsdale.

Fire

Paul Ledoux & David Young

Inspired by the lives of cousins, Jerry Lee Lewis and Jimmy Lee Swaggart, who take different forks on the same road of pride, lust, and greed.

	Razor Back, Arkansas. Inside Pinetop's Tippin' Inn, a sax begins to howl. CALE *and* HERCHEL, *with a bottle, run on.*
HERCHEL	I swear, Jimmy Jones don't get a better lock on his back door I'm gonna turn into a souse.
CALE	Daddy gonna catch you and whip your ass first.
HERCHEL	You keep on playing that boogie woogie in church, he gonna die of a heart attack long before he gets my britches down. *(laughing)*
CALE	Gonna take a lot more than Daddy to cut my water off, Herchel. Hell he can't even get this cat house shut down Sunday nights.
HERCHEL	I truly don't understand why you torment him so.
CALE	I torment him? He's been tormentin' me since the day I was born.
HERCHEL	Bullshit. He always treated both of us decent and you know it.
CALE	That's okay for you to say. He gave you the room with the window.
HERCHEL	*(laughing and handing* CALE *the bottle)* Growing up in a closet would make anybody want to bust out...
CALE & HERCHEL	...and boogie!
	They laugh again. CALE *drinks and hands* HERCHEL *the bottle.*

HERCHEL	You know what? You sounded great this morning.
CALE	I was great! Did you see the look on Daddy's face? Think he dropped a load in his drawers.
HERCHEL	Now Cale, you got no call to go talkin' about our Daddy like that. He's a religious man.

CALE *falls silent.*

HERCHEL	Besides, if Daddy's right, Jesus don't much like your taste in music.
CALE	Herchel, I learned to play piano in two weeks. It is a God-given gift.
HERCHEL	Well, I sure as hell don't know about that.
CALE	Well, I sure as hell do. Come on. *(heading toward the front door of the Pinetops)*
HERCHEL	Where you think you're goin'?
CALE	I am gonna slide on into Pinetops and sit in with that band.
HERCHEL	*(laughing) You* ain't gonna go playing in no whorehouse.
CALE	There ain't but two pianos in this town Herchel. One is in my daddy's church, the other is in this whorehouse.
HERCHEL	Well, if you're goin' in there, I'm goin' with you.
CALE	You confuse me, big brother! One minute you all hot on the salvation of my soul, the next you jumping up and down to go into a whorehouse in Darkie Town! *(laughing)* You hot boy. You want it.
HERCHEL	Which 'it' you mean?
CALE	Herchel, you're dying for a little taste of what a woman's got to give.
HERCHEL	You ain't no different.
CALE	Oh yeah, well all you doin' is lookin' and thinkin', I already done the deed.
HERCHEL	Bullshit... Who?

CALE	You got saliva in the corner of your mouth Herchel, you droolin'.
HERCHEL	Come on Cale. What you talkin' about?
CALE	Blonde gal heard the killer playing off the back of a pickup over at the fairgrounds. Next thing I knew it's dark, I'm on top of her and she is writhin' around like a shot snake.
HERCHEL	Where?
CALE	Wet grass out behind Bailey's Mill. Didn't even take my shoes off.
HERCHEL	I don't believe you for a second.
CALE	Where you think I got these stains? *(pointing to grass stains on his knees)* These pants ain't never goin' near a wash. They is holy relics now.
HERCHEL	You're lyin'.
CALE	Yeah, I'm lyin'.

They look at each other for a moment.

HERCHEL	So, what was it like?
CALE	Like pounding a piano harder than it can be done. *(whispering)* You never heard such grunting and groaning in your life. *(pause)* Know what else she done?
HERCHEL	What?
CALE	She sucked my ear.
HERCHEL	Sucked your ear?
CALE	Her tongue was hanging out to here...She was panting like an animal.
HERCHEL	Holy shit, ain't you scared of what's gonna happen?
CALE	God probably gonna make my dick fall off, is all. *(pause)* What are you looking at me like that for? Man you are as serious as cancer.

HERCHEL	In less than two weeks you are supposed to be coming with me to Beaumont Bible College, and there you stand braggin' on your lustful sins.
CALE	And there you stand drinking sour mash you stole out of the back of Jimmy Jones' store.
HERCHEL	There is a hell of a lot of difference 'tween stealing a bottle of whiskey and swimmin' in slime.
CALE	Jesus, sometimes you sound so much like Daddy I could puke.
HERCHEL	You gonna stick with Jesus?
CALE	Yeah I'm gonna stick with Jesus. He's my Saviour and my Lord just like he's always been, just like he's always gonna be.
HERCHEL	I want you to make a pact that you won't let Jesus down.
CALE	I'll make any kind of pact you want and double it.

HERCHEL *hauls out a knife.*

CALE	What in hell is that for?
HERCHEL	If we're gonna do it, we're gonna do it for real.
CALE	Any way you want.

HERCHEL *pricks* CALE's *thumb, then cuts his own.*

HERCHEL	Now you taste mine and I taste yours.
CALE	Why Herchel, I swear, this is ungodly.
HERCHEL	Not if it gets you on that bus to Beaumont it ain't.
HERCHEL	*(tasting* CALE'S *blood and vice versa)* Aunt Haddy told me that when you do this with somebody you are responsible for each other's soul forever and anytime you get asked your most awful secret by the one who shares the blood you got to tell 'em or you both go straight to hell.
CALE	Okay, that's the way you want it, let's mix it up.

> HERCHEL *and* CALE *put their thumbs together.*

HERCHEL   Now say after me: I promise...

CALE   I promise...

HERCHEL   To be with Jesus in the hereafter.

CALE   To be with Jesus in the hereafter — and with my brother in the here and now.

HERCHEL   And with my brother in the here and now.

CALE   And remember this night for as long as I live.

HERCHEL   And remember this night for as long as I live. So help me God.

CALE   So help me God.

> *Pause. Music begins to play in Pinetops.*

HERCHEL   So?

CALE   So?

HERCHEL   So, what's your most awful secret?

CALE   I already told ya. Look at them grass stains and think about it brother. I got a lustful demon inside of me, got to wrassle him, in this here whorehouse. *(heading for Pinetops)*

HERCHEL   Cale!

CALE   Come on brother, you want to stay a virgin the rest of your life? *(HERCHEL hesitates for a moment, then laughs and follows CALE into the whorehouse. The music swells, then fades)*

* * *

Published by Blizzard Publishing - trade paperback.

The Postman Rings Once

Sky Gilbert

The backroom of a bookstore in Red Deer, Alberta. Rupert and Andrew are young bookstore clerks who were caught by the manager kissing in the store the evening before.

> RUPERT *is working as* ANDREW*enters.*
> RUPERT *hears him, but only glances at him over his shoulder.* ANDREW *sees* RUPERT, *has no response, hangs up his coat and starts to creep out the door. He stops.*

RUPERT   Andrew?

ANDREW   *(after a pause)* Yeah. *(pause)*

RUPERT   Hi.

ANDREW   *(nervously)* Hi.

RUPERT   How are you feeling?

ANDREW   Okay *(pause)* I guess. *(pause)* I guess we're in trouble, eh?

RUPERT   Ya. *(pause)* Well...I'm in trouble more than you.

ANDREW   Oh. *(pause)*

RUPERT   I'm the senior staff member.

ANDREW   I see. *(pause)* Well I should get in trouble too. I mean I got drunk too.

RUPERT   That's nice of you Andrew.

ANDREW   Well. *(pause)* You got me drunk though.

> *They look nervously at each other.*

RUPERT   Yeah. *(pause)* I'm sorry Andrew.

ANDREW   There's nothing to be sorry for. It's my responsibility as
                  much as yours. Is Miss Slotnick mad?

RUPERT   Yea, well. She got pretty mad at me.

ANDREW   I'll tell her it's my fault too —

RUPERT   You don't have to do that Andrew —

ANDREW   Oh I think — I should it's true

RUPERT   That's really nice of you Andrew *(going to touch
                  ANDREW, who pulls away and stares)* What 's wrong.

ANDREW   Nothing. *(starting to leave)*

RUPERT   Andrew.

ANDREW   *(annoyed)* What?

RUPERT   There's something I wanted to say to you about last night...

ANDREW   *(angry)* Look. I don't want to talk about it —

RUPERT   But Andrew —

ANDREW   I tell you I don't want to —

RUPERT   But when Maud came in! we were —

ANDREW   *(furious)* We weren't doing anything. Look. I'll tell you
                  what happened last night. We got really drunk which was
                  really bad. And then, when we were trying to open the
                  mystery boxes, we fell on the floor and when Maud came
                  in that's what she saw. And that's all that happened. And
                  if you say anything else you're wrong. And if you tell
                  Maud anything else that you...made up, then I'll never
                  speak to you again.

RUPERT   Andrew, how can you —

ANDREW   I have to go and apologize to Miss Slotnick.

RUPERT   But...

ANDREW   Nothing happened. *(pause)* All that happened was that I
                  got drunk and acted...like I used to act. But that won't
                  happen ever again.

RUPERT   Why are you lying? *(pause)* Is it because you thought what we did was bad? I didn't think it was bad when we were doing it.

ANDREW   Rupert. *(pause)* We didn't *(with difficulty, he is pulled to* RUPERT *but resists)* do anything. Alright?

RUPERT   But...*(going to touch him)*

ANDREW   Don't. *(pause)* Please. *(staring at him)* Sorry Rupert.

ANDREW *hurries out.*

RUPERT   You liar. *(pause)* You're a liar. *(kicking box)* Shit. Stupid books. Stupid mystery books. Stupid *Postman Always Rings Twice*. Stupid Lana Turner. I hate you Lana Turner.

* * *

Available from Playwrights Union of Canada - copyscript

Homeward Bound

Elliott Hayes

The family is all home to hear the father, Glen, say he is in favour of euthanasia - his own, with his wife's support. Norris, the daughter is pregnant, not by her husband, Kevin, but most likely by her brother Nick's significant other - Guy, in his pre-AA days. Kevin and Norris have two sons and feels Norris should now have an abortion. Not your average evening with the folks.

KEVIN *has come in from the garage.*

NICK	Is it cold out there?
KEVIN	Getting there.
NICK	Would you like a drink to warm you up?
KEVIN	Any beer left?
NICK	How about a brandy?
KEVIN	*(shrugging)* If that's all there is.
NICK	'Fraid so. Till the champagne, anyway. *(going for drink)* So, you and Norris had a big fight.
KEVIN	She told you?
NICK	You know Norris.
KEVIN	She said she wouldn't. She made me swear I wouldn't bring it up. She said that she couldn't possibly face any of you, but I guess she just said that 'cause she wanted to bring it up first and prejudice you all against me...if that's possible under the circumstances...which I suppose it is, given the way your dad feels about me and the way Norris can make even the twins feel guilty.
NICK	Yeah. Well. You know Norris.
KEVIN	Did she tell you what it was about?
NICK	Not in so many words.

KEVIN	God damn it. She did, didn't she? Of course she did, because she said she wouldn't.
NICK	Well...
KEVIN	Damn her!
NICK	Calm down. *(handing him drink)* She didn't say anything...
KEVIN	I should have known she would tell all of you before I could get out. She wants me to feel worse than I already do.
NICK	Get out?
KEVIN	I think it's best, don't you? I mean, wouldn't you want to?
NICK	Hey, Kevin, look, honestly...
KEVIN	What do you think?
NICK	Me?
KEVIN	What do you think?
NICK	Well, it's really none of my business...
KEVIN	You're family. I mean, I know you're her family first, but you're still my family still.
NICK	I know, but...I don't want to interfere.
KEVIN	No. Really. I want your opinion.
NICK	You do?
KEVIN	Sure I do.
NICK	I'm flattered.
KEVIN	Well?
NICK	Well...
KEVIN	Look, don't be embarrassed. I'm not embarrassed. And hell, I'm the one who should be embarrassed, if anybody is going to be...And Norris should be too, of course, except she's not because she's, well, she's Norris.

NICK	I'm not embarrassed Kevin, it's just that...well...I don't know what to say.
KEVIN	I want your opinion.
NICK	Oh shit Kevin, I'm sorry...
KEVIN	Thanks.
NICK	Thanks?
KEVIN	I'm...sort of glad you're on my side.
NICK	Me? I'm not on anyone's side.
KEVIN	You know, even beside the point, I really do hate babies.
NICK	Babies?
KEVIN	Don't you?
NICK	Well, I...
KEVIN	I can't stand 'em. I mean, these guys are great and all, even though they've got this thing now about locking me out of the toilet. But that's O.K. I mean, the pediatrician says it's O.K. because it's part of their hangup with me being their dad and their wanting to be, like, artists. But they're not babies anymore. Thank God. I mean, I hate babies, don't you?
NICK	Well...yeah.
KEVIN	*(smiling)* Yeah?
NICK	Well, let's face it. I mean, I know you've had some and all...but they're boring, aren't they?
KEVIN	Boring?
NICK	Oh, I know they can't help it. Don't get me wrong. They don't know any better. But, I mean, it's the ripple effect that bothers me. And I don't mean grown men goo-gooing over a cradle — that's brief and relatively painless. It's like gas, actually.
KEVIN	You mean colic?
NICK	Pardon?

KEVIN	Colic.
NICK	Well, um, no, Kevin. What I really mean, is the way babies deaden whole circles of people. You know? Otherwise articulate adults suddenly say they're going to the potty, and insist that you applaud their offspring if it makes number 2.
KEVIN	*(proud)* The boys call it a B.M. now.
NICK	No kidding?
KEVIN	The pediatrician thinks it's best.
NICK	Well, he'd know, wouldn't he?
KEVIN	*(explaining)* Bowel Movement.
NICK	Right. I know.
KEVIN	Sorry, did I cut you off just then?
NICK	No, I was...I was...Never mind.
KEVIN	*(worried)* The twins are O.K. though, aren't they?
NICK	Oh. Yeah. *(beat)* They're great, Kevin.
KEVIN	It's just babies.
NICK	Right. Just babies.
KEVIN	They're so ugly.
NICK	Boring and ugly.
KEVIN	Right. Well, ugly.

* * *

Published by Playwrights Canada Press - trade paperback

Democracy

John Murrell

The American Civil War rages as two old friends, Walt Whitman and Ralph Waldo Emerson, meet and discuss their differing views on human nature and the nature of war. Whitman has taken two young soldiers under his wing; Jimmy has been blinded and wears a bandage over his eyes. He is also very near death but is either unaware of or denies this fact, though Walt knows Jimmy is dying

	Note: This scene can be done as a two-hander without PETE. *Intense but increasingly oblique sunlight.* PETE *is lying along a low sturdy branch of one of the larger shade trees.* WALT *is sitting in the shade on the ground, with his back against the same tree.* JIMMY *is stretched out on the ground, with his head in* WALT's *lap.* JIMMY *has been dictating a letter to his family.* WALT *has a small tablet of paper on the dry ground near him, and the pocket of his shirt, which he has put back on now, holds several sharp pencils. He writes fast, trying to record* JIMMY's *exact words.*
JIMMY	...and so we never got to the mouth of the Roanoke. Which is something I had hoped to describe to you. I know that the Hampsons' boy, Billy Hampson, saw the mouth of the Norfolk once, and all of us envied him for that. I dreamed about seeing the mouth of the Roanoke for two whole weeks before the Secesh caught up to us and shot us to pieces in our own camp. I feel like I could describe it to you, just from my dreams—Roanoke—the yellow brown water, widening out into meandering fingers, smaller and smaller fingers, then into threads that bubble over and hide under the spongy earth, sneaking their fastest way to the sea—not so much like a river at all — but like a big dirty brown piece of lace which the wind is moving —
WALT	Whoa up a bit, Jimmy. My hand's giving out on me.
JIMMY	I do feel like I've been there, Walt. It doesn't seem like just a dream to me. It seems less and less like a dream. But I never was really there, was I? Mouth of the Roanoke?

WALT

No. You boys didn't quite make it. *(still writing)* Hold on now. I'm just catching up. You might make your visit down there yet, one of these days. Mouth of the Roanoke?

JIMMY

Think so? Oh, I don't much mind whether I do or not anymore. I've seen as much as I'm ever going to see of it. I liked my dream though. Probably it wouldn't have really been much different, much better.

WALT

True. It might not have been nearly so nice.

> JIMMY *laughs, then coughs once.* WALT *finishes writing.* PETE *has started to hum the tune, "My Days Are Swiftly Gliding By", softly to himself.*

JIMMY

My friends, Walt and Pete, and me have come out to our place by a pond in the country. Nobody else knows about it though, so don't you tell a soul. Especially don't tell old lady Fanshawe. You know how she is. You know that, within a couple of hours, everybody in the whole county would hear about it and, within a week, the whole Union, I'm sure. And before you know it we'll have all sorts of odd folks swarming around our pond like a cloud of midges, all buzzing about how they were sent down here by some old woman named Fanshawe from Wisconsin.

> WALT *laughs.* JIMMY *pauses.* PETE *continues humming.*

JIMMY

(after a while) Out here by our pond, I feel a thousand miles away from Mount Pleasant Hospital, Mama, and from all the rest of that noise and smell in the capital — which I think I described pretty well to you, or my friend Walt did, in my last letter — which I do hope you have received by now. Today I feel a thousand miles away from practically everything and everybody. Except not from all of you, of course. I sent John my portrait as a soldier, wrapped up in the last letter. It was took before we left New York State, and I looked mighty handsome, at least to myself I did, when that picture was taken — I think you can tell that by my expression in it — and I hope that John will keep it on the little table between our beds. You tell Lucas and Mark I am scrounging up some other stuff to send to them, other rare treasures like my soldier portrait, so not to sulk. We know that Lucas will sulk, given half a reason. But he oughtn't to. He's too old for that now, and he is the handsomest of all your sons, when he's not

wearing that halo of gloom. The handsomest except for
one, I mean. And that one is away from home right now.

JIMMY smiles, pauses. WALT writes fast.

PETE   *(singing softly)* 'My days are swiftly gliding by...and I, a
lonesome stranger —'

JIMMY   'Pilgrim stranger,' Pete.

PETE   *(singing)* '....and I a pilgrim stranger...'

                  Pause.

JIMMY   *(prompting, singing.* 'Would not detain them as they
fly—'

JIMMY & PETE *(singing)* '...those hours of toil and danger...'

JIMMY   *(singing then fading)* '... For O we stand on Jordan's
strand ... our friends are ...'

                  Pause; then JIMMY starts dictating again.

And tell Dad not to — not to —

                  *Silence. WALT turns from the tablet, looks
                  down into JIMMY's face. Silence.*

— And tell Dad not to think about the war, or about Mr.
Lincoln's mistakes, or about me so much. This war is a
thing which happened to our country, and we ought to
have thought and thought hard before we let it happen, but
thinking and worry won't serve much purpose now. We
have to find our way back, by our feelings, to our
brotherhood. No, Mama, my friend Walt did not put that
last thought in here, truly — but I did learn something
about this from him, and I thank him for it. Tell Dad that
Walt says that Mr. Lincoln in his carriage looks just like
an upright old ingot of iron, streaked with rust, which
they keep hauling about — but it is an ingot which will
not weaken in a thousand more years. And tell Dad I
believe my lungs are on the mend now, they give me less
pain these past few days. I think I might be ready to head
for home any day now. And Walt fetches me nourishing
things to eat whenever he can — a jelly of tomatoes and
rhubarb, and a beef conserve almost as rich and clean as
yours, Mama — and he feeds me good words too — the
Bible and the exploits of the old Greeks and

Mr. Shakespeare and he brings me out into the sunshine — which is damper here than it is at home — but it is still the best healer, I think...*(stopping)*

> WALT *is scribbling as fast as he can.* PETE *is dozing as scene ends.*

* * *

Published by Blizzard Publishing - trade paperback

i

Liars

Dennis Foon

Jace is a teenager dealing with his father's alcholism.

JACE	*(entering)* Yoo hoo! Anybody home? Hi, Dad, how're ya doing?
FATHER	What'd you do with the screwdriver?
JACE	Nothing. I didn't see it.
FATHER	I'm fixing the TV set. Get me the screwdriver.
JACE	Did you look in the toolbox?
FATHER	Of course I looked in the toolbox, you idiot. Where else would I look?
JACE	I don't know.
FATHER	Where'd you put it!
JACE	What're you asking me for, I didn't touch it.
FATHER	Get me that screwdriver and my beer right now.
JACE	All right, all right.

JACE *comes back with the screwdriver and beer.*

FATHER	All right, that's my kid. Good work, boy. Two things a guy's gotta have. His beer and his screwdriver. Aren't you gonna have one?
JACE	Not right now.
FATHER	What's with you Jace, won't have a beer with the old man?
JACE	Okay.

FATHER	Atta boy. You're a good kid, Jace. You're all right. You found my screwdriver. Where was it?
JACE	In the toolbox.
FATHER	Right where I said it would be. Didn't I? Didn't I tell you where it was?
JACE	It was right where you said it would be...Dad —
FATHER	Yeah, what is it, I'm all ears.
JACE	I wanna ask a favour.
FATHER	Sure, what is it, son — you name it.
JACE	Can I have the car Saturday night?
FATHER	The car? You wanna borrow the car? Saturday night?
JACE	Yeah.
FATHER	No problem. It's all yours. I'm not using it. What's mine is yours, kid.
JACE	Thanks.
FATHER	You're very welcome. So what are you up to?
JACE	Gotta date.
FATHER	Oh yeah? Somebody new?
JACE	Yeah. Her name's Leonore. But I call her Lenny.
FATHER	Hey, I think you like this girl.
JACE	She's all right.
FATHER	Just like your old man, playing it cool — but I bet you got goosebumps lining your stomach.

They both laugh.

JACE	You think she knows I'm nervous?
FATHER	Doesn't matter, she'll like you for who you are.
JACE	I guess so.

FATHER   No sweat.

JACE   All right.

> *They slap hands. Pause.* FATHER *takes a long drink of his beer, then crushes the can.*

FATHER   Where's my screwdriver?

JACE   ...you just had it.

FATHER   What are you talking about? Where is it?

JACE   It was right there.

FATHER   Don't give me that crap, where'd you put it?

JACE   Here it is.

FATHER   You're always losing my stuff. That time you took my razor.

JACE   I was five years old.

FATHER   You steal my stuff.

JACE   I didn't know what I was doing.

FATHER   You never know what you're doing. How're you gonna make it in this world if you don't take responsibility!

JACE   I was five.

FATHER   How'm I supposed to shave without my razor? Get your own damn razor!

JACE   I've got my own razor, I don't need yours.

FATHER   You just stay outta my stuff. I don't do enough for you, you take everything? I looked all over the house for that damn razor. I was late for the interview. I didn't get the job. How'm I supposed to get work if everybody's always losing my stuff?

JACE   I didn't do anything.

FATHER   Get outta here. Get out! *(shoving* JACE*)*

JACE	You stupid drunk.
FATHER	What'd you call me?
JACE	You heard me.
FATHER	Come here and say it to me.

Pause. JACE *exits.*

Where's my screwdriver!

* * *

Published by Playwrights Canada Press - trade paperback

The Motor Trade

Norm Foster

Phil's wife has just left him, he is being audited by Revenue Canada, and his partner, Dan, wants to sell the car business. And it's not even noon yet. A raw, griity comedy set in the world of used cars.

PHIL	*(looking out the window)* Goddamn snow. Will ya look at the goddamn snow. I've never seen so much goddamn snow. Goddamn. We're not gonna move much iron today, Danny. No sir.
DAN	*(not really listening)* You don't think so?
PHIL	Well, take a look. You ever seen so much goddamn snow?
DAN	*(still reading)* No, I guess not.
PHIL	I guess not. Who's gonna go shopping for a car in weather lke this? And on a Saturday too. Our best day. Damn. Even our salesman isn't showing up for god's sake. Huh? It's ten-thirty and where is he? *(combing his hair)*
DAN	Hmm?
PHIL	Ted. Where the hell is he?
DAN	I don't know.
PHIL	He hasn't even called.
DAN	Probably stuck in the snow.
PHIL	Well, of course he is. Look at the goddamn stuff. I've never seen so much goddamn snow. I was in Greenland once - they didn't have this much snow. *(the phone on his desk buzzes and he answers it)* Doral Valley Motors, Phil Moss...Yessir. Uh-huh. You were in when? — Tuesday. And what were you looking at sir?...The Pontiac. Well, which Pontiac, sir. We've got about a dozen Pontiacs on the lot right now....The Pontiac LTD. That's a Ford, sir....Yes. Honest mistake. Yessir, I remember you now.

Yes.You're not sure what the price was? Well, lemme check it for you. *(rustling paper)* Uh..Twelve five, sir... Beg your pardon? Eleven three? Hang on. *(rustling paper again)* Yessir, you're absolutely right. It is eleven three. My mistake. I was looking at an old price list. Right....Warranty? Yessir, that comes with the famous Doral Valley curb and gutter warranty. *(covering the mouthpiece and speaking to* DAN*)* Once it's over the curb, you got her. Yessir...Uh-huh. We sure do. What kind of car would you like to trade in? A 79 Chevette. How much could we give you for it? Well, that depends, sir. How much gas is in it?...Look, I'll tell you what. Why don't you come in on Monday and we'll talk? Right. We'll look forward to seeing you sir. You bet. Bye-bye. *(hanging up and going to table to pour coffee)* Well, at least the day isn't gonna be a total loss. Guy's a walkover. He was in Tuesday looking at the 86 LTD. I quoted him eleven three and he didn't even try to talk me down to a skinnier deal. We should just throw him out front there and use him for a welcome mat. You want another coffee?

DAN   No thanks.

PHIL   Donut?

DAN   No.

PHIL   God, ever since I quit smoking, all I do is put stuff in my mouth. Gum, coffee, donuts. I can't get enough.

DAN   It's oral gratification.

PHIL   Hmm?

DAN   That's what it's called. Oral gratification.

PHIL   Hey, I'm just talkin' about coffee and donuts here.

DAN   That's what oral gratification is. You're satisfying your need for a cigarette by putting other things in your mouth.

PHIL   *(beat)* Yeah, but just coffee and donuts.

DAN   Right.

PHIL   Right. *(taking a bite)* You think I'm putting on weight?

DAN   Who you?

PHIL	Yeah, what do you think? Can you notice it?
DAN	Naw.
PHIL	You sure?
DAN	A pound or two maybe. It's nothin'.
PHIL	That's what happens when you quit smoking. You gain weight.
DAN	Greenland? When were you in Greenland?
PHIL	What?
DAN	You said you were in Greenland.
PHIL	Yeah. Last year when I was in England. You remember.
DAN	That was England. That wasn't Greenland.
PHIL	Yeah, but on the way back the plane had engine trouble and we had to put down in Greenland. You remember that.
DAN	Greenland?
PHIL	Yeah.
DAN	I thought it was Iceland.
PHIL	No, it was Greenland.
DAN	I thought you told me Iceland.
PHIL	No.
DAN	I mean, Greenland's — not even on the way, is it?
PHIL	Well, that's where we put down.
DAN	No, your flight path would probably take you over Iceland then Newfoundland. I don't think you'd go anywhere near Greenland. You sure it wasn't Iceland?
PHIL	Hey, what am I, Charles-fucking-Lindbergh? It was cold and there was snow. Figure it out.
DAN	It was probably Iceland. I mean, Greenland's up there too, but you'd probably miss Greenland altogether.

PHIL   Fine. All I'm saying, Mr. Rand McNally, is that there
                was a lot of snow wherever the hell it was, all right?

DAN   *(still reading)* Probably Iceland.

                        The phone buzzes and DAN answers it.

DAN   Doral Valley Motors. Yeah, Ted, yeah, I know. Is it
                what? *(putting hand over phone, to PHIL)* Guy lives half
                a mile away and he wants to know if it's snowing here
                too...

PHIL   *(leaning into the phone)* No, Ted, it's sunny and warm
                here, ya goddamned idiot!

DAN   Yeah, that was Phil. Uh-huh.... Right. Okay, whenever
                you can make it. We'll see ya. *(to PHIL)* He's shovelling
                his car out. Says he'll be here as soon as he can. *(going
                back to the paper)*

PHIL   Yeah, he's probably usin' the snow as an excuse to jump
                the ole skin train one more time.

DAN   Who, Ted?

PHIL   Sure. Him and the wife? All aboard!

DAN   No, I don't think so. Ted's pretty conscientious. If he
                could get here, he'd get here.

PHIL   Hey, I'm conscientious too. Doesn't mean I don't like to
                get the ol' lugnuts tightened once in a while. God, I'll tell
                you what I'd like right now. A cigarette. This is the
                toughest time you know. With that coffee in the
                morning? I mean, a cigarette with your morning coffee is
                better than sex.

DAN   You must be having sex with the wrong women.

PHIL   Hey, at least I'm having it. Of course, you know what
                they say. Sex is like Bridge. If you don't have a good
                partner you'd better have a good hand. Well, you'd know
                all about that, wouldn't you? Huh?

DAN   Thank you.

PHIL   Well, I mean, good God. I don't know how you do it,
                Dan. I honest to Christ don't.

DAN	Don't get started, Phil, alright?
PHIL	Well, really now, when was the last time you had your ticket punched?
DAN	What?
PHIL	Come on, when?
DAN	What's it to you?
PHIL	I'm worried about you. A man goes that long without it, it's not normal. I mean, if it was me, I'd be looking twice at well-groomed sheepdogs by now.
DAN	Well, it's not you, so try and get over it.
PHIL	Well, I feel like I have to look out for you, you know?
DAN	Well, you don't.
PHIL	I could set you up if you want.
DAN	No thanks.
PHIL	You don't want me to?
DAN	No.
PHIL	Okay, but I know a divorced mother of three, drives a loaded Le Mans, gets a fat alimony check every month, and she's into motorised implements, you know what I'm sayin'?
DAN	Gee, and she hasn't been snapped up yet?
PHIL	Fine. Make fun. But, don't say I didn't offer. *(beat)* Hey, I'm using a new aftershave today. Did you notice?
DAN	No .
PHIL	Yeah. Ten years an Old Spice man, today Mr. Ice-Blue Aqua Velva. *(moving to* DAN*)* Take a whiff and see what you think. *(leaning over)*
DAN	Not bad.
PHIL	So, tell me the truth. If you're a woman, and you smell this on me, you're gonna want to jump me, right?

DAN   Oh, come on.

PHIL   No, tell me.

DAN   Get out.

PHIL   Come on.

DAN   I can't answer that.

PHIL   Why not?

DAN   Because I've always wanted to jump you.

PHIL   You see what I've been telling you? You've been without it for too long. *(looking out the window)* God, look at it out there.

DAN   *(looking out)* Yeah, she's comin' down all right. *(back to paper)* Oh, God.

PHIL   What?

DAN   Here's Jerry's obituary.

PHIL   Oh, no.

DAN   *(reading)* Henderson, Jerry. Suddenly at his home on Thursday, January 23rd.

PHIL   The poor bastard. He was one of the best, you know that?

DAN   Beloved husband of Mary. Dear father of Lois and Nestor.

PHIL   Nestor. Why in the hell would Jerry do that? Name his kid Nestor. I never understood that.

DAN   It was Jerry's grandfather's name.

PHIL   Oh, but still. Good God. Nestor.

DAN   Resting at the Goodfellow Funeral Home. Funeral — Sunday, eleven a.m. at the Franklin Cemetery.

PHIL   Good luck in this weather. They're gonna have to drag him up there behind a goddamned Skidoo.

DAN   That's all it says.

PHIL	Hmm?
DAN	That's all it says. They mention his family and his funeral.
PHIL	So, what do you want them to say?
DAN	Well, they should say something about him.
PHIL	Like what?
DAN	I don't know. Something that tells you what kind of a guy he was.
PHIL	He was the kind of guy who liked spanking his secretary with a ping pong paddle? You want that in there?
DAN	No, I mean...well, they should say what he did with his life.
PHIL	And what was that?
DAN	Well, he...Jesus, he ran that dealership for thirty-five years. Doesn't that count for anything?
PHIL	He was a car salesman, Dan. He wasn't Ghandi.
DAN	That shouldn't matter.
PHIL	Do you remember that?
DAN	What?
PHIL	The time we walked into his office unannounced and he had what's her name across his knee? What was her name? Terry! Terry something. And he's got her across his knee, her skirt hiked up, ping pong paddle up in the air and in we walk. *(laughing)* And there they are, both of them just staring at us in shock. And Jerry says...he says a spider went up her skirt and he was killing it for her. And you say...you say, 'Damn, I guess that means we're in for some rain now.' *(laughing uncontrollably)*
DAN	*(laughing a little too)* Come on, Phil. The man's dead. Have a little respect. *(laughing more)* Spider.
PHIL	Oh, God. Stupid bastard. Don't get me wrong though. I loved Jerry. You know that. I loved the guy. I wonder whatever happened to her. Great legs.

DAN　　　　　　　It's still not right though.

PHIL　　　　　　　What isn't?

DAN　　　　　　　A man dies and the only thing they remember about him
　　　　　　　　　　is that he had a wife and two kids.

PHIL　　　　　　　Come on, Dan. What else did he do? He ran a car dealership.

DAN　　　　　　　Well, that's what we do. Isn't that anything?

PHIL　　　　　　　Sure it is but...

DAN　　　　　　　Well, why can't' they put it down? Owned Henderson
　　　　　　　　　　Motors. Just put that down.

PHIL　　　　　　　Danny, it's the family that writes these things up. I mean,
　　　　　　　　　　if they thought his being in the motor trade was
　　　　　　　　　　important, they would've put it down.

DAN　　　　　　　What, you think they didn't think it was important?

PHIL　　　　　　　Well, how the hell should I know? I'll tell you this much
　　　　　　　　　　though. If I'm his son, and I got a name like Nestor, I'm
　　　　　　　　　　not even goin' to the funeral.

DAN　　　　　　　*(almost to himself, looking at paper)* They shoulda said
　　　　　　　　　　more than this.

PHIL　　　　　　　Yeah, well, nothing you can do about it now. Man, I sure
　　　　　　　　　　owe him a lot. We both do, huh? I mean, he hired me
　　　　　　　　　　when I was goin' nowhere. I had no experience, nothin'.
　　　　　　　　　　Jerry taught me everything about this business. And then
　　　　　　　　　　he loans us the money to buy this place. Guy was a saint.
　　　　　　　　　　(looking out the window) Will you look at that? We've
　　　　　　　　　　got a blizzard outside and the strip joint across the street is
　　　　　　　　　　packed. Look at it. The lot's full. Now, explain that to
　　　　　　　　　　me. I mean, in the first place, who wants to watch
　　　　　　　　　　strippers at ten-thirty in the morning, huh? I mean, the
　　　　　　　　　　woman's up there shakin' it with the Tim Horton's coffee
　　　　　　　　　　in her hand. She's half awake for chrissake. What the
　　　　　　　　　　hell's the attraction? Jesus. *(taking a sip of his coffee)*
　　　　　　　　　　You wanna go over?

* * *

*Published in "The Motor Trade & The Affections of May" by Playwrights
Canada Press - trade paperback*

Zastrozzi

George F. Walker

A revenge melodrama inspired by Shelley's novel in which Zastrozzi, the master criminal of Europe, engages in a relentless quest of retribution against his double, the saintly, deluded Verezzi. Victor is Verezzi's tutor and protector.

In an inn.

ZASTROZZI   Where's my wine? I called for that wine an hour ago. I warn you it is in your best interest to keep me drunk. I am at my mellowest when drunk. Innkeeper!

VICTOR   *(off)* Coming, sir. *(entering)*

ZASTROZZI   Who are you?

VICTOR   I own this inn.

ZASTROZZI   No. I've met the owner.

VICTOR   The former owner. I won it from him in a card game last night.

ZASTROZZI   Congratulations. Put the wine down and get out.

         VICTOR *puts the wine down.*

VICTOR   You are the Great Zastrozzi, aren't you?

ZASTROZZI   I am a lodger in your inn.

VICTOR   Are you ashamed of being Zastrozzi?

ZASTROZZI   If you were to die in the near future would many people attend your funeral?

VICTOR   No.

ZASTROZZI   Then save yourself the embarrassment. Get out.

VICTOR	I heard that Zastrozzi once passed through Paris like the plague. Leaving the aristocracy nearly bankrupt, their daughters all defiled and diseased, the police in chaos and the museums ransacked. And all because, it is said, he took a dislike to the popular French taste in art.
ZASTROZZI	A slight exaggeration. He took a dislike to a certain aristocratic artist who happened to have a very willing daughter and one painting in one museum.
VICTOR	And did Zastrozzi kill the artist, rape his daughter and destroy the painting?
ZASTROZZI	The daughter was not touched. She had syphilis. Probably given to her by the father. The painting was not worth destroying. It was just removed from the illustrious company it had no right to be with. *(taking a drink)*
VICTOR	But the artist was killed.
ZASTROZZI	Yes. Certainly.
VICTOR	Why?
ZASTROZZI	To prove that even artists must answer to somebody.
VICTOR	And what has Zastrozzi come to this obscure place to prove?
ZASTROZZI	Zastrozzi is starting some new endeavour. He is going to murder only innkeepers for a year.
VICTOR	I am not afraid of you.
ZASTROZZI	Then you are stupid. *(pausing)* And you are not an innkeeper.
VICTOR	They say that all Europe has no more cause to fear Zastrozzi. They say that for three years he has been single-minded in a search for revenge on one man and that all the rest of Europe has been untouched.
ZASTROZZI	They think and say only what Zastrozzi wants them to think and say.
VICTOR	They also say that any man can cross him, that any woman can use him. Because the master criminal, the Great Zastrozzi, is in a trance.

ZASTROZZI	Ah. But then there are trances...*(drawing his sword and doing four or five amazing things with it)* ...and there are trances. *(putting the sword to* VICTOR's *throat)* Now, who are you?
VICTOR	*(stepping back, afraid)* Your revenge upon Verezzi will be empty.
ZASTROZZI	Who is he to you?
VICTOR	I'm his tutor.
ZASTROZZI	His what?
VICTOR	Tutor. I teach him things.
ZASTROZZI	Is that so. And what, for example, do you teach him?
VICTOR	How to evade the man who wants to destroy him.
ZASTROZZI	You are the one responsible for stretching my search to three years.
VICTOR	Yes.
ZASTROZZI	Interesting. You don't look capable of having done it. You look ordinary.
VICTOR	I am.
ZASTROZZI	No. In your case the look might actually be deceiving. But we'll soon find out. Where is your weapon?
VICTOR	I don't have one.
ZASTROZZI	Then why the innkeeper disguise? You must be here to intervene for your student.
VICTOR	Intervention doesn't have to be violent.
ZASTROZZI	I'm afraid it does. Haven't you been reading the latest books? The world is in desperate need of action. The most decisive action is always violent.

> ZASTROZZI *repeats this last sentence in German.*

VICTOR	Interesting. But all I'm saying is that I didn't think killing you would necessarily have to be the only way to stop you. I thought I could try common sense with you.
ZASTROZZI	You were wrong. Try something else.
VICTOR	Verezzi is insane.
ZASTROZZI	I don't care.
VICTOR	But revenge on an insane man can't mean anything.
ZASTROZZI	Wrong. I don't share the belief that the insane have left this world. They're still here. They're just hiding.
VICTOR	But he thinks he is a visionary.
ZASTROZZI	Well perhaps he is. I don't care about that either. That's between him and his God. This matter is between him and me.

Pause.

VICTOR	I know why you seek revenge on Verezzi.
ZASTROZZI	No one knows!
VICTOR	I know of the crime that he and his father committed upon your mother.
ZASTROZZI	Ah yes. The crime. What version have you heard?
VICTOR	The real one.
ZASTROZZI	Is that so?
VICTOR	I was a friend of his father. I was away studying. Hadn't seen him for years. Had never even met his son. A letter arrived. He said he was dying. And asked if I would protect his son who would probably be in danger.
ZASTROZZI	And the letter described what they had done?
VICTOR	Yes.
ZASTROZZI	What did you think?
VICTOR	It was horrible, of course.

ZASTROZZI	Describe exactly what you mean by horrible.
VICTOR	Bloody. Vicious. Unforgivable.
ZASTROZZI	Wrong. Not even close. Horrible is when things proceed unnaturally. When people remain unanswerable for their actions.
VICTOR	But the letter also told me why they had done it. This woman's son had killed my friend's daughter. Verezzi's sister.
ZASTROZZI	No. It wasn't me.
VICTOR	Then who was it?
ZASTROZZI	Never mind. But even if I had killed her then the quarrel would be with me. Not my mother. That is usually the way with revenge, isn't it?
VICTOR	You couldn't be found.
ZASTROZZI	I was away. Studying. I was called back to examine my mother's corpse. And the father's letter actually did describe what they had done to?
VICTOR	Yes.
ZASTROZZI	Imagine that. How could he bring himself to tell anyone. I thought he was a Christian.
VICTOR	It was a confession, I think.
ZASTROZZI	Are you a priest?
VICTOR	I was at the time.
ZASTROZZI	And you left The Church just to protect Verezzi?
VICTOR	It doesn't matter why I left The Church.
ZASTROZZI	Yes. That's correct. Only two things should matter to you. That Verezzi killed my mother in a horrible manner. And that I, her son, have a legitimate claim to vengeance.
VICTOR	But he has no memory of the crime. He never has had. He must have blocked it out almost immediately.

ZASTROZZI	I don't care. I seek revenge. Revenge is a simple matter. You shouldn't have turned it into such an issue by hiding him from me for all this time.
VICTOR	But there's something else, isn't there?
ZASTROZZI	I beg your pardon.
VICTOR	I think there's another reason altogether why you want to destroy Verezzi.
ZASTROZZI	What is your name?
VICTOR	Victor.
ZASTROZZI	No. You are not an ordinary man, Victor. But you would be wise to become one within the next few hours.
VICTOR	When are you coming to take him?
ZASTROZZI	I am here now. Are you going to run off again?
VICTOR	No. He won't leave. He's waiting for his followers. Listen. I don't care much for violence. But to get to him you will have to go around me.
ZASTROZZI	I have already done that. And I didn't even know you existed.
VICTOR	How?
ZASTROZZI	Never mind. Concern yourself with this. If what I plan doesn't work I will not be going around you or anyone or anything else. I will be coming directly at him. And if you are in the way you will be killed. Now go away. I'm tired. Tired of the chase. The explanation of the chase. Of everything. Of you specifically at this moment.

> ZASTROZZI *turns around.* VICTOR *pulls a knife from inside his shirt, raises it to* ZASTROZZI's *back, and holds it there. Finally* VICTOR *lowers it.*

ZASTROZZI	Go away.

* * *

Published by Playwrights Canada Press - trade paperback

Heroes

Ken Mitchell

Heroes is not only a satire based on Superman and the Lone Ranger but is a study of heroes in crisis. Each of these characters has grown beyond the two-dimensional comic book and suffers the impact of the "real" world. This world has aged them, changed them, and now forgotten them. The heroes also discover that their former side-kicks — Lois Lane and Tonto — have become the new heroes.

	SUPERMAN *is seated on a chair, his arms folded high on his chest, almost formally. He stretches, yawns, and suddenly leaps dramatically to his feet, flinging his cape back. He goes to the magazine table, flips perfunctorily through a couple of magazines, and throws them down again. He wanders about the room, makes a tentative leap in the air. Suddenly, for nothing better to do, he makes a great display of flexing his right bicep. While in this posture, he hears someone at the entrance, right, and leaps with a magnificent bound to his seat, resuming his heroic pose.*
	The LONE RANGER *enters, looking tense and high-strung. He glances around quickly, looking for an ambush. There is only* SUPERMAN.
RANGER	*(touching his hat)* Afternoon.
	SUPERMAN *ignores him, except for one flick of the eyes.* RANGER, *almost casually, checks his revolver, and sits down cautiously on the opposite side of the Chief's door. He suddenly seems very tired, tilts his hat back. He lifts his mask-like spectacles — to rub his eyes. He sees* SUPERMAN *look at him, and quickly lowers the mask again. They sit silently.* RANGER *speaks finally.*
RANGER	It is not easy to stable a horse in downtown New York.
SUPERMAN	I suppose not.

RANGER	Take my advice.
SUPERMAN	Hm?
RANGER	Don't ever try it. Finally had to leave him in a parking lot. *(defensively)* Well, I couldn't just tie him to a parking meter, could I?
SUPERMAN	You can't leave him by himself?
RANGER	Certainly not.
SUPERMAN	Kinda stupid, is he?
RANGER	*(bristling)* Silver is not stupid!
SUPERMAN	A bit — ornery?
RANGER	Do you mind if we change the subject?
SUPERMAN	Okay, okay! *(pause)* So — you're in the horse business, huh?
RANGER	No, I am not in the 'horse business.'
SUPERMAN	What's with the weird costume, then?
	RANGER *looks at his clothes, then at* SUPERMAN's, *rather pointedly. He does not reply.*
SUPERMAN	Cows?
RANGER	No.
SUPERMAN	Sheep?
RANGER	No!
SUPERMAN	*(pause)* Pigs?
RANGER	No!
SUPERMAN	Sor-r-r-ry! *(pause)* It's a bit — passé, isn't it? The boots and everything.
RANGER	All sorts of people wear clothes like this.

> RANGER, *getting irritated, snatches a magazine and snaps through a few pages. He is trying to think of a comeback.*

RANGER   May I ask what you're doing here?

SUPERMAN   Here?

RANGER   In this office.

SUPERMAN   *(curtly)* Business.

RANGER   What kind of business?

SUPERMAN   *(long pause)* What's the mask all about?

RANGER   Huh?

SUPERMAN   *(very clearly)* Mask?

RANGER   Are you trying to say you don't know?

SUPERMAN   *(pretending to think)* Batman!

RANGER   *(through clenched teeth)* Are you here on official business?

SUPERMAN   *(enjoying himself)* Who wants to know?

RANGER   The Lone Ranger wants to know!

SUPERMAN   *(pause)* Who?

RANGER   Lone Ranger! Lone Ranger! What the heck do you think this mask is for?

SUPERMAN   Oh, I dunno — you see a lotta funny sights downtown these days.

> RANGER *leaps to his feet, snatches a couple of cartridges from his gun belt, pushes them in* SUPERMAN's face.

RANGER   Look! Look at these!

SUPERMAN   *(non-committal)* Interesting.

RANGER   Interesting? They're solid silver!

SUPERMAN   Some kind of dum-dums, are they?

RANGER	They're my own special bullets!
SUPERMAN	But why — silver?
RANGER	*(taken by surprise)* Well, it's a kind of...trademark.
SUPERMAN	Oh. *(pause)* Oh! A horse called Silver! That mask! You're...
RANGER	*(with some satisfaction)* The Lone Ranger.
SUPERMAN	Right! A fiery horse with the speed of...
RANGER	Light!
SUPERMAN	Yeah. A cloud of dust and a hearty...*(looking slyly at RANGER)*...Giddy-ap?
RANGER	*(frostily)* Hi-yo Silver, away!
SUPERMAN	Yeah, I remember now. *(shaking his head)* Man, that's a long time!
RANGER	What?
SUPERMAN	That musta been, what? Fifteen, twenty years...?
RANGER	For your information, I've spent the last three weeks chasing a gang of desperate outlaws!
SUPERMAN	Train-robbers?
RANGER	*(pause)* Dope peddlers.
SUPERMAN	You don't say? *(friendlier)* Where's your, um, buddy?
RANGER	*(with the proper dignity)* I ride alone.
SUPERMAN	Oh, come on! Otto or whatever his...
RANGER	His name is Tonto.
SUPERMAN	Otto. Tonto. Pronto.
RANGER	And he is not my 'buddy'. He is my -- faithful Indian companion.
SUPERMAN	*(laughing)* He's what?

RANGER   You wouldn't understand. Easterners never do.

SUPERMAN   Whuddaya mean — Easterner?

RANGER   *(not above sarcasm himself)* From — the — East.

SUPERMAN   Listen, pal. This might be a little hard for you to follow, but I've got a lot of territory to cover...I serve the world!

RANGER   The world?

SUPERMAN   Yeah — the world.

                    Gestures a globe.

SUPERMAN   International. You know?

RANGER   *(suspiciously)* You sound like one of those anarchists.

SUPERMAN   *(incredulous)* What?

RANGER   You are implying there's something wrong with the good old U. S. of A., right?

SUPERMAN   Jesus. How long have you been out in Texas, anyway?

RANGER   Arizona.

SUPERMAN   Arizona.

RANGER   *(pause, with steely intent)* I believe we were discussing you.

SUPERMAN   Look, pal! I'm not wearing a mask! I got nothing to hide.

RANGER   How about that red cape? I suppose it represents something?

SUPERMAN   Represents?

RANGER   *(just getting warmed up)* Are you domiciled in this land of liberty and enterprise?

SUPERMAN   Huh?

RANGER   Do you live here?

SUPERMAN   Yeah, in a way.

RANGER   *(grimly)* You are evading my questions!

SUPERMAN   No, I'm not! I just — well, I stay with a friend of mine.
                Clark Kent!

RANGER   You stay with a male friend?

SUPERMAN   Sort of. Clark is a reporter for...

RANGER   Male — right?

SUPERMAN   Yes!

RANGER   And this little — home of yours is in the East, right?

SUPERMAN   Jesus Christ! Is all this...?

RANGER   Right?

SUPERMAN   ...relevant?

RANGER   *(pause)* I could tell you were a fruit, the minute I laid eyes
                on that outfit.

                         SUPERMAN *looks at his costume in surprise.*

RANGER   They'd laugh you out of every town west of the
                Mississippi.

SUPERMAN   They would not!

RANGER   Try it and see.

SUPERMAN   I been west of the Mississippi hundreds of times.
                Thousands of times!

RANGER   Did you take your — friend along? Clark Kent?

SUPERMAN   Yes. No! He has to stay in — Metropolis.

RANGER   Metropolis, eh?

SUPERMAN   He works there.

RANGER   I never heard of it.

SUPERMAN   *(trying hard)* You wouldn't have.

RANGER   *(pause)* Still, I will say it's...colourful.

SUPERMAN	What?
RANGER	Well, that bikini. The cape. The monogrammed shirt...
SUPERMAN	Monog...! That's my symbol!
RANGER	I see. 'S' for symbol.
SUPERMAN	*(dangerously quiet)* Do you know that with a single breath, I could blow you right through that wall?
RANGER	Well, you've been doing your darndest for ten minutes now.
SUPERMAN	Do you realize that one blow from this — fist of steel could send you into orbit around the moon?
RANGER	*(unimpressed)* A hazard I could learn to live with.
SUPERMAN	You're starting to piss — me — off, fella!
RANGER	*(satisfied with his victory, standing up to ease the tension)* Have you been waiting here long?

SUPERMAN *refuses to answer.*

RANGER	*(cajoling)* Aw, come on. There's no point in sulking. If we gotta water at the same trough, we might as well pretend to be neighbourly.
SUPERMAN	Do you mind laying off the hillbilly metaphors?
RANGER	Pardon?
SUPERMAN	Save it for your — fans!
RANGER	Suit yourself. I was only trying to pass the time of day.
SUPERMAN	*(pause)* Fifteen minutes!
RANGER	Pardon?
SUPERMAN	I was waiting — fifteen minutes!

Pause.

RANGER	What did you mean about my fans?
SUPERMAN	Fans?

RANGER   You said — save it for my fans.

SUPERMAN   *(bored)* Did I?

> *Pause. The telephone behind the Chief's door*
> *rings three times. SUPERMAN listens intently.*
> *RANGER tries to hear, too, but can't.*
> *SUPERMAN finally shakes his head in disgust.*

SUPERMAN   So where's your 'faithful Indian companion'?

RANGER   Oh, he's out at the silver mine. He can't stand the East.
                Couldn't drag him here with a herd of mustangs.

SUPERMAN   Did you say silver mine?

RANGER   Yeah.

SUPERMAN   You guys own a silver mine?

RANGER   Yeah. That's where these come from.

SUPERMAN   You mean that's all you do with it?

RANGER   Do with what?

SUPERMAN   Man, do you know how much silver is worth these days?

> *This sends RANGER off into one of his standard*
> *speeches.*

RANGER   Oh, yes! I do know its worth. In fact, that material value
                which you attach to it is what we seek to destroy -- by
                constantly employing these shining bullets as weapons in
                the fight for justice, and for decency, and for freedom.
                (stabbing the air) By eradicating the root of all evil from
                existence, we will preserve our founders' heritage and ...

SUPERMAN   You don't have to tell me, pal. Ever since I got to this
                planet, it's been fight, fight, fight — just to keep a little
                law and order.

RANGER   *(pleasantly surprised)* You mean — you too are engaged in
                the eternal battle against evil and perversion?

SUPERMAN   *(modestly)* In my own little way.

RANGER   There aren't many of us left these days.

SUPERMAN   It gets lonely sometimes.

RANGER   *(pause, checking his watch)* Hope that parking lot attendant is reliable.

SUPERMAN   I wouldn't trust one with a stale sandwich.

RANGER   *(alarmed)* Maybe I better go check...!

SUPERMAN   Oh come on. Where's he going to go with a horse?

RANGER   *(agreeing)* Yeah. *(pause, a bit puzzled)* That's strange about the fans.

SUPERMAN   What is?

RANGER   That's what he said, too. 'Save it for your fans.'

SUPERMAN   Who?

> RANGER *looks around cautiously, flicks his thumb at the Chief's door.*

RANGER   Him.

SUPERMAN   He invited you here?

RANGER   Yes.

SUPERMAN   All the way from Texas?

RANGER   Arizona. He telephoned.

> SUPERMAN *seems shaken by this; put out, distracted.*

RANGER   What is it?

SUPERMAN   Oh, nothing. Nothing. *(pause, suddenly)* You ever get — premonitions?

RANGER   *(startled himself)* Premonitions? What about?

SUPERMAN   Well, I...dunno. *(pause)* Had a kinda funny thing happen on the way over here — from Metropolis.

RANGER   Like what?

SUPERMAN	I guess it was over — Baltimore I happened to look down, and there was this house on fire. In the suburbs. There were all these people, a family, screaming from the windows, so I swooped down to help.
RANGER	*(too politely, not believing a word)* Oh?
SUPERMAN	There was a little baby! And an old guy, must have been eighty! They wouldn't have stood a chance!
RANGER	I suppose not. *(long pause)* What exactly do you mean, you swooped down?
SUPERMAN	Well I was in a rush, see, flying over and...
RANGER	You were flying over.
SUPERMAN	Yeah, and all this smoke curling up. Man, I flew right through it.
RANGER	Let me get this straight. You were flying along in this balloon, or airplane or whatever, and you just happened to look down and see...
SUPERMAN	No, no! I was flying — all by myself!

RANGER *begins flapping his arms like a bird, and caws like a crow.*

SUPERMAN	You see I've had the power of flight since...*(turning to RANGER)* Okay, knock it off, hayseed! *(turning away)* Anyway, when I -- landed, they...all started to laugh. They said to -- kiss off. It was a big joke! What are you grinning at?
RANGER	Well -- flying! That's a bit far-fetched, isn't it?
SUPERMAN	No more than those goddamn silver bullets!
RANGER	Eh?
SUPERMAN	I don't expect some dumb cowboy to know this, but I — am Superman!
RANGER	*(suppressing a laugh)* Who?
SUPERMAN	Superman!

RANGER*'s laugh runs down in the silence.*

RANGER   All right...'Superman', what are you doing in here? In my Chief's office?

SUPERMAN   Your Chief's office?

RANGER   Yes.

SUPERMAN   Say, how do you earn your money, anyway?

RANGER   Well, I don't...I mean, Tonto looks after that side of things. *(pause)* Probably makes a few bucks selling beadwork and — stuff.

SUPERMAN   Beadwork, huh?

RANGER   Sure! There's good money in — well, how do you make money? Put on some kind of — flying circus?

SUPERMAN   Clark gets a good salary at the Daily Planet. It keeps us in groceries.

* * *

Published in "Six Canadian Plays" by Playwrights Canada Press - trade paperback

male ∞ *female*

Marcia Bennett and Frank Adamson in the 1987 Five & Dime production of
Bat Masterson's Last Regular Job.
Photo by Aaron Schwartz.

Life Without Instruction

Sally Clark

A play based on the life and trial of Artemisia Gentileschi, a 17th Century Italian painter. In her youth ,she is raped by her art instructor, her father's best friend. She then sets out to deliver a rare and deliberate revenge.

ARTEMISIA	*(entering)* How do you do Signore Tassi. *(completing a curtsey and looking around)* Where's Tutia?
TASSI	No need to be so formal. I'm not your mathematics teacher. I'm your art teacher. And art is life. Is that not right?
ARTEMISIA	I don't have a mathematics teacher.
TASSI	Don't be so literal. Art is life. Would you agree with that?
ARTEMISIA	I hadn't thought about it.
TASSI	You should. Lesson No. 1: Think. Agostino. *(holding out hand)*
ARTEMISIA	Oh- I-ah- my father will think I'm being rude if I call you by your first name. Have you seen my chaperone?
TASSI	No. I haven't. Lesson No. 2: Your father is not the only man in the world. Here is another. *(holding out hand)* Agostino Tassi. And your name?
ARTEMISIA	You know my name. She should be here.
TASSI	Your name.
ARTEMISIA	Artemisia Gentileschi. But everyone calls me Bella.
TASSI	Give me your hand.
	ARTEMISIA *gives it reluctantly.*
TASSI	*(fondling her hand)* Artemisia. What a beautiful name.
ARTEMISIA	Yes, it's from the Greek goddess of the hunt. She —

TASSI | Yes yes, I know all that. Artemisia, you must learn that when a man says something nice, you don't suddenly talk his ear off. If someone gives you a compliment, take it. Because they're going to be few and far between. So- you say 'Thank you.' We'll try it again.

ARTEMISIA | Why should they be few and far between?

TASSI | You're no beauty.

ARTEMISIA | I'm not?

TASSI | No, of course not. You look shocked. You've been paying too much attention to your father. Fathers see with different eyes. Do you know why your father hired me?

ARTEIMSIA | To teach me drawing.

TASSI | No. To teach you perspective.

ARTEMISIA | Yes. Drawing and perspective.

TASSI | Don't be sullen. Perspective isn't just drawing. It's a way of looking at the world. Everyone agrees that they will learn to look at the world in the same way and when you learn to see the way everyone else does, then that's perspective.

ARTEMISIA | I thought perspect —

TASSI | Parallel lines meet at the horizon.

ARTEMISIA | I thought parallel lines never met.

TASSI | As I said, I'm not your Math teacher. That is one of the rules of perspective.

ARTEMISIA | But it's wrong!

TASSI | You think you're very important. If you were standing in a meadow 100 feet away fron a man and he looked at you, from his point of view you would be very small and not important at all. That's perspective. So when I tell you you're a big ugly girl, believe me. Because that also is perspective. An objective point of view.

ARTEMISIA | Why are you so mean to me?

TASSI	I hate to see someone go through life deluded. Now, let's look at some of your work. *(starting to pull "Susannah and the Elders" out)*
ARTEMISIA	No! *(placing herself in front of it)*
TASSI	Why not?
ARTEMISIA	I don't want to show you my work.
TASSI	Don't be spoiled. There are worse things in life than being a big lump. Are you going to get out of my way or do I have to move you myself?

ARTEMISIA *doesn't move.*

TASSI	All right. *(grabbing her and picking her up as she struggles, then placing her to one side)* You're better looking with a bit of colour to your cheek. Don't get enough excitement at home. *(looking at painting)* I don't know why you didn't want me to see it. It's quite a good painting.
ARTEMISIA	I know it's a good painting.
TASSI	Is that a fact.
ARTEMISIA	Yes. It is. And if you don't mind, I'd like you to look at something else. *(going to it)*
TASSI	I do mind. And it's not as good as you think it is. The two Elders are ridiculously placed. They're almost on top of her. Wait a minute. You've changed his face.
ARTEMISIA	How would you know. You've never seen it before.
TASSI	*(peering at it)* And you've never seen me before. But if that's the case, why am I in your painting?
ARTEMISIA	That's not you!
TASSI	No? *(moving in closer)* Have you been spying on me, Artemisia?
ARTEMISIA	No.
TASSI	I'm flattered that you decided to immortalize me. I had no idea you found me that attractive.

ARTEMISIA   I don't. In my painting, you're an Elder.

TASSI   So, you work from life.

ARTEMISIA   Pardon?

TASSI   Well, that's me. I don't look at all old there. And that's your father. You've made him look old. And a bit dim, too. Do you think your father's stupid?

ARTEMISIA   Of course not!

TASSI   I think he's stupid. I wouldn't let a man like me near my daughter. So — if that's him and that's me, then that beautiful naked woman must be you. You look a lot better with your clothes off.

ARTEMISIA   That's not me!

TASSI   The face is yours and those hands are definitely yours. Huge. So, I presume the rest is you. Cowering in naked splendor from those two old men. What are you afraid of, Artemisia?

ARTEMISIA   I'm not afraid of anything.

TASSI   You've painted me and your father as conspirators plotting against you. Do you really think your father lusts after you?

ARTEMISIA   Of course not!

TASSI   Why did you paint him that way?

ARTEMISIA   I just used his face. Stop reading meaning into it!

TASSI   What a beautiful body you have. The skin is milky. And that breast...*(running finger along painting and looking at her)* Exquisite. You're blushing, Artemisia.

ARTEMISIA   No, I'm not.

TASSI   Yes. You are. You see, the skin here has a rosy glow to it. *(running a finger along her cheek)* Not like the skin here. *(running finger down and around neck)* You've captured your skin tone very well. Oh. Blushing again. It's funny. You portray me as a man lusting after you and here I am, suddenly obsessed with your body. There is a power in your painting, Artemisia.

ARTEMISIA   Is there?

TASSI   You like it when I talk about your art. *(kissing her neck)*

ARTEMISIA   It's what you were hired to do.

TASSI   Maybe I was hired to do something else. *(kissing her passionately)*

ARTEMISIA *is too surprised to resist.* TASSI *puts his hand up her skirt and she tries to push his hand away. They struggle.* TASSI *pins* ARTEMISIA *down and yanks her skirt up.*

ARTEMISIA   NO! *(struggling and screaming)*

TASSI   *(clapping hand over her mouth)* Your father's left you here alone. Surely that should tell you something.

ARTEMISIA *bites his hand.*

TASSI   OW! *(loosening his grip on her)*

ARTEMISIA *tries to get away.* TASSI *grabs her, stuffs a paint rag in her mouth, pins her down and rapes her.*

* * *

Available from Playwrights Union of Canada - copyscript

Dead Serious

Doug Greenall

Terror strikes an isolated resort when employees find a guest brutally murdered. Tracey begins to doubt her brother's innocence as the killings continue, despite the presence of other likely suspects, because of his reliance on a childhood game which has now become pathological.

	Late at night. TRACEY's room. She is sleeping. A bit of light spills in from outside. He moves to the bed and shakes her.
SEYMOUR	*(lowered voice)* Tracey... Tracey...
	TRACEY rolls toward him, waking.
TRACEY	What is it? *(pause)* What is it?
SEYMOUR	It's back.
TRACEY	Oh, no...
SEYMOUR	Remember. Remember how good it could be...
TRACEY	No, Seymour. No.
SEYMOUR	I dream about it. I dream about the good ones. The really good ones. Remember...
TRACEY	Seymour...
SEYMOUR	I dream about you and me doing it still.
TRACEY	Listen to me. This is not going to start again.
SEYMOUR	Oh, god, it could be so delicious...
TRACEY	It was just a game, Seymour. It got out of control.
SEYMOUR	That's when it was the best.
TRACEY	It's over. We've lived without it for seven months.

SEYMOUR	And I've felt dead inside.
TRACEY	You know what we did.
SEYMOUR	That's why I'm so goddamn scared.
TRACEY	You've got to get help.
SEYMOUR	You know, for me, I don't think it ever went away. It feels like a thing that's separate from me. Like I have no control over it.
TRACEY	If you can't stop it you've got to go to town and see a doctor. *(pause)* You hear me?
SEYMOUR	Yeah.

TRACEY *touches him, hugs him.*

TRACEY	We don't need the game. We can live without it. It started hurting, Seymour. Even before the accident, it was hurting us. There were a thousand little signs, little voices, saying, 'quit'. The accident wasn't the first time one of us went too far.
SEYMOUR	I know. I know.
TRACEY	Maybe when it started it was fun. Creative. I've thought a lot about why we started. But it doesn't matter. I can analyse it forever. Say it was loneliness or isolation. Or blame it on Mom. But when it comes down to it — it was us. We started it. We have to stop it.
SEYMOUR	I know.
TRACEY	The three weeks I spent in this room after the accident were the blackest weeks of my life. I thought about everything. Every detail. I wanted to go back and change things so desperately.
SEYMOUR	Oh, Tracey...*(putting his arm around her)*
TRACEY	And now Donald is dead. We both need some reality to hang on to.
SEYMOUR	Yeah.

TRACEY	I talked to Ted today. *(as* SEYMOUR *moans)* Now don't. For me, it helped. We talked about death and what it means. I felt better about Donald. And Mr. Forbes too.
SEYMOUR	Look. I think there's something I should tell you about Ted. I can sense that you're starting to fall for this Regenon stuff.
TRACEY	I'm not falling...
SEYMOUR	*(cutting her off)* The other night I saw something very scary. Now maybe you won't think this is a big deal, but when I saw it, it terrified me.
TRACEY	Go on...
SEYMOUR	I'm walking back to my cabin and I hear this chanting. It's coming from Ted's cabin, right. So I walk over and I look in the window. And there's him and Mom — and they're naked — standing on either side of the table. There's all these candles burning on the table and the dresser while they're standing there doing this chant. Now I was right ready to take off except for one thing — something was moving on the table. So I moved closer to get a better look...and there was this animal on a board...some small animal, thrashing. It looked like it was nailed to the board. And while this poor animal is thrashing and bleeding, they're standing there chanting.
TRACEY	Get out. Out. I don't need this shit.

SEYMOUR *rises to leave.*

TRACEY	*(stopping him)* You think I'm stupid? I know the game. I can smell it.
SEYMOUR	Why don't you let me walk out of here then? You're so sure it's a game. I'm worried about Mom. And maybe about you too. And I'm not stupid either. If I was gonna play the game, I wouldn't walk in here, announce the game is coming back, and then start playing it again.
TRACEY	Regenon is not like that.
SEYMOIJR	How do you know? How do *you* know? I saw what I saw.
TRACEY	It sounds like some kind of witchcraft. That I don't believe.

SEYMOUR	I don't know what it is — but it scares the hell out of me.
TRACEY	Don't do this to me. If this is a lie it's really unfair. Tell me the truth. Please.
SEYMOUR	I wish it was a lie, Trace. I really do.
TRACEY	Oh, god...

SEYMOUR *embraces her* .

* * *

Available from Playwrights Union of Canada - copyscript

A Short History of Night

John Mighton

In this play about the life of the famous astronomer *Johannes Kepler, and is a disturbing parallel between modern and mediæval thought, the painfully shy Kepler is wooing his future wife.*

                                        Lights up on BARBARA *sitting nearby.*

BARBARA   How's your Aunt Kunigard?

KEPLER   Dead.

BARBARA   Katherine?

KEPLER   She too is dead.

BARBARA   Sebaldus?

KEPLER   She was skillful and intelligent, but married most unfortunately, lived sumptuously, squandered her goods and is now a beggar.

                                          Pause.

BARBARA   How's your father? He was always nice to me.

KEPLER   Saturn in seven made him study gunnery. He has many enemies and ran the risk of hanging. So he fought in Holland. A jar of gunpowder burst and lacerated his face. He's in exile.

KEPLER   *(taking out a knife)* This is all he left me.

BARBARA   You've had a difficult life.

KEPLER   I take comfort in the stars. When the storm threatens us with shipwreck, we can do nothing more noble than fix the anchor of our studies into the ground of eternity. *(pausing)* God has chosen me to receive the insight of the creation plan.

                                          Pause.

BARBARA	You're very young.
KEPLER	Nineteen.
BARBARA	And God told you this?
KEPLER	Yes.
BARBARA	In a dream?
KEPLER	No. In a mathematical proof.

Pause.

BARBARA	Are you hard working?
KEPLER	To excess.
BARBARA	Do you expect riches?
KEPLER	No.
BARBARA	Love?
KEPLER	No.
BARBARA	Fame.
KEPLER	I expect nothing of that sort.
BARBARA	You don't seem very happy.
KEPLER	I don't look for such happiness as the foolish lovers of the world experience, but such as the good and faithful servants of Christ wait for. A human consolation is in vain.

Pause.

BARBARA	You should have joined the ministry.
KEPLER	I tried. They wouldn't let me.
BARBARA	Why not?
KEPLER	They said I am too opinionated.
BARBARA	How unfair.

KEPLER
I have often incensed my school fellows against me.
Once, out of fear, I was driven to betray them. I argue
with men of every profession for the profit of my mind. I
am like a dog worrying a bone — I cannot help gnawing.
I hate many people exceedingly and avoid them.

BARBARA
(after a pause) Come and sit down. It's a beautiful
evening. Look at the stars.

BARBARA
(as KEPLER sits beside her) What's that one called?

KEPLER
Where?

BARBARA
The little one. Beside the North Star. I've often watched it.

KEPLER
I cannot see. My eyes are weak.

BARBARA
(laughing) A nearsighted astronomer.

KEPLER
I see with the eye of my mind.

Pause.

BARBARA
I'm sorry you're so unhappy. I like you. My father likes
you. You should visit us some time. I have a wonderful
family and I would do anything to please them. Especially
my father. He's always singing. When I was a child he
used to throw me up in the air and catch me. He said he'd
throw me right up into heaven...How far is heaven?

KEPLER
Two thousand, four hundred and fifty million miles.

BARBARA
How did you figure that out?

KEPLER
There are five perfect bodies that can be inscribed between
the earth and the five planets. The tetrahedron, the
hexahedron, the octahedron, the dodecahedron and the
isocahedron. God loves Geometry. I deduced it from their
dimensions.

Pause. BARBARA takes his hand.

BARBARA
We're alone here.

KEPLER
Yes.

BARBARA
Did you like it?

KEPLER
Like what?

BARBARA   Don't be coy.

KEPLER   It was necessary.

Pause.

BARBARA   It's late. I'm cold. Where's your comet?

KEPLER   I can hardly predict it to the minute.

BARBARA   I can't stay much longer. My father is expecting me.

KEPLER   Alright.

BARBARA   We'll see each other tomorrow?

KEPLER   Yes. I'll bring your father's horoscope.

Pause.

BARBARA   My father has known your family for some time. He's appalled by your poverty, but recognizes your promise as an astrologer.

Pause.

BARBARA   I like you. We've known each other for three months. You seem noble and trustworthy, which is rare. Your features aren't unpleasing. And we share the same faith...If you asked me to marry you, I wouldn't refuse.

KEPLER   You'd have me?

BARBARA   I could do worse.

KEPLER   I have to consult my charts.

BARBARA   Alright. But don't keep me waiting too long. I have plenty of prospects.

KEPLER   I won't.

BARBARA *exits.* KEPLER *looks at the sky.*

✳ ✳ ✳

Published in "Possible Worlds & A Short History of Night by Playwrights Canada Press - trade paperback. Winner-1992 Governor General's Literary Award for Drama

Midnight Madness

Dave Carley

Wesley and Anna haven't seen each other since they both quit high school years ago. Their reasons for quitting were as different as they were, or so it seemed, until they discover plenty they never knew about each other in the bed department of Bloom's furniture store.

WESLEY	It was my theory that I'd come back in the next life, well, as a big stud. Like Billy, only with the ability to eat without scratching. It's a common theory of afterlife. You get reincarnated upwards: rooster to cow, cow to Wesley, Wesley to — big stud. So when I gave up religion I had to face the bitter truth: I wasn't ever going to reincarnate. I would never be a sex god in my next life. And, if I only had one life to live that meant I only had one body to live it in — I joined the Y the next day.
ANNA	It shows.
WESLEY	Huh?
ANNA	You look a lot better than you did in high school.
WESLEY	Bull.
ANNA	I'm not kidding. Your shoulders are really broad and —
WESLEY	Stop it okay.
ANNA	I just said I thought you were looking —
WESLEY	I heard you —
ANNA	It was a compliment.
WESLEY	*(moving away)* Look. Do you want a bed? I'll sell you a bed.
ANNA	Excuse me for living.
WESLEY	*(pause)* Sorry. I thought you were making fun of me.

ANNA	By saying you looked good? *(shaking head)*
WESLEY	Sorry. *(pause)* Why'd you come here?
ANNA	I smell a trick question. Because I want to buy a bed?
WESLEY	No, why'd you come back to Ashburnham? You didn't have to, so why did you?
ANNA	That's not very loyal to the town that bred and raised you.
WESLEY	I just mean you could've stayed in Toronto, there's lots of people there. Unmarried ones. Jude's always got a party or something on. You could've moved Jason down there.
ANNA	I didn't have a social life in Toronto, so I'm not losing anything by moving here. Mom's here and I think it's healthier in Ashburnham. If the kid and I had to make a go of it in Toronto we'd be locked away in some high-rise out in the suburbs and Jason'd be into God knows what. Which he's into here, no doubt, but on a more modest scale.
WESLEY	I still don't understand why you came back.
ANNA	Aw, I don't like sounding like the holy martyr all the time, but I'm here because Jason's here. I'm not uprooting him any more than I have to. He'll be finished high school in six years — if he wants to move then we will. But he's got to have roots somewhere and his, well, they're here.
WESLEY	But if the roots aren't good.
ANNA	I don't think I heard that. *Bad* roots?
WESLEY	I didn't mean bad, I meant not good. I mean, not good as in not-good-different, I think.
ANNA	You'd better explain.
WESLEY	I guess I mean I wonder if letting Jason have roots like you say is going to make up for well, him being denied a father.
ANNA	That's a neat little judgmental turd. I 'denied' him a father?
WESLEY	I meant life denied him. Events. Same way I got gypped.

ANNA	And now it's 'gypped'.
WESLEY	I meant sort of —
ANNA	I think you meant gypped. That's what you said.
WESLEY	That guy in law school — Albert — he would've married you.
ANNA	Oh. I'm supposed to get married so Jason can have a father.
WESLEY	You said Albert loved Jason. They had a bond. Do we have to talk about this —
ANNA	I want to tell you something. People get married because they love each other, not because they happen to love the same third person.
WESLEY	You might have come to love Albert, in time.
ANNA	Not as a life partner. No.
WESLEY	But you're not sure.
ANNA	Of course I'm not sure. That's something you're never sure of.
WESLEY	Some people seem to know.
ANNA	What the living hell would you know. You're a goddamn Presbyterian nun! Look. I have been through hell and back for that son of mine. I've been through hell to become a lawyer — school, school, more school, articling, bar ads, part-time jobs and every extra minute, every free minute I had I came home and spent it with Jason. No matter how much I wanted to go out with my girlfriends, or out on a date...no matter how...
WESLEY	You didn't have to become a lawyer.
ANNA	You're right. I could've sold beds.
WESLEY	There's nothing wrong with selling beds.
ANNA	There's something wrong with hiding under them. I'm sorry, I'm having a real problem here. You can't stir your fanny out of this place to save your life but me, I'm supposed to forget any aspirations I might have — I'm

supposed to marry some guy I don't love — what's the use. You're not the first one to say I've gypped him. Aren't you going to tell me I should've put him up for adoption? I get that thrown at me too. Well, you don't have the right. You just don't have the right. Not you, not this town, not anyone. Look at you. Where the hell do you get off judging me. I'd've thought that you, of all people, you, *Weirdley,* you'd be above that. You're pathetic. No sale. No sale. I'm history.

    ANNA *exits.* WESLEY *stands frozen, shocked.*

WESLEY   Anna. Anna. *(louder)* Anna! Wait! *(running after her)* Anna! Don't go! Anna! Anna! Jesus. Jesus Christ, she's gone. *(running to window, trying unsuccessfully to pull it open so he can yell after her)* Get back here dammit! You can't walk out — open, come on, open — *(looks)* Where is she! Anna! Anna! *(now angry, directing it at objects as he returns to main part of room. He might rip diplomas off walls, kick pillows etc.)* Aw to hell with it, you're just like everybody else, so go to hell. Go to hell Anna Bregner! I hate you, I hate you all... I hate this place. *(pause)* I'm through. I'm through. No more Bloom's, no more Bed Department, no more beds, no more goddamn swags, no more cannonball, no more brass... *(reaching desk, pulling out letter-opener, beginning to stalk the waterbed)* So. So. No one wants you eh. You've been up here a little too long eh. Well it's time you earned your goddamn keep. Time we put you to good use. Maybe we'll just forget our little Midnight Madness Sale, maybe we'll have ourselves a Water Damage Sale! Time to die my undulating little friend. *(raising letter opener)* Speak hands for me! *(pausing, poised to stab, lowers)* Aw shit. *(sitting on bed)* They never give me a chance. They never give me a goddamn chance... *(looking up to see* ANNA, *who has returned to the room)* Anna.

ANNA   *(coming over)* Are you okay?

WESLEY   You came back.

ANNA   Wes — are you —

WESLEY   Yes. No. I don't know. You came back, I thought you went.

ANNA   I never left. Are you *sure* you're okay? *(as* WESLEY *nods)* You sounded —

WESLEY	No, I was —
ANNA	It's not a crime to get mad.
WESLEY	Sorry. *(beat)* Why am I apologizing? You stormed out of here and never let me finish what I was trying to say. We were having a good time and then whammo, out you go, and I'm all alone *(snapping fingers)* just like that, I'm alone. You have any idea what that's like?
ANNA	Yes.
WESLEY	No. No you don't, you don't have a clue, it's easy for you to run out of here, you've got someplace to run to. You've got people, your Mom, Jason...What have I got? I'll tell you what my life's like. When there's a symphony night I buy two tickets. I show up at the high school, they hand me my tickets and I shrug and say, 'My friend's sick, I only need the one.' So they won't know. I've only got one pillow on my bed — why would I ever expect a guest head? Some nights I lie there and look at the map I've got up on the wall beside my bed and I count all the dots that are cities and I wonder, 'How many Wesleys are there in this goddamn country? How many others are lying there, alone, wondering what'd be like to have a real human being breathing beside them...' In the winter I don't shovel the walk. Why would I? The only ones using it are me, the neighbours' kids flogging chocolate bars, Jehovah's Witnesses. Winter progresses, there's just this one deepening groove, one person wide, one neat path to my door that I follow up and down, up and down, until thaw...One skinny little path...
ANNA	I understand.
WESLEY	How could you!
ANNA	There's more that one kind of lonely. You've got one kind, I've got another. I've got a family but I don't have anyone — to talk to — you know — like an adult, a friend...So what do I do with the first one I meet? I blow my stack. I got downstairs — oh I just feel sick about what I said, Wes, I'm truly sorry.
WESLEY	For what?
ANNA	Come on, for being a witch, for saying —

WESLEY	Everything you said was true. I am pathetic. That was a good word. You must take me for the biggest idiot in the world.
ANNA	That's not what I think at all.
WESLEY	I can never say what I'm thinking. Not when it's important. I want to do something or say something and it just doesn't come out. I wanted to tell you I admire you. For coming back here, for facing everyone, for never letting things get you down, or screw you up, for being brave.
ANNA	That's a laugh.
WESLEY	You've raised a son on your own and done it well. That's brave. I could never have done that!
ANNA	Who says I've done it well. I've been an absentee parent. Sure — Jason's a good kid — right now — but what's to stop him becoming a mess later? I don't know if I've — I've been around him enough to instill any values —
WESLEY	Sure you have —
ANNA	Enough to keep him out of trouble? Don't admire me for being a successful parent. The jury's still out on that one. And I'm not brave. I'm terrified. I don't know if the kid and I can get it together and he's all I've got. Jason is it. No, I'm not brave...*(touching* WESLEY, *a smile)* We have a lot in common, you and I. We're both lonely, we're both scared. Maybe it is harder for you. You live alone, you work here alone. And this place, this room, it's kind of a time warp. I don't mean that negatively, just that —
WESLEY	It's only one more day.
ANNA	But all those years.
WESLEY	I chose it. At least I think I chose it. You make your bed...

* * *

Published by Blizzard Publishing - trade paperback

Flux

Pete Soucy

Jill has been living in a new relationship with Jaqueline for a week after leaving her long-standing boyfriend Claude. She has returned for the last of her things.

	CLAUDE *has answered the door and* JILL *enters. He stares at her inquisitively.*
JILL	*(pause)* What?
CLAUDE	You rang the doorbell.
JILL	Oh. Yes. I stood there for a moment wondering about that myself. Guess I felt I should, somehow.
CLAUDE	Uh huh. *(silence)* How's Jaqueline?
JILL	She's fine.
CLAUDE	You're getting along okay?
JILL	Yeah.
CLAUDE	How okay?
JILI	What can I say? *(pause)* She's clever. Stimulating, resourceful, brutally sincere...
CLAUDE	Good, good, that's good. That's how she struck me at the library that day. Frank. Resourceful. *(beat)* The, uh, apartment's big enough and, well, no major problems? With the plumbing, or anything.
JILL	Enough room for us. Everything seems to function okay.
CLAUDE	Good...good.
JILL	*(beat)* Claude, I know this is difficult. God knows I have moments myself...

CLAUDE	No Jill, I told you before, it's fine. I can empathise with your situation. Really. The...emotional transition you're going through. And I accept it fully. Honestly, I do. You know me. I'm not confined to the conventional male psyche. I can even appreciate your needs, and I support you...*(as she gives him a look)* Really. And what's more, I think Jacqueline understands that as well.
JILL	Yes, she does. We've talked about it.
CLAUDE	You have?
JILL	Yes.
CLAUDE	What did she say?
JILL	Nothing, really.
CLAUDE	Nothing?
JILL	*(pause)* She says you're full of shit.
CLAUDE	What?
JILL	She says 'he doth protest too much', and that you're just overcompensating for the real psychological trauma caused by this rupture in your already fragile, sexist mindset.
CLAUDE	What?
JILL	She says that you're feeling socially and emotionally castrated at the moment, and that you'll probably want to get laid silly in order to reaffirm your Cro-magnon manhood.
CLAUDE	No!
JILL	And she also thinks that your energetic support of the women's movement is just a political prerequisite for survival within the artistic community.
CLAUDE	That's not fair! Political prerequisite. That's old stuff! C'mon, Jill!
JILL	Maybe.
CLAUDE	Oh, I don't belive this!
JILL	It's just what she thinks.

CLAUDE	Oh yeah? What do you think? *(pause, as she won't answer)* Give me a break! That bitch was going to say that anyway.
JILL	That what?
CLAUDE	She can't even grant me the slightest potential for empathy? What, do none of us care?
JILL	I'm not sure.
CLAUDE	Jesus, Jill she's got you believing that?
JILL	I make my own statements.
CLAUDE	Since when?
JILL	Since always.
CLAUDE	Come on Jill. What you say usually depends on who you've been with all day!
JILL	*(beat)* That's not true.
CLAUDE	It's true. You've never really decided what you think about anything. Have you?
JILL	*(pause)* Well maybe I haven't had to. *(beat)* Maybe I've always been backed up no matter what I thought. *(silence, then as she starts to leave)* At least it's good to know there is an end to your understanding. Don't start apologizing until I'm gone, will you? *(exiting)*
CLAUDE	*(beat, to the door)* I'm sorry, Jill.

***

Available from Playwrights Union of Canada - copyscript

Sanctuary

Emil Sher

Every week, June — an emotionally abused woman — retreats to a secluded spot in a park for some time alone. For a year, Philip has watched her from a distance. He introduces himself on the very morning when June has come to scatter her husband's ashes. In this scene, June asks Philip to help her recreate her husband's drowning.

JUNE	I killed him.
PHILIP	Sorry?
JUNE	My husband. I killed him.
PHILIP	You told me he drowned. This winter. They had to wait for the ice to melt.
JUNE	He did drown. But I still killed him. I could have saved him, but I didn't. It's as good as killing him.
PHILIP	You don't know if you could have saved him. Not saving someone isn't the same thing as killing them.
JUNE	We were walking on a lake. Sometimes, it could be like that. You know, peaceful. I'm walking and walking. You can barely hear your own footsteps, the snow is so soft. Then I realize I've been walking on my own. He did that sometimes. Stopped walking next to me and waited for me to notice. And it's true, I wouldn't always notice right away. Sometimes I get lost in my own world. I turned around. He was way back. Way back. And he waved at me. Only this wasn't a 'Wait-for-me' type of wave. It was like he was blowing me off. You know, a kind of shrug with his hand. *(imitating the movement)* Then he turns around and disappears. Just like that. Like he dropped off the edge of the earth. *(long pause)* Would you do me a favour?
PHILIP	Sure.
JUNE	Would you sit over there and wave your arms?

PHILIP	Sorry?
JUNE	Please. *(standing and pointing to a large, flat stone upstage right)* Over there. Can you just sit behind that stone for a minute?
PHILIP	Okay.
JUNE	Now just kind of wave your hands back and forth.
PHILIP	What?
JUNE	Please. Wave your hands back and forth.

> PHILIP *moves his hands tentatively.*

JUNE	Faster.

> PHILIP *moves them faster.*

JUNE	A little more frantic.

> PHILIP *complies, and begins to thrash wildly.*

JUNE	Not too frantic. Ease up. That's it. Good. *(composing herself)* Run back. That's what your instincts tell you. You don't think. You don't have time to think. You just run. *(to PHILIP)* Keep waving. I reach the spot where he's fallen through the ice. And he doesn't look too good.
PHILIP	I can imagine.
JUNE	You can't imagine! You weren't there. Okay. Okay. Stop waving and grab onto the ice.
PHILIP	Ice? What ice?
JUNE	Help me out here. Can't you pretend that stone is a piece of ice? I thought artists were good at making things up.
PHILIP	Yes, well we are. What do you want?

> JUNE *walks over and plants* PHILIP's *arms over the boulder, so that it looks like he's hanging on for dear life.* JUNE *walks back to stage left.*

JUNE	'June!' he says, like I'm the eighth wonder of the world. 'June!' Can you say that?

PHILIP	*(weakly)* June.
JUNE	No, no! It wasn't like that. Look, your balls are clinking like ice cubes, your legs are long gone, and all you can come up with is 'June'? *(imitating his weak version)*
PHILIP	Listen. Maybe this isn't the best time to be doing this. I'm not sure I should be...
JUNE	It is. It is the best time. It's the only time. Stay. Please. Just say 'June' with more feeling.
PHILIP	June!
JUNE	That's better. After a couple of Junes, he says, 'Oh, babe, thank God you're here.' Try that.
PHILIP	*(stiffly)* Oh, babe, thank God you're here.
JUNE	Not bad. Try it with more — relief. Yeah, real relief. More of a just-in-the-nick-of-time type of thing.
PHILIP	Oh, babe, thank God you're here.
JUNE	And I say, 'I'm here'. He hangs onto the ice and just sort of catches his breath. I imagine he must have been pretty tired and cold at this point.
PHILIP	*(head down on the stone so his words are muffled)* I imagine.
JUNE	Then he picks up his head and says, 'Crawl on your stomach.'
PHILIP	Crawl on your stomach.
JUNE	'Or you might fall in, too.'
PHILIP	Or you might fall in, too.
JUNE	Good. That's really good. So I get down on my stomach and start to crawl. *(doing just that)* It's cold, really cold. But I keep crawling. I'm about half way there when he says, 'Easy, June. Nice and easy.' Say it.
PHILIP	*(wooden)* Easy, June. Nice and easy.
JUNE	You had it, Philip. You just had it. Don't lose it. Not now.

PHILIP   Easy, June. Nice and easy.

JUNE   Again. *(crawling)*

PHILIP   Easy, June. Nice and easy.

JUNE   Perfect. A couple more 'Easy, June's.

PHILIP   Easy, June. Easy. Easy. *(beginning to get carried away, making sound effect)* Easy, girl. Nice and easy. Good girl.

JUNE   Okay, okay! *(pause)* I stop. Right there on the ice, maybe ten feet away from him. I can't go any further. I hear him, I hear him say, 'You're good to me, you're good to me.' I hear him, but it's like I don't hear him. I feel real cold and very alone. Like there's no one else in the world except me and this hole in the ice about ten feet away. And I get this feeling inside, as cold and solid as the ice I'm lying on, that if I get too close to that hole I'll be sucked right into it, that it'll swallow me whole and freeze over, sealed shut, and no one will ever know I'm somewhere underneath, alive. So I just lay there, real still, not making a move. Then I hear him again. And it's like he's crying. 'What's wrong? What are you doing? What the hell are you doing? What's the matter with you?' Try that.

PHILIP   What's wrong? What are you doing? What the hell are you doing? What's the matter with you?

JUNE   No, no! More desperate.

PHILIP   What's wrong? What are you doing? What the hell are you doing? What's the matter with you?

JUNE   For God's sake, Philip, the man was holding on for dear life. I was his lifeline, his saviour, his final hope, and I wasn't moving.

PHILIP   *(with gusto)* What's wrong? What are you doing? What the hell are you doing? What's the matter with you?

JUNE   I didn't move. I should have moved, I know that, but I didn't. If I moved, I would've been swallowed by that hole. I know it. So I didn't move, and I saved my life, instead of saving his. I heard him, yelling and desperate. He grew more tired. I heard it in his voice. Weaker and weaker. And he started to cry. That wasn't the worst of it.

JUNE   I heard sounds, terrible sounds. Sounds I'd never want to hear again. His fingers scraping across the ice, trying to cling on. There was no other sound in the world except my husband's hands grabbing ice. And then I didn't hear a thing. Nothing, except the sound of my own breathing. Silence. White silence. *(long pause, getting up on her knees)* I killed my husband.

* * *

Available from Playwrights Union of Canada - copyscript.

In the Cards

Caroline Russell-King

A reluctant psychic's powers cause her no end of trouble in her romance with the man she knows she is going to marry even though he is fighting it tooth and nail.

RIVKA, *also called Barbara, and* ROBERT *are on a Ferris wheel, stuck at the top*

RIVKA   Look you can even see the school from here.

ROBERT   *(uptight).* Do you realize that we're the only ones that got on this Ferris wheel?

RIVKA   *(changing the subject)* Oh, look, is that Sam and Joe and Tim Bakerson? Hi, guys!

ROBERT   Why would they only put us on the Ferris wheel when there's a whole line-up down there?

RIVKA   I really don't think I should have eaten all that cotton candy. It was too sweet.

ROBERT   *(a little panicked)* It's stopped. He's stopped it with us right at the top.

RIVKA   Maybe it's broken.

ROBERT   Then he should call up to us and tell us how long we're going to be up here.

RIVKA   I'm sure it'll be fine.

ROBERT   *(calling down)* Hey, hey, hello, down there.

RIVKA   He knows we're up here, Robert.

ROBERT   You're not at all worried. *(beat, looks at her suspiciously)* Why aren't you worried, Barbara?

RIVKA   *(flippantly)* Oh, I'm just not.

ROBERT	Something's going on.
RIVKA	*(softly)* I paid the man.
ROBERT	YOU PAID THE MAN TO KEEP US UP HERE?
RIVKA	Yes.
ROBERT	Why?
RIVKA	I wanted to talk to you in private.
ROBERT	In private?
RIVKA	Yes, this is private.
ROBERT	This is not private.
RIVKA	Don't be upset with me.
ROBERT	I'm not upset.
RIVKA	You are. It's the first time I've heard you sort of panicky.
ROBERT	I'm fine.
RIVKA	You look kind of ill. It was the cotton candy wasn't it?
ROBERT	I just went on this thing because you kicked up such a fuss. I said I'd wait for you on the ground. I even offered to win you one of those ridiculous stuffed animals as consolation for going up alone.
RIVKA	Oh, my god, you're afraid of heights.
ROBERT	*(he is).* No, I'm not.
RIVKA	Why didn't you tell me?
ROBERT	How long is he going to keep us up here?
RIVKA	Only fifteen minutes.
ROBERT	Fifteen minutes!
RIVKA	I didn't know. I'm sorry. It seemed like a good idea at the time.

ROBERT	Everyone's looking up. *(looking down and the swing tilts)* Uaaah.
RIVKA	I thought it would be neat to be up here and I just wanted to talk to you alone.
ROBERT	We couldn't be alone in my car. No, you want to be alone with fifteen hundred people.
RIVKA	I thought we could have a quiet, romantic talk.
ROBERT	You want romantic? I love you. There, now tell the man to let us down.
RIVKA	Do you know, that's the first time you've told me you love me without undressing me.
ROBERT	Is that what's bothering you? You think I don't love you. I loved you when I was undressing you. I love you now, I'll love you even more when we're on the ground.
RIVKA	How much?
ROBERT	What do you mean, how much?
RIVKA	How much do you love me?
ROBERT	I'll tell you how much I love you when you tell me how much I have to pay to get us down.
RIVKA	Do you love me lots?
ROBERT	Lots and lots. Can we go now?
RIVKA	In a minute, I promise.
ROBERT	Barbara, you've got sixty seconds before I shout obscenities and threats down to that man. Now, what is it you want to say?
RIVKA	Robert, I love you.
ROBERT	Great, that only took two seconds.
RIVKA	I haven't finished yet.
ROBERT	Go ahead. *(looking down)* Uh.

RIVKA	Look into my eyes. Don't look down, just pretend we're sitting on a bench.
ROBERT	We are sitting on a bench, four thousand feet in the air.
RIVKA	I told you, I thought it would be romantic.
ROBERT	We'll see how romantic you feel when I throw up.
RIVKA	*(faster)* It's just that I love you and you love me, but I know that you're going away to Calgary in the fall. What will we do?
ROBERT	We'll write, we'll phone each other. You'll see me when you can. I'll come up on weekends.
RIVKA	Can't you think of any alternatives?
ROBERT	Barbara, I'm going away to join the police force.
RIVKA	Maybe I could go with you?
ROBERT	Oh, I don't think that's practical.
RIVKA	Maybe if you asked me to marry you?
ROBERT	*(taken aback)* Marry you?
RIVKA	Yeah, what do you think?
ROBERT	I didn't think about it.
RIVKA	So think about it now.
ROBERT	We've only been going out for a week.
RIVKA	Doesn't it seem like we've known each other longer, much longer?
ROBERT	*(taken aback)* You're not going to keep me up here until I propose, are you?
RIVKA	No.
ROBERT	So I don't get it. Why are we up here?
RIVKA	Well, Daisy was proposed to in a hot air balloon and I thought that was just the most romantic thing so

ROBERT	So you couldn't find a balloon, so you got a Ferris wheel.
RIVKA	I didn't know you didn't like heights. You should have told me.
ROBERT	It never came up. This is Stettler. We don't even have a highrise.
RIVKA	*(beat)* So?
ROBERT	So? What?
RIVKA	So, what do you think about us getting married?
ROBERT	Are you proposing to me?
RIVKA	I'm trying to get you to propose to me.
ROBERT	I'll think about it.
RIVKA	Think about it now. *(taking his hand)* We wouldn't spoil our wedding night being nervous, we've already practiced that bit.
ROBERT	*(still annoyed)* Yes, we have.
RIVKA	I'd be a great wife — honest, and mother.
ROBERT	Mother? You're not, er, are you?
RIVKA	No.
ROBERT	Oh, good. I just had a flashback of us sitting in a sandbox.
RIVKA	*(giggling, surprised)* You remember that?
ROBERT	It scarred me for life. I was really upset. I told my mother, who laughed at me and proceeded to tell all the neighbours and they all laughed at me.
RIVKA	I'm sorry.
ROBERT	You said you knew we were going to get married, so we might as well get it over with.
RIVKA	It was a feeling I had.

ROBERT	As a kid you feel hot, cold, hungry, you don't feel married.
RIVKA	More like a dream then.
ROBERT	A dream.
RIVKA	Yeah, I saw you much older. You're going to lose your hair you know, but it's okay, I'll still love you. Anyway, there's you and there's me in this house with a teenager, a boy. I think he's our son. We're about forty.
ROBERT	Yeah, what do you look like?
RIVKA	Gorgeous still.
ROBERT	Not wrinkled, or fat?
RIVKA	No, I promise.
ROBERT	Okay.
RIVKA	Okay?
ROBERT	I'll marry you.
RIVKA	You will?
ROBERT	Sure.
RIVKA	You didn't propose to me, yet how do you know I'll say yes.

* * *

Available from Playwrights Union of Canada - copyscript.

Sacred Hearts

Colleen Curran

In the midst of a crisis over having given her daughter up for adoption, Bridget experiences a miracle. Is it a miracle, as the townspeople fervently believe, a psychic occurrence, or Bridget's way of dealing with her guilt?

> BRIDGET *is tending a flock of sheep on a hill in a small Quebec town.* EVAN, *who runs the local newspaper, pays a visit.*

EVAN   *(calling off)* Hello up there.

BRIDGET   Go away.

EVAN   *(arriving)* Too late.

BRIDGET   Why does everyone think they can come up here?
                 This is my work space.

EVAN   It is open space.

BRIDGET   That needs a big fence.

EVAN   An electric one. And maybe a few attack sheepdogs. What
                 a view.

BRIDGET   Where's your wool?

EVAN   No, I don't need a wool alibi today. I'm here on official
                 business.

BRIDGET   You figure an interview with me will boost circulation?

EVAN   It's quite a story.

BRIDGET   Just the one you've been waiting for.

EVAN   Don't be like that. You expect me not to write anything
                 about it just because we're friends?

BRIDGET   I don't expect you to come out with a Special Edition.

EVAN   That was Gretchen exaggerating.

BRIDGET	Oh. So the stuff about you trying to prove it's fake is made up too?
EVAN	No. I am investigating all possibilities.
BRIDGET	It makes a better story. Even if it means devastating all the people who go to the shrine.
EVAN	I don't see you up there everyday. Maybe I could get your reaction to a couple of things.
BRIDGET	No.
EVAN	Father Phil gave me his.
BRIDGET	Did he?
EVAN	Do you think he could be behind this?
BRIDGET	Oh you're pathetic, you really are.
EVAN	He might have used you.
BRIDGET	What?
EVAN	By setting you up. You were the perfect person to witness it.
BRIDGET	Get out. Get off my hill.
EVAN	He's always been unhappy about being here.
BRIDGET	So he staged this event to get back at everyone?
EVAN	No, to get himself sent somewhere else. Or to get attention. He's stuck here. He might as well be important and influential.
BRIDGET	How can you be so cynical?
EVAN	How can you be so naive?
BRIDGET	He's not that kind of man.
EVAN	He's already been interviewed on national television.
BRIDGET	By Gretchen. You were too.

EVAN	And what did he do? Did he say 'I cannot pass judgment on this occurrence' the way priests are supposed to? No, he said 'It is a miracle' and then started naming off his causes.
BRIDGET	And how did he pull off this miracle all by himself?
EVAN	It's only a theory, right now.
BRIDGET	Got any more? Wbo else do you suspect?
EVAN	The village. Do you know how much money this sort of event generates?
BRIDGET	So, if it wasn't Father Phil it, was the Town Council? Lead by Violet Leahy, I guess.
EVAN	They're possibilities, I said.
BRIDGET	You must have more than three.
EVAN	Yes.
BRIDGET	But you won't consider the most impossible one of all. It might be something you can't explain away.
EVAN	No. I don't believe in miracles.
BRIDGET	What do you believe in, Evan?
EVAN	I don't believe that I was chosen to receive messages from above.
BRIDGET	It's not like that.
EVAN	They might be using you.
BRIDGET	They're not. Why do you want to prove something as terrible as that?
EVAN	Because if I can't, there's only one possibility left.
BRIDGET	And what's that? If it wasn't natural causes and it wasn't a miracle or Father Phil or the village, who was it?
EVAN	*(pausing)* You.
BRIDGET	Me?

EVAN	You told me you cracked up once.
BRIDGET	I did. I never thought you'd use it against me.
EVAN	I didn't want to. I mean, I'm not.
BRIDGET	But you might have to, right, if you can't prove anything else? Maybe you'd like to tell everyone about the baby I gave up for adoption?
EVAN	You see how difficult it is for me?
BRIDGET	You'd actually include that in a story?
EVAN	If I'm going to write an honest story, I'd have to. I'm a journalist.
BRIDGET	Oh God. You're a prize.
EVAN	The statue that turned toward you isn't just any statue, it is one of the Blessed Virgin Mary. And she has all these complicated religious connotations for you. Especially in terms of being pure and perfect.
BRIDGET	And because of this I went up and turned the statue around? I must be pretty strong.
EVAN	I didn't say you did it, categorically.
BRIDGET	But how could I turn the statue? Uncategorically?
EVAN	Severe trauma and stress often causes manifestations. It's a psychic phenomenon.
BRIDGET	Oh really? And what caused my severe trauma and stress?
EVAN	This need to be pure.
BRIDGET	And why did I feel that I wasn't pure?
EVAN	Because of you and me.
BRIDGET	WHAT?
EVAN	*(lowering voice)* You and me.
BRIDGET	You and me what? Nothing happened.

EVAN   It almost did.

BRIDGET   No it didn't.

EVAN   I'm a married man, you felt guilty about that.

BRIDGET   So that's why this happened? I went to the statue of Our Lady and said, 'Please forgive me. I'm interested in a married man and I almost made him be unfaithful to his marriage vows,' and this activated my psychic powers?

EVAN   Maybe.

BRIDGET   Oh that's a terrific story, Evan. Run it on the front page.

EVAN   I can't involve me. I mean, I won't run that.

BRIDGET   You must think you're pretty wonderful. Because the minute a woman rejects you, no matter how good the reason, there must be something really wrong with her.

EVAN   No.

BRIDGET   Or was I the first woman who didn't fall for your 'If I wasn't married' approach?

EVAN   Yes. I mean no. I'm not good at affairs. I never had one before. I still haven't. I am a very married man. Saturday was the closest I ever came to cheating on my marriage. Honest to God.

BRIDGET   Well, I'm sure glad you didn't succeed.

EVAN   Me, too. I mean, if I had, look at what a wreck I am now.

BRIDGET   I am so sorry for your wife. You're such a hypocrite. You told me that you respected the fact that I was such a spiritual person. But the moment something happens that proves you're right, I'm a freak. And I'm crazy. I thought you were so. . .I thought you could be a friend.

EVAN   Look, I'm trying to understand this—

BRIDGET   No, you're trying to tear it down and take whatever's left and make it fit so that you don't feel rotten about nearly cheating on your marriage with a woman who's a religious maniac. You can tear it down all you want, you can weasel around and try to destroy this miracle but all you're going to get is speculation. You can't believe in anything greater than yourself. Go write your story, Evan and put out your Special Edition. But I promise you something.

EVAN What?

BRIDGET If you include any information about my baby I will make sure that everybody finds out what almost happened the night I told you. Go. Hurry up, Evan. You've got a deadline to meet.

* * *

Published by Playwrights Canada Press - trade paperback.

Gravel Run

Conni Massing

A wildly dysfunctional family plans a small-town wedding for a prodigal daughter, Leona, who comes home after a five-year absence with her fiancée, Len.

> LEN *and* LEONA *at the dining room table writing their vows.* LEN *is dressed in blue jeans, plaid shirt and brand new cowboy boots.*

LEN   To have and to hold?

LEONA   Sounds like real estate.

LEN   But I've always liked that. How about cherish?

LEONA   Cherish till we perish —

LEN   Leona...

LEONA   To have and to hold is fine.

LEN   Well if you're not happy with it —

LEONA   It's fine. Alright. Are we still having this Kahlil Gibran reading?

LEN   No, not necessarily. Your Mama suggested a poem.

LEONA   Oh no...it's not *The Cremation of Sam McGee* is it?

LEN   Of course it's not —

LEONA   She loves that poem.

LEN   It's a...traditional piece which...equates marriage with a good cake recipe.

LEONA   Yeah?

LEN   I know it sounds hokey but it's really quite clever. The ingredients it takes to make a good marriage and a good...cake. What makes a good cake rise and —

LEONA   *(quoting)* 'The beauty's in the batter when a love cake' s in the making. What makes it sweet and so complete —' Oh for crying out loud, Len. She's got you sold on having Lydia Harmon sing *My Best to You* at the bloody signing of the register and now this —

LEN   She's a friend of the family —

LEONA   She can't sing! She was kicked in the throat by a cow —

LEN   She what?

LEONA   Oh never mind. She sings like an angel. But this poem —

LEN   I think it's kind of important to her. I'm not sure but I think she might have written it. She wants Sarah to recite it at the reception.

LEONA   God help me, I wish I'd never mentioned her. Now that Mama thinks Sarah's coming she's really gone into high gear. It's not my wedding anymore — it's a homecoming party for Sarah.

LEN   We don't have to decide right now, about the poem.

LEONA   I hope not. So where were we?

LEN   Cherish, to have and to hold.

LEONA   Oh, right.

LEN   You still haven't forgiven me, have you?

LEONA   Do you want the bit about 'till death do us part'?

LEN   Leona, I'm sorry about dragging that tree into the house.

LEONA   What are you sorry about? Did I say anything? It's just a hunk of birch, Len.

LEN   It's gone now. I put it in Billy's truck.

LEONA   Fine.

LEN   *(after a pause.)* What was Nelson Eddy like, Leona?

LEONA	Why?
LEN	I know we agreed but I just...I'd like to know.
LEONA	He wore tight jeans.
LEN	Yeah?
LEONA	Yeah.
LEN	Leona, it's important to me.
LEONA	He smelled like whisky and *Export A* cigarettes. It was a nice smell. He had lashes an inch long. Curly lashes. And he wore tight jeans.
LEN	Is that why you...fell in love with him?
LEONA	Len...
LEN	Please.
LEONA	Alright. I guess I liked...he'd do anything for a nickel. He was always on the edge of doing something unacceptable. He was wild.
LEN	He sounds rather...imposing.
LEONA	He had an awful temper. He had a signet ring that was all scratched from him banging his fist into walls. He had green eyes, like a cat, only they were huge. And lips. Big, purple lips that tasted like whisky and cigarettes. But mostly whisky.
LEN	He was a drinker.
LEONA	No, Len. He wasn't a 'drinker'. Not anymore than Billy's a drinker. *(pause.)* He was a lot like Billy actually. Quite a lot.
LEN	Billy can drink, alright.
LEONA	But you can't, can you? A little too much hooch makes you dig up graveyards and sing songs that don't belong to you.
LEN	You see — you're still mad.
LEONA	You were never meant to know —

LEN   Know what? That you had a boyfriend in high school?
                    That seems to me a pretty standard confidence between
                    two people who are getting married —

LEONA   Oh, that ain't the half of it.

LEN   So what's the other half of it? *(pause, as* LEONA *doesn't
                    respond)* Billy said Nelson Eddy was killed in a hunting
                    accident.

LEONA   An accident?

LEN   Well yes...

LEONA   Then you know all about it. He was killed in a hunting
                    accident.

LEN   Because he wasn't wearing a red hat.

LEONA   *(laughing)* That's right. That's what Papa said. And Papa
                    would know.

LEN   Wait just a minute here —

LEONA   I left town shortly afterwards. Three hours later.

LEN   Now hold on, Leona. You're not accusing your own father
                    of —

LEONA   I never accused anybody of anything. Rest in peace — good
                    riddance. The only person I talked to before I left was Mama.

LEN   What?

LEONA   He had a big mouth. Big lips, remember? One of the things
                    I liked best about him. He used to pull into that driveway
                    singing *Bee-Bop* at the top of his lungs. When he wasn't
                    singing he was talking. It wasn't a good quality in this
                    family. If you know something you keep it to yourself.

LEN   Your mother was telling me, she used to wait up for you.
                    She worried a lot —

LEONA   Look, Len — the less you know the better off you'll be.
                    Rest in peace. Nelson Eddy just wasn't well liked around
                    here.

LEN   He was well liked by you and Billy.

LEONA	We...had a hell of a good time.
LEN	*(after a pause.)* Why did you fall in love with me?
LEONA	You were...different from anyone I'd ever met before. You'd never farmed a quarter section, gone to a drive-in, or de-horned cattle...
LEN	Leona, I like it here.
LEONA	I'm glad, Len. A nice place to visit.
LEN	It's peaceful.
LEONA	Are you crazy? I've hardly slept since we've been here.
LEN	It's simple. Things are simpler —
LEONA	I keep having nightmares — not the scary monster kind — the slow, creepy ones where everything quietly goes wrong.
LEN	I really like your family. And they like me —
LEONA	I had one last night that Mama stood up in church and disowned me. 'She's not my daughter — we're not paying for this.' People started jumping through stained-glass windows —
LEN	Leona, you're not listening to me. I said I like it here. I wouldn't mind staying for a while. I wouldn't mind —
LEONA	Len, are you serious?
LEN	I mean it —
LEONA	You're getting sucked into the centre of the house —
LEN	I know what's happening to me — I like it. You didn't think I'd fit in, did you?
LEONA	Oh you're fitting in alright. You're — where did you get those clothes anyway?
LEN	Mama bought the shirt for me and I bought the jeans —
LEONA	What the hell's happening to you?

LEN	Why did you bring me here if you didn't think they'd like me?
LEONA	I wanted Mama to — I wanted her to stop worrying — I wanted to make her happy —
LEN	Well she's happy, isn't she?
LEONA	Oh sure — she's delirious.
LEN	Well if you're having second thoughts, I guess now's the time to say.
LEONA	I'm having second thoughts about the damn three-ring circus. It's not our wedding —
LEN	Then whose wedding —
LEONA	I just want — darn it, Len. I know all the conventional wisdom about weddings being for the parents. But this is different. This is all for Mama and I don't think she even knows it. This wedding —
LEN	This wedding or this marriage?
LEONA	The wedding, Len. For God's sake, you know what I mean. That poem and the Legion Hall and — oh never mind. I'll be fine as soon as we get out of this goddamn house, as soon as Mama...*(pause)* You've changed, that's all.
LEN	So have you. You're unhappy. But I'm having fun. And I think your mother would appreciate it if we didn't rush off after the wedding.
LEONA	Yes I know. I know she'd appreciate it.
LEN	*(after a pause)* Where were we then? The vows.
LEONA	What? Oh...I don't know.
LEN	Till death do us part. How do you feel about that?

* * *

Published by Blizzard Publishing - trade paperback

Martha Ross and Robert Morgan in the 1987 Theatre Columbus
production of *The Anger in Ernest and Ernestine.*
Photo by Amir Gavriely.

The Anger in Ernest and Ernestine

Robert Morgan, Leah Cherniak, Martha Ross

*In this surrealistic play, Ernest and Ernestine live a perfectly ordered existence,
but when cracks appear in the veneer, their repression gives way to dark,
humourous rage.*

> *Moving day in the new basement apartment, an
> empty packing box is on the table.* ERNEST *and*
> ERNESTINE *enter and come down the stair unit
> which slowly swings down as they make their
> descent. They both carry more boxes,* ERNEST
> *carries a broom.* ERNESTINE *takes a tissue box
> and places it on the table then crosses to the
> cupboard shelves to put away books, bowls,
> paper towels, etc.* ERNEST *takes the tissue box
> from the table and puts it in his box.*

ERNESTINE   I love our basement home Ernest.

ERNEST   It's like a dream Ernestine.

> *They rub noses and coo "widgy widgy woo".*

ERNEST   It's so warm. Snug as a rug on a bug. Snug as two rugs
on two bugs ahuggin'.

ERNESTINE   I can't believe I'm going to see you every day.

ERNEST   Every day. Day after day. *(more cooing)* I'm going to put
my hammer up here on the shelf sweetie.

ERNESTINE   *(joyfully resuming her unpacking)* Uh-huh.

ERNEST   And the new broom close by...

ERNESTINE   Uh-huh.

ERNEST   And the cereal right here in the bookshelf...and your
teapot over...What's this?

ERNESTINE   Sweetie they're teabags.

ERNEST	Sweetie you should always take the teabags out of the teapot.
ERNESTINE	Oh sweetie, Aunt Mildred always said you're supposed to leave them in. That way the teapot gets a nice roasty flavour of tea over the years.
ERNEST	That's tannic acid. Tannic acid is really bad.
ERNESTINE	Oh?
ERNEST	You should always, always take the teabags out of the teapot. It's not good sweetie, it's bad.
ERNESTINE	Oh of course, sweetie. That Aunt Mildred!
ERNEST	So, I thought I'd put your teapot up here on the shelf.
ERNESTINE	I thought, sweetie, we should keep it in the cupboard.
ERNEST	In the cupboard?! Okay. *(more cooing)* We need more shelves. Your things would fit here and my things would fit here but together they don't fit.
	They both laugh nervously. ERNEST unwittingly puts the hammer back into the box he is holding. He then places the tissue box on the top shelf, turns and sees a package of cigarettes on the table.
ERNEST	What's that?
ERNESTINE	It's my cigarettes, sweetie.
ERNEST	You don't smoke them?
ERNESTINE	Well, I didn't bother to tell you Ernest because I smoke maybe one cigarette a year on very cold nights.
ERNEST	I guess you won't have to worry about that in this place. Boy oh boy, this furnace really chugs out the heat!
	ERNEST *takes off his jacket-sweater and goes to hang it on the coatrack.*
ERNESTINE	I'll just put them away for that one nice cold winter night sweetie.

> ERNESTINE *"hides" her cigarettes in the*
> *cupboard then takes the tissue box from the shelf*
> *and puts it back on the table.*

ERNEST   I'll just put this empty box in the closet sweetie.

ERNESTINE   Oh Ernest, I thought that we could put all the coats on the
coatrack, and the sweaters in the sweater drawer.

ERNEST   What a good idea!

> ERNESTINE *takes the sweater-jacket towards the*
> *bedroom.*

ERNEST   Where are you going with my jacket?

ERNESTINE   This? This is a sweater.

ERNEST   What? No, no sweetie, that's my jacket.

ERNESTINE   Isn't that funny, I was sure it was a sweater.

ERNEST   This? *(taking his jacket-sweater)* No, it's my good jacket.
I've had it ever since I was in Boy Cubs with Mr. Garlic.

> ERNEST *hangs his jacket-sweater on the*
> *coatrack and moves the tissue box back to the*
> *shelf. He turns and becomes transfixed, staring*
> *into space.*

ERNESTINE   Ernest? — Ernest! — ERNEST!

ERNEST   What? *(both jumping)* Oh, I'm sorry sweetie, I forgot you
were here. It's like a dream.

ERNESTINE   Ernest, what were you looking at?

ERNEST   Oh, I was thinking I could paint a window. This is my
first basement home and I think I'll miss the windows,
but I could paint one for myself...with the sun streaming
in, the rain and the lightning, the leaves changing colours,
antelope running free.

ERNESTINE   Oh Ernest, I was so lucky to meet a man like you!

ERNEST   Ah, me too sweetie.

ERNESTINE	Ernest, I have a little something for you, for us. Close your eyes — No peeking — Come sit down. *(running to the closet)*
ERNEST	*(sitting)* Can I open my eyes now?
ERNESTINE	Not yet sweetie. *(placing a gaudy artificial plant on the table)* Okay you can open your eyes now.
ERNEST	Golly. Boy oh boy, look at that.
ERNESTINE	Do you like it sweetie?
ERNEST	Yes, oh yes. It's so darn colourful.
ERNESTINE	I like it because it doesn't pretend to be anything that it's not.
ERNEST	No, look at that, it doesn't pretend. It just sits there. You don't have to water it.
ERNESTINE	No.
ERNEST	Won't grow, won't ever change. Where're you gonna put it?
ERNESTINE	Are you sure you like it sweetie?
ERNEST	Yes, oh yes!
ERNESTINE	Well, I thought maybe it could go right here. *(crossing to cupboard and putting the plant on the top shelf)*
ERNEST	Would you look at that!
ERNESTINE	What?
ERNEST	There must be, how many places are there in our basement home?
ERNESTINE	Well, I suppose...
ERNEST	2000. Over 2000! And you picked the perfect spot!
ERNESTINE	Oh!
ERNEST	Sweetie, you're an artist.
ERNESTINE	No Ernest, you're the artist.

ERNEST   Ernestine you have art in you.

                    Strange sounds erupt. ERNESTINE *realizes it's
                    the furnace.* ERNEST *stands transfixed, staring at
                    the plant. As the sounds grow louder and more
                    ominous the furnace begins to glow. Steam
                    seeps from the furnace and its pipes.*

ERNESTINE   Ernest it's the furnace.

ERNEST   Hmmm?

ERNESTINE   It's the furnace Ernest. ERNEST!

ERNEST   It's the furnace Ernestine. To your stations!

ERNESTINE   What do we do Ernest? What do we do?

ERNEST   *(grabbing the furnace manual hanging above the furnace)*
                    We look at the book that the landlord left. We must
                    follow the rules calmly, methodically, thoroughly, step
                    by step.

ERNESTINE   Ernest we have to do something!

ERNEST   Step by step. First step: 'Get the hammer.' Get the
                    hammer sweetie.

                    ERNESTINE *looks in the cupboard.*

ERNESTINE   There is no hammer.

ERNEST   Of courses there's a hammer, I put it right up here on
                    the...where's my hammer?

                    ERNESTINE *kicks the furnace.*

ERNEST   No, No! Step two: 'Get the ratchet.'

ERNESTINE   What's a ratchet?

ERNEST   What's a ratchet?

ERNESTINE   What's a ratchet?

ERNEST   A ratchet is a ratchet.

ERNESTINE   Well what does a ratchet look like?

ERNEST   It looks like a ratchet.

ERNESTINE   Well good for it!

ERNEST   Don't 'good for it' Ernestine, just get it! Calmly go and get the ratchet that looks like a ratchet!

> ERNESTINE *pulls the widget on the furnace.*

ERNEST   No, not the widget!

ERNESTINE   What's a widget?

ERNEST   That's a widget!

ERNESTINE   How am I supposed to know what a widget is?

ERNEST   Don't pull the...

ERNESTINE   I don't know what the...

ERNEST   Dddd —

ERNESTINE   I —

> *The commotion of the furnace subsides. Pause.*

ERNEST   Boy oh boy.

ERNESTINE   Whew wee.

ERNEST   I guess we fixed it.

ERNESTINE   Yeah we did Ernest.

ERNEST   Good thing we followed the rules.

ERNESTINE   Yeah, good thing we followed the rules and I pulled the widget.

ERNEST   Boy oh boy. *(coming towards each other and meeting)* These old beasts can be pretty temperamental. Pretty temperamental.

* * *

Published by Playwrights Canada Press - trade paperback

Kristallnacht

Richard Epp

Fritz has spent most of World War II in a P.O.W. camp for German soldiers near Medicine Hat, where he is trying to erase the memory of his involvement in Kristallnacht, the night of shattering glass. Allowed to work for a local farmer, he forms a close relationship with Laura Ferguson, a young woman impatient to leave her "ordinary" life behind.

	Evening. LAURA *and* FRITZ *are sitting on the porch. They have been there for some time.*
FRITZ	*(reading from the newspaper)* Oh how pleased and thrilled was Sally, When the Captain got so pally; But, alas, the romance ended — We all perspire, but she offended. *(to* LAURA*)* Somebody selling soap. *(as* LAURA *doesn't respond, he goes on)* Early Blizzard Sweeps Sask. *(to* LAURA*)* Should I read that one? *(silence again)* Getting cooler, alright. *(reading)* Grade One Class Buys Victory Bond. The grade one class of Elm Street School yesterday signed their names to a victory bond. Six-year old Corrie Gibney, spokesman for the patriotic group, said they bought it...
LAURA	...To make sure that bad man Hitler doesn't come to Canada. I read it.
FRITZ	The stars over Canada tonight...
LAURA	*(simultaneously)* We should have gone to the movies.
FRITZ	Eh?
LAURA	The movies. Every evening it's the same thing.
FRITZ	Ja. Oh, no good?
LAURA	No. What about the stars over Canada tonight?
FRITZ	Nothing. Same as last night.
LAURA	Nothing ever changes. The war drags on; the world keeps passing me by.

FRITZ	No word from *The Star Weekly*?
LAURA	Your story was too dull. If I were over in Europe they'd pay attention. The wire service would be sizzling with my bylines. All the action, from both sides. Tom was there; he saw it. Riding a bomber. The thrilling life of a gunner.
FRITZ	Dangerous, too.
LAURA	The gunners hate those little window bubbles, perspex they're called. They get all scratched up from polishing and up high they frost over. So Tom flies with it open. Keeps his head low, crammed in there behind the guns.
FRITZ	It's the same in a tank. Crammed.
LAURA	The cold air makes the guns freeze up, so you use antifreeze gel. If you use too much the guns jam completely. Cold on the hands, too. Take your gloves off, your fingers freeze; keep them on, you can't shoot. All the while you're watching for the shadow of an enemy fighter. You drop your load in Happy Valley, make a split-ass turn for the Channel, 'Let's take her home, boys, balls to the wall!' *(becoming silent)*
FRITZ	Maybe when the war is over he comes home.
LAURA	Who'd want to come home to this? Potatoes. Mountains of potatoes. Silage corn, for Pete's sake.
FRITZ	You can make good schnapps with corn.
LAURA	Oh, that changes everything.
FRITZ	Okay, you are bored. I will tell you a story.
LAURA	Thanks, but...
FRITZ	Once upon a time in a German prison camp...*(whistling or humming a line or two of the German anthem)*
LAURA	Don't whistle that dumb song.
FRITZ	It's *Deutschlandlied*.
LAURA	I know what it is and it's verboten here.
FRITZ	Did I ever tell you what we do at the camp?

LAURA *is not interested, but* FRITZ *continues.*

FRITZ	Our band, you know, they are not supposed to play that song at concerts. Only official occasions, which means funerals.
LAURA	What band?
FRITZ	Listen. One time they take a concert program to the guards for approval. They don't have to, but it's part of the fun. And it was there on the list — the German National Anthem, only it was called Haydn's *String Quartet, Number Seventy-Six.* When the band begins to play the guards are sure surprised. 'It's just Haydn,' everybody says, 'number seventy-six.' *(pause)* You can play that trick only once.
LAURA	It's a hideous song — Germany above all else in the world.
FRITZ	Sure, the words they use now — pretty strong stuff. But the music is still good.
LAURA	It's in our hymnbook at church.
FRITZ	When it's played I feel a link with the past, with heritage, with the real Germany. Hitler, well what can we do about that?
LAURA	You elected him.
FRITZ	Not me. It was the time. Everybody was fed up to here with inflation, taxes, stupidity. The Worker's Party was going to give us back our self-respect. And he was so convincing. I heard him once at the rally. It is extraordinary, you know, the power he has. I came away thinking I had heard God. We were going to make the world over again. And my own pride, woo, boosted way up. I was twice the man I was before. Afterwards I ran straight to a shop and bought my mother a portrait of Adolf Hitler. She hung it in her bedroom so she could see it when she said her prayers. First thing I do when I get home is find that picture and tear it into a thousand pieces.
LAURA	Who knows what we'll do after the war?
FRITZ	I do. There is a dream gets every day clearer in my mind. Do you know who's in that dream?

LAURA	Who?
FRITZ	You.
LAURA	Me?
FRITZ	You will be my wife.
LAURA	Your w...what?
FRITZ	My wife. Sure. I was going to ask you.
LAURA	To marry you?
FRITZ	Yes.
LAURA	You're not serious.
FRITZ	Sometimes.
LAURA	I mean, goodness, Fritz, I'm your friend.
FRITZ	Good friend.
LAURA	I guess I've never thought of you and me as anything more or less than friends.
FRITZ	I thought young ladies dreamed of marriage.
LAURA	Did you?
FRITZ	Don't they?
LAURA	Among other things. Like seeing the world.
FRITZ	It's nothing special, the world. Here in the spring it is so green. Once I looked through the fence toward your farm and saw rows and rows of green and rich brown — the way the earth was meant to be. It was after a rain.
LAURA	You told me there was nothing to see. Miles and miles of nothing.
FRITZ	I was so blind 'til I met you.
LAURA	Oh, dear.
FRITZ	I have surprised you.

LAURA   Just a little. Fritz, Alfred, who can say what we'll feel like
               after...the end.

FRITZ   I know. I'm coming back here. I'm going to fill out the
               papers as soon as I get home.

LAURA   You want to come back here?

FRITZ   It's good here. There is food, land, dreams.

LAURA   There are always dreams. Don't take them too seriously.

FRITZ   That's not what Laura Ferguson Hill believes.

LAURA   Besides, you have a mother and father who miss you.

FRITZ   A man leaves his family when it is time. I want to stay.
               So I hope the war is over soon. I'm pretty good tanner or
               maybe there is a small farm to start with.

LAURA   Wait a minute.

FRITZ   Best of all, there is you.

LAURA   No, it's not me you want.

FRITZ   I think so.

LAURA   Food, land, dreams.

FRITZ   That, too.

LAURA   Rows and rows of green.

FRITZ   Back home will be nothing left.

LAURA   Boy, you are really something, you know that? It's finally
               coming out. You're an opportunist, that's what you are.

FRITZ   Op...?

LAURA   You can't lose. If the war had gone better for you you'd
               have marched back home whistling *Deutschlandlied*. As it
               is you just kiss your country good-bye. 'Sorry, I got osser
               plans.' Boy, you are a heck of a patriot, you are!

FRITZ   No, you don't understand.

LAURA	I do understand. You want everything handed to you. You want to marry me because you have no ambition. *(beat)* I'm going inside.
FRITZ	Wait a minute!
LAURA	*(going)* 'I thought young ladies dreamed of marriage.'
FRITZ	Laura *(calling after her through the screen door)* ...We'll talk about it later.

* * *

Available from Playwrights Union of Canada - copyscript.

Communication

F. David Peat

An exploration of a relationship from first encounter to break-up. This is a relationship based upon communication and miscommunication; upon words and their interpretations and misinterpretations; upon the difference between saying what you mean and meaning what you say. At this point in the play the cracks have begun to show and words are turning into weapons.

At a fast-food restaurant.

SHE	Would you say I was fat?
HE	Fat? No you're not fat. *(pause)* Not *fat.*
SHE	Well would you say I was thin then?
HE	Er...
SHE	No seriously. I'm serious. Would you say I was thin?
HE	Thin? You could say...not exactly thin but...
SHE	Go on.
HE	Well, you're...just right.You're...erm, nicely built.
SHE	Built? .
HE	No...not exactly, more...
SHE	Well built?
HE	No. I didn't mean anything like that. You're just, well...you're just right — not too fat, not fat at all and er...not too thin. Well you couldn't exactly say you were skinny, could you? You're not emaciated. Not one of those anorexics.
SHE	Just right?
HE	That's it. *(laughing)* Just right. Just right for me.

SHE	So I'm not as fat as that woman over there.
HE	God no...she's really fat.
SHE	Just right. Well...now...that other one, the one going over to that table.
HE	Look, I've told you...you're not fat. She's fat...just look at her. This is ridiculous.
SHE	All right. Well tell me then. Point someone out. Go on, point to someone who looks just like me. Someone that's just right.
HE	No...that's stupid. I can't...I mean, I can't find someone that looks exactly like you.
SHE	I didn't say exactly...just someone who looks approximately like me. *(pause)* Well? Go on.
HE	Well...er...No, this is crazy.
SHE	There's no point to my trying is there? There's no point to my going on a diet...not if you won't tell me. I just want to be objective about it all.
HE	Objective?
SHE	Yes, objective, scientific, detached.
HE	Oh well, in that case. Let me see...hang on...that one over there, the one just coming in the door. The blond with the white sweater.
SHE	The tight white sweater?
HE	Yes, she looks pretty good doesn't she? She's about your shape.
SHE	And I look like that, do I ?
HE	What? Er...well not quite then...er not exactly.

SHE God, what's the point. I wonder why I don't let myself go for good, wear polyester suits and tennis shoes. God I knew you'd say that, I knew you'd pick her. Go on then, buy me a Whopper and a double order of French Fries. I may as well give up all together. I don't know why we go out together. I don't even know why we're even sitting here.

HE But what did I say?

***

Available from Playwrights Union of Canada - copyscript

Fair Game

Karen Wikberg

Janet is a ruthless business woman; devotion to the deal comes before all else. Gordon, her husband and all her friends are shocked by her actions. Only her young artist lover shares her passion and vision.

JANET *is casually dressed.* GORDON *enters from hallway, straightening his tie.*

JANET	Your meeting's at eleven, right? You'd better get going.
GORDON	Good morning honey. Any coffee?
JANET	There. *(indicating coffee in container on dining table)*
GORDON	Thanks.
JANET	That was extremely inappropriate!
GORDON	I bet you're dying to know how much I won. Come on, guess. *(getting no response)* Three thousand, one hundred and fifty-six smackeroos. Impressed?
JANET	You ruined her birthday!
GORDON	I told the truth.
JANET	Oh god! *(starting to read the paper)*
GORDON	You know Jake Brown is retiring?
JANET	Who cares?
GORDON	Fifty-five years old. He and his wife set out next week. They're sailing to Mexico. All the way down the coast. Sounds good, doesn't it?
JANET	Aren't you a little young to plan your retirement?

GORDON	I don't think sailing is really for me. I'd like a little cabin — maybe on Saltspring or even one of the smaller islands. Wouldn't that be great? Chopping wood — growing our own vegetables.
JANET	I can't imagine anything more boring.
GORDON	*(laughing)* I knew you'd say that.
JANET	Well, why on earth would you want to retire early? Don't you like your work? Doesn't it mean something to you?
GORDON	Some of it. I'd still do the work that mattered to me.
JANET	Don't tell me. Land claims and oil spills.
GORDON	What is wrong with that?
JANET	Nothing! I'm happy for you. I like to see you be as involved in your work as I am in mine. I couldn't stand living with someone who just hung around waiting for me to get home.
GORDON	I want a family.
JANET	What?
GORDON	I think we've waited long enough. I want a child, Janet.
JANET	Oh Gordon!
GORDON	We always said we'd consider it. Talk about it. And when we were both ready...
JANET	I'm not ready.
GORDON	You're not getting any younger.
JANET	This isn't fair.
GORDON	You know what I think? You're never going to let us have a child. You don't want to give up what you've got.
JANET	I will not bring a child into this world just to stick it in daycare or have someone else spend twelve hours a day with it. I'm not interested.
GORDON	Well, I guess that's the bottom line — right there.

JANET   I've got a lot on my mind right now.

GORDON   I guess you do.

Long pause.

JANET   I want to talk to you. But not like this. I don't want us to be angry with each other.

GORDON   Sorry. Hey! Maybe we should go down to your office. Have a proper discussion. Keep our personal feelings out of it.

JANET   If you're not going to be reasonable...

GORDON   Tell me. Go ahead. I'm listening!

JANET   What's wrong with you?

GORDON   I know all about him. That Dan character. God! How could you do it?

JANET   Oh no.

GORDON   You must think I'm a complete fool.

JANET   How did you...

GORDON   It doesn't matter. How long has this been going on behind my back? How many others that I don't know about?

JANET   This has never happened before!

GORDON   I'm supposed to believe that.

JANET   Yes! I wouldn't lie about it. Whatever we've had we've always been honest with each other.

GORDON   That's over obviously.

JANET   I didn't tell you because...I certainly didn't enjoy having an affair behind your back.

GORDON   Well! Now it's in front of my face. Better?

JANET   I didn't want you to know, because I didn't want you to think that it was the cause of a problem between us.

GORDON   Tell me it's not the cause.

JANET	It happened! I'm not the kind of person who has a frivolous affair on the side.
GORDON	But you did.
JANET	Yes. I did. I walked right into it.
GORDON	You're trying to tell me it's symbolic?
JANET	Yes.
GORDON	Bullshit! We had a marriage here. Sure...I've always let you go your own way, but...
JANET	'Let' me?
GORDON	You know what I mean. It's not as if you've been stuck in the kitchen baking cookies.
JANET	Oh, for god's sake!
GORDON	We had no problems! We've been doing fine, until this guy came along.
JANET	Gordon! I cheated on you! If something like this could happen — what do you think it means?
GORDON	It means this guy has come along and screwed up a perfectly good marriage.
JANET	We've drifted apart...
GORDON	More like a landslide.
JANET	Yes! You're right!
GORDON	I don't want you to ever see him again.
JANET	*(sighing)* It doesn't matter whether I see him again or not.
GORDON	It does to me.
JANET	We have to face this.
GORDON	I love you.

JANET   I love you too. I just don't want to be married to you anymore.

GORDON   Oh.

> GORDON *pauses and then exits, leaving* JANET *alone.*

*** *

Available from Playwrights Union of Canada - copyscript

The Butcher's Apron

Charles Tidler

In this dream comedy, August Strindberg falls in love with the young feminist theatre critic, Frida Uhl, and they attempt to forge a new kind of marriage wherein the Feminist and the Superman may co-exist as partners, lovers, and equals. But through an experiement in alchemy, Strindberg has become two people and his doppleganger is out for blood.

At a restaurant table, AUGUST *has paper, and a pen in hand.*

AUGUST   Let us compose, together, the rules of modern marriage.

FRIDA   We two will never be stifled, August?

AUGUST   Never. We shall discover life anew each day. We shall never stand still.

FRIDA   I know nothing about housework.

AUGUST   I don't want you for a wife in order to clean a house. There are maids for that.

FRIDA   I have no talent for diapers.

AUGUST   We shall engage a nurse.

FRIDA   I don't cook.

AUGUST   We shall engage a cook.

FRIDA   Three servants already. But they must be paid, and, without my father, I have no money, only debts.

AUGUST   Me, too.

AUGUST *and* FRIDA *laugh.*

Let's do this. Rule number one. We shall live in three rooms. One for the gentleman...

FRIDA   One for the lady...

AUGUST	Yes. And one for the marriage *(pause)* Rule number two. Catering.
FRIDA	Three. Each to have a door which can be locked. *(pause)*
AUGUST	Four. One may close the door now and then behind one's own thoughts and feelings. *(pause)*
FRIDA	Five. One needs time to think of the other person.

> *Pause.* AUGUST *signs with a flourish, then hands the pen and paper to* FRIDA.

AUGUST	Agreed?
FRIDA	Only five rules?
AUGUST	A pentagram of marital bliss.
FRIDA	Agreed.

> FRIDA *signs.*

AUGUST	Our marriage must never be like, like, like the other. Ohh...

> *Pause.*

FRIDA	Have you any news of your children?
AUGUST	Their mother forbids them to write to their father. Can you imagine such a woman?
FRIDA	I would like to see a photo of your children. Have you got one?
AUGUST	Of course I have. Right here. *(short pause)* Well, I thought I had them right on top here. Never mind, I'll find them. *(rummaging in his bag)* Here they are. *(giving them to her)*
FRIDA	Oh, they're beautiful children. How generous you are, August, to give me your children. Who's this?
AUGUST	*(taking the photo and turning it over and reading)* That's Karin. She wants to be a teacher. And this is Greta. She wants to marry and become a mother. And ...
FRIDA	He's beautiful.

AUGUST	Hans. He wants to be a chemist doing research to prove his father's theories.
FRIDA	How old is Hans?
AUGUST	Five or six...six.
FRIDA	Do you think we could have him?
AUGUST	Hans?
FRIDA	Yes. Do you think his mother would give him up, and we could raise him?
AUGUST	I don't know. She's a very selfish woman.
FRIDA	The world belongs to the man who has such children.
AUGUST	*(taking the photo and beginning to cry)* I don't know where they live.

Pause. FRIDA *reaches out and touches* AUGUST.

FRIDA	Poor stranger.
AUGUST	Well I...I suppose we should go.
FRIDA	Yes, my husband.

AUGUST *puts the photos away. He looks about, taps a spoon against his glass.*

AUGUST	Well, where's the waiter so we can go?
FRIDA	We may go, my husband.
AUGUST	Not until I've paid the bill, we can't.
FRIDA	I invited you, and I paid the bill.
AUGUST	You did?
FRIDA	Yes.
AUGUST	I don't know the customs of Vienna, but here in Berlin, and in Sweden, it's a disgrace for a man to let a lady —
FRIDA	You were my guest.

AUGUST	Don't you understand the sort of reputation you've given me? The names the waiter will hurl upon my back?
FRIDA	Stop acting like a child.
AUGUST	I gave you my heart across this table. You have abused your power, and now must expect the usual fate of a tyrant.
FRIDA	What have I done? Does it make any difference whether I entertain at home or in public? What do I, what do we, the supermoderns, care for custom, or, worn-out conventions?
AUGUST	My heart. Return it immediately.
FRIDA	You're not the man I thought you were.
AUGUST	I demand my heart.
FRIDA	Your fierce wildness has evaporated.

AUGUST *snatches* FRIDA's *bag away from her.*

AUGUST	Give it to me!
FRIDA	You don't love me. You love love.
AUGUST	I love love, very well. You, however, love my disordered affairs because they give you the upper hand in the battle of the sexes for the triumph of the individual ego. *(opening* FRIDA's *bag, getting a package, and putting it into his own green bag)* It belongs to me.
FRIDA	It is undone. We are haters.
AUGUST	Yes, we are enemies. *(getting up from the table)* Good night. *(exiting)*
FRIDA	Good night. *(exiting)*

*** *** ***

Available from Playwrights Union of Canada - copyscript

White Biting Dog

Judith Thompson

In this winner of the Governor General's Literary Award for Drama, which pushes against the boundaries of naturalism, Cape, a suicidal young man is rescued by a white dog which gives him a mission: to save his father from imminent death. His mission flounders until the dog's owner, Pony, comes along and helps him by bringing his reluctant mother back into the family.

	PONY *is heard singing, off. She enters, continuing to sing until she notices* CAPE *when he says 'Hello.'* CAPE *speaks after he has heard the word 'dog' for the second time.*
PONY	Your eyes do shine so bright and clear my dear my Queenie dear 'cause you're my dog my doggie dog I love ya sooo I always will 'cause your eyes do shine so bright and clear my dear my Queenie dear and I hope you never shed a single tear my Queenie dear 'cause you're my dog my doggie—
CAPE	Oh my God! Oh my God that's it this is it she's here - *(running out of the house)* It's — it's — a GIRL!! I guess an angel, kind of a...Hello!
PONY	Oh!
CAPE	I...heard you sing!
PONY	Oh...
CAPE	Don't be...embarrassed it was...what — what— *(intending to ask* PONY *what the answer is, he suddenly realizes that maybe she is* only *a girl)* What — are — you — doing out after — curfew?
PONY	Curfew? There's no curfew here!
CAPE	Yeah but that guy, that guy that strangled the cheerleader, he's still loose!
PONY	I'm not afraid of some weasel. Who are you?

CAPE   I'm...you *know*?

PONY   No.

CAPE   I'm *the guy*. That lives...here. Who are you?

PONY   Just a girl.

CAPE   *Just* a girl?

PONY   I think so.

CAPE   I don't — think so, I think — I mean — if you're just a
                girl what are you doing wandering the streets singing
                songs to a dog?

PONY   Well, to tell you the truth, I'll be honest with ya, I was
                lying on my fold-out in my furnished bachelor on Albany
                and I got this UNRESISTIBLE urge to get up and go out
                for a walk. And when urges like that come along, I listen
                to them so I did. I just walked where my feet took me.

CAPE   — and they took you *here*?

PONY   Well. I don't feel like walking any further.

CAPE   So you don't *know* where you're going? *(realizing PONY
                is an unknowing agent of the dog)*

PONY   Not particularly.

CAPE   You're so brave!

PONY   Ha. You obviously don't know me very well.

CAPE   What, what do you mean?

PONY   I mean that when you've done one-fifty down Thunder Bay
                Road and ya've jumped out and picked up an S.I.D. and
                watched him die right in front of your nose, going out for
                a midnight stroll is tiddlywinks. See?

CAPE   S.I.D.—

PONY   It stands for sudden infant death, and it is a very tragic
                thing.

CAPE   Oh. You — you were an ambulance man?

PONY	Only for four years.
CAPE	Only.
PONY	You want to watch me. I'm sarcastic.
CAPE	You saved lives then, you — you saw the m-m — *(using his face and body to indicate the word 'movement')*
PONY	You better believe it. Heck my first day on we get a call from this Chinese family downtown, eh, so we walk into the house and this kid takes us to the bathroom and ya know what we see? This old Chinese guy sittin' on the toity bleedin' from every hole in his body; nose ears dink mouth, everything, just pourin' out blood, so my supervisor looks at me and she goes 'That's cute.'
CAPE	Didn't all the blood make you queasy?
PONY	Who me? You kidding, dissection was my favourite subject.
CAPE	Yes? Why's that?
PONY	I don't know. It always made me feel — I don't know, like I was a top model or something.
CAPE	You — *(trying to keep her there)* — name. Name, what is your name?
PONY	Daid, Pony. *(hitting herself)* I mean, Pony Daid.
CAPE	I'm Cape, Cape Race. Does — does that sound — familiar to you?
PONY	Sure. I even been there. Are you from there?
CAPE	Where? Oh, Cape Race? No. No.
PONY	Well how come you're named for it?
CAPE	'Cause, 'cause you know why? 'Cause I am the way the word sounds, I think. Do you — think?
PONY	I can see that.
CAPE	You're the first person who could. Hey! Why did you leave the ambulance business?

PONY	I'm not at liberty to say.
CAPE	Oh please?
PONY	Swear you won't reveal it?
CAPE	Swear.
PONY	Speeding.
CAPE	They fired you for speeding an ambulance?
PONY	They fired me 'cause they knew I was gonna quit and their pride was hurt.
CAPE	Why, why were you gonna quit?
PONY	'Cause it was a bum operation. Like I'm an order-oriented person, eh, a neat bar my Dad even called me, and this was the slackest outfit I ever saw. Something you'd think would be the tightest, and it was the slackest. Nobody gave a fig! So I said to myself, 'Pony, if you want order you're gonna have to be your own boss and that's all there is to it.'
CAPE	So now, you save lives on your own?
PONY	Kinda. I got my own fix-it stand, for things though eh, not people, up at the mall, out in Mississauga.
CAPE	Ah...would you — would you like to come in?
PONY	What, for a — tea?
CAPE	Tea? Sure, sure I can make tea.

Pause.

PONY	Um — just in case you're a bad guy, although I don't think you are, I think I should tell you that I have been trained by this Vietnam vet — Herb.
CAPE	Hey! Hey you think I'd hurt you? My life is in your hands!
PONY	Pardon?
CAPE	Just a — manner of speech — ah — well! Here it is!

PONY   Well. This is quite the — bare room.

CAPE   Yeah? Oh yeah we — Pap and me keep breaking things — a couple of oxes.

PONY   Oh, I like a clean room — although I do like the occasional knick-knack. Nice clock. Hey, ya dropped your mitten.

CAPE   P-please put that back.

PONY   Why?

CAPE   He ah — Pap wants it there he — it's been there for over a year, do you believe it? Ever since the — ah — the old duck dropped it when she left — left. He — he thinks it'll bring her back or something.

PONY   Poor guy. Is he a little—

CAPE   He — he's dying. In fact, he is going to die tonight, if nothing stops him. But you — you know that, don't you?

PONY   Well — there is a kind of a creepy feeling...Also if I do say so you're acting a little — shook up.

CAPE   Yes, yes I'm very shook up.

PONY   I don't blame you, eh, I'd flip out if anything happened to my old man.

CAPE   You understand?

PONY   Oh yeah, like I'm wild about my dad, just wild. He's very interesting you know. He collected mice!

CAPE   Mice! He was a mouser?

PONY   Kinda. He'd spend all Sundays with them, building run-wheels and such. Huh. He had two hundred and twenty-six at one time. Freaked the mum right out.

CAPE   How many now?

PONY   None any more. My dad had to gas them. Not meanly, though. He's the projectionist for Kirkland Lake, where I'm from. Us kids really lucked out, eh, got to watch every film fifteen, sixteen times.

CAPE   Look, I can't beat around anymore I — listen — if you think I'm nuts just leave, but — I have to ask — are — are you here — to help us?

PONY   What, you and your dad?

CAPE   Yes.

PONY   Well, not that I was personally aware of. I guess I could be.

CAPE   Okay, I'm gonna spill the whole boodle — as I said, if you think I'm insane — just walk away. But every word is pure truth.

PONY   I'll believe you.

CAPE   Okay. See, I was a lawyer, married, making money, everything was — in place; only trouble was, I have a disease, where I hated — I hated living so much my teeth were ground down to baby teeth. One day it got so bad that I had no choice; I went to the Danforth Bridge, climbed up on the wall, and I was just about to kill myself when I saw a dog, a white dog, just sitting there. And then a real miracle happened — the dog — the dog spoke. She told me that I was JUMPING TO HELL.

PONY   A white dog?

CAPE   Yeah, a small white dog with bu-blue eyes.

PONY   I don' t believe it.

CAPE   You've got to!

PONY   No, I mean I believe what you say, but I'm freaking out because *I* had a white dog, like that, she was probably the being to which I was very closest of all, Queenie, and I *know* she had ESP in her, things happened all the time, and then just last month she died then I get this overpowering urge to come here?

CAPE   The — the dog told me that to save my father was my only hope; if he lives, I'm cured, now you've come along, and you, you've saved lives!

PONY   Boy. Boy I knew something important would happen to me sooner or later. 'Cause — well — I feel shy to say it, but — well, I — yeah. I admit it, I'm a psychic!

CAPE   Yes?

PONY   Yeah! Like this isn't a very good example, but up in
        Kirkland, whenever I wanted the traffic light to change, I'd
        just squeeze my bumcheeks together, eh, hard as I could,
        till I almost passed out but it worked, it worked every
        time.

CAPE   Well!

PONY   Oh, I did bigger things too...well I never used it to save a
        human life, but I, a couple times I found out how to save
        them.

CAPE   You did?

PONY   Yeah. All I would do is, I would concentrate on the
        question 'How do I save them?' like a trance and then an
        answer comes out. It's worked three times. One was
        Queenie. That's my dog. I hooked right into her mind and
        she told me what was wrong! Another was a private
        matter to do with my brother Wade's wife, Linda, and one
        was when Chrissy Pilon was missing and I took them
        right to the house where he — the guy — had her. Now
        they could have all been like a coincidence, but—

CAPE   No, they weren't. They weren't at all. You — are —
        here...to save our lives! You have...

PONY   I knew it! I knew I'd do something special more than work
        in a mall!

CAPE   Could you go into your trance now, he's very bad.

PONY   Um sure, I don't mind but — this feels so — kinda —
        normal, you know? I — like I wonder if we could have
        something for the — underneathness?

CAPE   Oh yes! Sure. *(turning out lights; moving to his drums
        and drumming)* How's that?

PONY   That is excellent. You keep on doing that, and I'll just
        concentrate real — Oh yeah, keep up that drumming,
        that's —

CAPE   His name is Glidden, Glidden Race.

PONY   Glidden — Race...okayyy — mm-mm...

> PONY *holds her breath, sways. They both almost go into a trance. The drumming is spectacular.* PONY *shudders and says in the voice of* CAPE'*s mother.*

PONY   Oooooooooh that's lovely darling could you just do the inside of my arm, oh God that is delicious I just made a lovely thick fanny burp.

> CAPE *jumps up, turns on the lights.*

CAPE   Ahhhhh' What — what what was that?

PONY   I don't know, I didn't even hear me, but whatever you heard, that's what it is. It's what the answer is, I know, I feel it.

CAPE   But but but that — that was my — my mother my oh. That was her voice. That was my mother's voice. *(almost vomiting)*

PONY   Jeeps. You obviously don't get on with your mum.

CAPE   But her words came out of your mouth, didn't they? What does that mean?

PONY   It means her coming back is the only thing gonna save your dad.

CAPE   What?

PONY   I know it, I can feel it in my feet. Oh yeah, when I get it that way it's always right, right as anything.

CAPE   That means I — I have to convince her somehow to come back for good?

PONY   Yes. Yes it does.

* * *

Published by Playwrights Canada Press - trade paperback

The Saints and Apostles

Raymond Storey

This is a contemporary love story about Michael, a world weary director, and Daniel, bright and insightful beyond his tender years, who is HIV infected. A warm and human tale about the ultimate fear of intimacy that re-examines modern relationships and the power and limitations of love. In this scene, 'The Martyrdom of Saint Rita', Michael has come to visit his mother, something he tries to avoid doing.

> RITA *is on her apartment balcony near the airport.*
> MICHAEL *joins her and they drink wine.*

RITA   How's Madeline?

MICHAEL   The same.

RITA   You don't want any of this ivy, do you?

MICHAEL   No.

RITA   I can cut some slips.

MICHAEL   I'm no good with plants.

RITA   Well, you couldn't kill ivy.

MICHAEL   So you said about that Christmas Cactus, and what I did to it was grisly.

RITA   Ivy's like a weed. It just grows and grows. And grows and grows. And grows and grows. Maybe Madeline would like some.

MICHAEL   No plants, no pets, no thanks. We don't have the nurturing skills to grow mould on cheese, so let's drop it, okay?

RITA   I just thought you'd like some ivy. Top me up, will you, barbender. You were at a concert?

MICHAEL   Yeah.

RITA   Who's in town?

MICHAEL	What?
RITA	Who was playing?
MICHAEL	The symphony.
RITA	Oh, I thought you meant a real concert, like Julio Iglesius, or something.
MICHAEL	Remember my grade two teacher?
RITA	Grade two teacher — how would I remember your grade two teacher?
MICHAEL	Mr. Carnegie.
RITA	Oh, good lord love a duck — him.
MICHAEL	Used to say he looked like Robert Kennedy.
RITA	I haven't thought of him in years. I never said he looked like Robert Kennedy.
MICHAEL	You did so! I remember you telling Daddy.
RITA	Maybe one of the Kennedys. Not Robert. A cross between Bobby and Teddy, maybe. More like Teddy, only thinner through the face...
MICHAEL	He works at the mall now.
RITA	Which mall?
MICHAEL	The thingmee mall where we bought the wine.
RITA	Mr. Carnegie?
MICHAEL	In a shoe store. I'm sure it was him.
RITA	I guess he's not teaching any more then. That doesn't surprise me a bit.
MICHAEL	Why not?
RITA	It just doesn't surprise me that Mr. Carnegie is not teaching anymore. That's all.
MICHAEL	Why?

RITA   Well...enough said.

MICHAEL   You didn't say a thing.

RITA   Well, I think he was...you know.

MICHAEL   No, I don't.

RITA   Oh, quit your playing dense. You know what I mean. He was kinda...funny. And it doesn't surprise me a bit that he's working in a shoe store.

MICHAEL   What are you saying?

RITA   You could just tell by looking at him.

MICHAEL   You said he looked like a Kennedy.

RITA   Like Teddy a little, but thinner.

MICHAEL   A gay Kennedy? Mother, please.

RITA   It wasn't what he looked like, it was how he acted. Nervous sorta.

MICHAEL   Nervous? Who wouldn't be? A classroom full of hyper seven-year-olds? That would make Charles Bronson twitchy.

RITA   He wasn't twitchy. And he was no Charles Bronson. Teaching grade twos? A man just didn't teach grade two. They just didn't. And he was kinda...well, nervous. Wouldn't ever look you in the eye hardly. Unless you nearly hit him over the head.

MICHAEL   Which, of course, you did.

RITA   I hate this weather, I am just sticking to myself.

MICHAEL   How old would he have been then?

RITA   Look at this head of mine. I got the hair from beyond the grave. One more permanent and I'll be bald.

MICHAEL   Twenty-five?

RITA   Should quit bleaching it — let the whole goddamn mess grow out.

MICHAEL	Mom?
RITA	Coulda been twenty-five. Younger, maybe. Mighta been his first teaching job. I can't remember.
MICHAEL	Remember that pageant? The end of the year pageant?
RITA	Which one? Grade two?
MICHAEL	We did this thing out of a book that Mr. Carnegie had. I think it was called, *Holidays Of the Year*, or, *Every Day's A Holiday*, or something like that. I forget that part.
RITA	Let's plug the cork back in this bottle and go down to the pool. I gotta man's bathing suit in my drawer — that somebody left behind. Should fit you well enough for all that's gonna see you from this building.
MICHAEL	Everybody in the class got their own holiday. Mr. Carnegie was up to October by the time he got to me. I was hoping for Hallowe'en, but no such luck. Columbus Day. It was an American book. I'd never even heard of Columbus Day.
RITA	I'm sweating.
MICHAEL	October 12th is Columbus Day. And on that day in 1492...
RITA	Let's at least go in where it's air-conditioned.
MICHAEL	Do you want to hear the rest of this story?
RITA	Not if it's another poor little Michael story, no, I don't.
MICHAEL	But this isn't. It's a poor little Rita story. We — the grade twos — we were doing this thing at the front of the class. It was hot, the windows were open. All the mothers were squatting in rows on these little teeny chairs, low to the ground. Sitting there knocked-kneed fanning themselves with mimeographed programs. For some reason, you weren't there. Mr. Carnegie was chording on the piano, and you weren't there. He'd lined us all up at the front of the room and I'm watching the parking lot, through the window. Caroline Fusco's halfway into 'Easter' when you pulled in — driving the two-tone Chevy two-door demonstrator that Daddy brought you home from the lot. The '61 with the mint green body and the dark green top, and the white wall tires.

RITA	That was a sporty little car — good pick up. I liked that little car.
MICHAEL	It's the world's longest minute. You don't get out of the car. You push up your hair at the back, as if you want to feel a cool breeze on your neck.
RITA	He wouldn't let me keep it.
MICHAEL	Some kid is launching into the 4th of July and you still aren't out of the car. You pull down the sunviser and look in the little check-it-out mirror and you slash on some more lipstick. And you push open the door and pull yourself out.
RITA	He never let me keep anything.
MICHAEL	By now, Mr. Carnegie is introducing, 'Labour Day'. You're picking your way through the gravel in the parking lot like you're picking your way through a mine field, wearing a white sleeveless sweater and a straight white skirt, no stockings and you're wobbling on white high heels. You stop to fish a stick of Dentyne out of your purse. I'm only seven, I don't know what that means yet, but I do know that when you wobble on your heels, your breath is going to smell like Dentyne.

> October 12th is Columbus Day,
> And on that day in 1492
> He landed here,
> In the western hemisphere
> I'm glad he made it...Phew!

	And all of the other mothers laughed and clapped and laughed, and in you trip tip-toe at the back of the room, after I was done.
RITA	Somebody's been throwing bottles and garbage off of these balconies. They're talking about closing the pool if whoever it is doesn't knock it off.
MICHAEL	You went and stood beside Mr. Carnegie. You must have apologized, did you? For being late?
RITA	Somebody down there could get hit with something and get hurt. It would be a shame to close it in this heat.

MICHAEL   And you said something funny to him or something.
                 Whispered some funny little Dentyne words into his ear
                 and laughed. And Mr. Carnegie jerked his shoulder up to
                 his ear, as if he was trying to wipe something off it, and
                 he looked down at the keys and kept chording and kinda
                 leaned away — leaned as far as he could away from you.

RITA   Is this what you came here for today, Mickey? You drop
                 in out of the blue to...to what? Did you wake up this
                 morning and decide you wanted to come out here and stick
                 pins in me? What do you want?

MICHAEL   To visit.

RITA   Honest to God, Mickey. Can't you even imagine what it
                 feels like to want somebody to love you?

MICHAEL   Daddy loved you.

RITA   He loved me. You're right, he did. What the hell do you
                 know about it? You don't even know the meaning of the
                 goddamned word.

MICHAEL   Probably not.

MICHAEL *exits.*

* * *

Published by Playwrights Canada Press - trade paperback

Coyote City

Daniel David Moses

*In this funny and mysterious look at Native people moving into the city, a
ghost, a Coyote story and impossible love draw a reserve family into the depths
of the Silver Dollar bar. In this scene, it was troubling for Thomas, a minister,
and a friend of the family, to meet Clarisse, the fallen woman who seemed to
know all about his past. She is sheltering both Thomas and his charge Lena
from the night and the city. He begins to trust her which is not wise since all
Clarisse cares to see is Lena being innocently and passionately in love.*

	A telephone rings. A spot reveals THOMAS, *shoeless on the edge of the couch. Another spot reveals* CLARISSE, *seated nearby on the floor, eating a sandwich from a plate.*
CLARISSE	Let the thing ring.
THOMAS	You aren't going to answer it?
CLARISSE	The machine will take care of it.
	The ringing stops.
THOMAS	It could be of some importance.
CLARISSE	Naw. Besides, I got visitors in from out of town, right? Can't you relax, Father Tom?
THOMAS	I want to offer you my thanks, dear lady.
CLARISSE	Clarisse. Call me by my name. Clarisse.
THOMAS	All right, my dear — Clarisse. I'm sorry I misjudged you. You've been an angel of mercy to us.
CLARISSE	You sure you don't want more to munch? You still look a bit wasted.
THOMAS	No. This will suffice. Clarisse. Thank you. It was an eventful drive.
CLARISSE	Can I get you something else, sweetie? You thirsty? How about something to drink?

THOMAS	No. No, thank you, dear lady — Clarisse.
CLARISSE	Lady Clarisse? I like that. Like hair lightener or something? Ha. I wish you'd un-lax. I'm known for putting fellows at ease.
THOMAS	I apologize. I'm so concerned —
CLARISSE	Oh, she'll be okay. She was just hungry.
THOMAS	I don't think you understand, Clarisse.
CLARISSE	Just a couple of bruises on her arm. All she needs is a nap.
THOMAS	No, I'm not speaking of her flesh. It's her spiritual condition.
CLARISSE	Spiritual condition?
THOMAS	Lena isn't well. This young man she's after. Her mother and I are afraid she's possessed.
CLARISSE	Is that so? I don't think there's nothing wrong with being in love.
THOMAS	You don't understand, Clarisse. This Johnny. He came here alone a year ago and —
CLARISSE	A year! And they're still after each other's bods. That's great. That's adorable. Oh hell, I got to drink to that. You got to drink to that too. Come on. We both have to drink to that.
THOMAS	No, not for me, thank you.
CLARISSE	You sure?
THOMAS	Yes, nothing. Clarisse, please. About this Johnny she's looking for. The boy, he was killed six months ago. Yes. He's dead. Buried.
CLARISSE	Really? I guess you did your duty. The funeral?
THOMAS	Well, no. The remains were transported out west. That's where he was from.
CLARISSE	Where'd you say he bought it? Got killed.

THOMAS	*The Silver Dollar.*
CLARISSE	So that's why she's heading there?
THOMAS	Yes, he called her to come last night on the telephone.
CLARISSE	Really?
THOMAS	Yes, I'm afraid he's allianced with the evil one.
CLARISSE	That sure would fit.
THOMAS	It's more than I have strength for. I know that now after the accident. Clarisse, help me convince her to go back home.
CLARISSE	Her mother didn't like him?
THOMAS	Oh he was a wild boy. You know what they're like out west.
CLARISSE	Ya, I do.
THOMAS	You must help me. Convince the child what madness this is. Her soul is in peril tonight. She almost destroyed our bodies today.
CLARISSE	That's real interesting, Reverend. I guess I could help, but you're going to have to tell me all about it. I don't have much spiritual experience. I'm not exactly a nun.
THOMAS	Let he who is without sin cast the first stone.
CLARISSE	I'll take that as a compliment. So come on. Let's drink to our partnership.
THOMAS	No, please, I don't drink.
CLARISSE	Don't drink? Really? Oh sweetie, you can't tell me that. I can see by looking at you that's not true. That nose almost glows in the dark
THOMAS	No, please, Clarisse. I've given it up.
CLARISSE	Nobody ever gives it up. Reverend Tom, you have to down at least one. For luck. We'll need luck, won't we, to beat the devil?
THOMAS	I could use water or something.

CLARISSE   Oh you're not getting into the spirit of it.

THOMAS   No, thank you, dear lady. My flesh is weak.

CLARISSE   You're not that old, Tommy. I can tell. See. *(tickling him)* You've got reflexes. Oh relax. And look at this stuff. Come on. Look at colour. This is good quality. Pure. Better than holy water. You don't use that stuff, do you? Here, take a sniff. *(spilling)* Oh sorry. I'm sorry. I didn't mean to. What a waster. You all right? I'll get a towel.

THOMAS   Never mind the towel. It dries fast.

CLARISSE   I'm sorry, Reverend.

THOMAS   It does smell good.

CLARISSE   All in a good cause. Against the devil. Here we go. There you are. Cheers.

THOMAS   *(drinking)* Cheers.

CLARISSE   Okay. That went quick. Did we hit the spot or what? Clarisse knows what's good for the tired traveller. More? But we didn't do it right. We didn't toast to luck or whatever. It won't work unless we do it right.

THOMAS   No, please.

CLARISSE   Oh, come on. Come-on-come-on-come-on-come-on. *(tickling him)*

THOMAS   All right. All right.

CLARISSE   Okay. Here we go. You make the toast. Wait a sec. Okay.

THOMAS   All right. May we defeat the evil that threatens the child Lena's soul. May we be victorious in the coming struggle. May the poor child find happiness and return —

CLARISSE   To Lena's happiness. So tell me details. Tell me about this nutso love affair. You said a whole year?

THOMAS   Her mother's very concerned.

CLARISSE   I've heard mothers can get like that. Did she hate his guts?

THOMAS   She was glad the boy left, when he went away to work.

CLARISSE	Did Lena moon away over him?
THOMAS	Yes. She stayed in her bed for months. After he died. So many tears she shed. No one knew how to replenish her.
CLARISSE	I wish I could fall in love.
THOMAS	But this was like a disease, a madness. This is what it's like when the devil's involved. This is what he does to destroy our hope. Our boys kill themselves and our daughters act like...
CLARISSE	Would you call him a demon lover?
THOMAS	The boy was from out west. I hear they're still pagans out there. I suspected him from the start. I could see it in his eyes. A spirit like an animal's.
CLARISSE	I'll drink to that. Here. Let me fill you up.
THOMAS	Thanks. I didn't say anything about it. But I watched. I watched him close.
CLARISSE	I think I would too. Cheers.
THOMAS	I didn't want her worrying. But she couldn't help it, after the child got sick. I told her, Martha, be patient. All things come to those who wait.
CLARISSE	But what about the boy?
THOMAS	But Martha just worried, worried inside herself. Patience is a virtue, I told her.
CLARISSE	Heck, Reverend, I'm about to lose all what's left of my virtue. What about the sweethearts?
THOMAS	I said to Martha, 'We must pray. Let us pray for Lena'.
CLARISSE	Come on, Tommy, tell me about Lena and Johnny.
THOMAS	And you know, she seemed to take some comfort in it. We got down on our knees and prayed. Heavenly Father, hallowed be thy name.
CLARISSE	You're driving me to drink.
THOMAS	And I didn't mean to do it, but we were there, down on our knees together, praying, and I came to the knowing that

my eyes were open and I was watching her lips moving as she prayed. I was drinking it in, the way her little pink tongue moved, making the words. I didn't care at all what she was saying. I didn't care at all.

CLARISSE   You got a crush on the old doll?

THOMAS   She trusted in me and in my heart I betrayed her.

CLARISSE   Oh that's so sweet, Tommy.

THOMAS   My heart sank with shame inside my chest.

CLARISSE   Oh come off it, Reverend. What's the big problem? It's adorable.

THOMAS   We were praying for her daughter. For her poor daughter's soul.

CLARISSE   Reverend Tommy, Lena's a big girl. She can take care of herself.

THOMAS   And all I could feel — lust. Lust. I wanted to die.

CLARISSE   You're just a guy, Tommy. Just a man. *(kissing his cheek)*

THOMAS   Don't do that.

CLARISSE   What's the matter?

THOMAS   You shouldn't do that to me.

CLARISSE   You un-clean? Oh cheer up, Tommy. It don't mean a thing. Not a thing.

THOMAS   Only a whore could say that. Only a whore.

CLARISSE   I'm not arguing with you, Reverend.

THOMAS   I'm — thirsty. Clarisse, do you hear? I'm thirsty.

CLARISSE   You've had enough.

THOMAS   Give me that.

CLARISSE   No more till you settle down. You got to tell me more about —

THOMAS	Give it to me!
CLARISSE	Ow! Don't you think you should slow down a bit?
THOMAS	I'm thirsty. And this hits the spot. What kind of whore are you, anyway? I'm the one who's supposed to say what's sin.
CLARISSE	It's okay with you, it must be okay I guess.
THOMAS	It's okay with me, lady, okay by me. God I been thirsty. Look at it. Look at that colour. Like dawn. Hey, where you going? You're not going to leave me high and dry, pretty lady? Lady Clarisse.
CLARISSE	Guess not. Guess I could stay a little bit longer.
THOMAS	A little bit longer? Hell, woman, what kind of whore are you? You're supposed to be in service, in service to the devil.
CLARISSE	Listen, Reverend, I don't do charity work.
THOMAS	You're pulling me down, you're making me fall.
CLARISSE	Back off, Reverend. Back off.
THOMAS	Come on, whore, whore of the city of darkness. Come on. Just a little kiss. Give me some tongue.
CLARISSE	Sorry, Father. No pay, no play.
THOMAS	Oh what a temptress you are. What a red woman, an evil woman.
CLARISSE	You're really into this aren't you?
THOMAS	Lady. Pretty Lady. Pretty Lady Clarisse. Handmaid of Darkness.
CLARISSE	Oh brother. Here. Here's the extra bottle. *(exiting)*
THOMAS	Thank you, Dark Lady. Thank you.

* * *

Published by Williams Wallace Publishers- trade paperback

Ever Loving

Margaret Hollingsworth

Three war brides from England, Scotland, and Italy travel to Canada in 1945 and their lives and relationships with their husbands interweave with the fabric of the Canadian experience — the hopes, fantasies, disappointments and the grim realities of life in a new land.

> CHUCK *and* LUCE's *apartment, Halifax 1952.* CHUCK *is playing and singing* "Mona Lisa". LUCE *is packing a suitcase.* CHUCK *stops playing and looks at* LUCE.

CHUCK   No mi ami.

LUCE   Speak English. I cannot stand your terrible Italian.

CHUCK   You do not love me, you bitch.

LUCE   Love?

CHUCK   Love.

LUCE   *(amused)* I took your name — only for love would I take such a terrible name.

CHUCK   You think that?

LUCE   Rotten flesh?

CHUCK   Basta! Ascoltate! Basta!

LUCE   Speak English.

CHUCK   I have the right to speak Italian.

LUCE   Then speak it well. *(pause)*

CHUCK   Why didn't you say you didn't want my name?

LUCE   Why didn't you say you intended to live all your life in Halifax?

CHUCK   There's nothing wrong with Halifax.

LUCE   No? Sure is nothing wrong. Is not even possible to drink
               wine in a restaurant, is possible smoke opium, but is not
               possible drink wine - is hypocrite town - no culture.

CHUCK   Why didn't you say what you wanted before you came?

LUCE   Many things I did not know how to say Chuck. No...was
               not language. Not English, not Italian...how to make you
               understand...How to make you hear when you do not
               know how to listen. *(pause)* Not listen to words but
               (reaching down inside herself; then gives up, shrugging)
               Ach — the whole what you are is...Canadian.

CHUCK   You think you corner the market in sensibility because
               you're some high-class dago bitch? Mussolini was an
               Italian.

                         LUCE *shrugs.*

               I was ashamed, you know that? When I was in Italy, I
               always said I was a Maritimer. Canada may be a desert but
               at least we don't breed thugs. Black shirts!

LUCE   You breed only bores!

CHUCK   What's that supposed to mean?

LUCE   It means I am going to Toronto.

CHUCK   For the two hundredth time — n...o...no.

LUCE   *(quietly)* It means...I cannot wait for you any longer
               Chuck. I am more than thirty years old. Time is passing
               — too much time. I am older than you.

CHUCK   You never would have been a singer - you know that.
               That's why you came here in the first place, you were a
               second-rater and you knew it. That's why you'd never go
               off to study when I gave you your chances. That's why
               you made out you were going off your head.

LUCE   So this time I go. Maybe this time I do go off my head...
               this time I go as far as I can. I find out what is inside me.

CHUCK   No...no. I won't let you.

CHUCK *empties* LUCE's *suitcase. She picks it up calmly.*

LUCE   I have already accepted to go. You cannot stop me! *(pause)*

CHUCK   Okay, so okay. We'll make it Toronto. You win.

LUCE   No. No. No. No. I see now —

CHUCK   What do you see?

LUCE   That you have no ambition. Only dreams. Dreams and compromises.

CHUCK   So you don't compromise eh? You refuse to talk Italian. You refuse to even acknowledge where you're from and you take a job as a hostess on an Italian radio show in a city you say you hate. That's not a compromise?

LUCE   It will not be for long. Soon I get into another show... maybe television.

CHUCK   Television? This time next year it'll be dead.

LUCE *shrugs, continues to pack.* CHUCK *watches, helpless.*

Listen, *Loose.* It's not too late — we could still have a kid ...I'm making good money. The old man's getting old now — he keeps asking, now that mama's gone. He's got money put aside — wants to make an investment — he was talking about maybe opening up a coffee bar. Well, you could learn to bake. We could hire someone to look after the kid...

LUCE   I already have a kid. *(smiling at him)*

CHUCK   Well, what am I? How am I supposed to make you stay? How long would you be gone for?

LUCE   Maybe not for long...*(snapping the suitcase shut)*

* * *

Published by Coach House Press in "Willful Acts "- trade paperback.

The Wedding Script

Don Hannah

An English rock star must marry to avoid deportation so his housemate, Louise agrees, the transsexual landlady oversees, and the long-standing boyfriend, Bob, gets on his knees — to propose!

	BOB *and* LOUISE *are in their mid 30's. Morning. A back yard deck in Riverdale, Toronto.* BOB *has just arrived. He paces nervously about and plays with the plants, pinching them back and pulling off dead leaves.*
LOUISE	Sure you don't want a coffee?
BOB	No, thanks, I don't have enough time. But I have to talk to you.
LOUISE	Yes. If you have something to tell me, I'll be reasonable.
BOB	I know I was unreasonable last night. I've calmed down, and...and I wanted to say that...Look, I know there are easier fellows to put up with than me. I'm a disappointment.
LOUISE	Oh, Bob
BOB	No, wait. Wait till I'm finished, done, please. I wanted to say that I understand why you needed this little break where we aren't living together right now. It's hard for me to appreciate the kind of potential you feel I have. I don't feel it anymore and I don't think I'm being unreasonable when I say that the world won't let me make a go of things. I just have...
LOUISE	Wait, Bob, please, I can't, I just can't handle it right now if you start talking about bad karma.
BOB	I would never talk about bad karma and you know that. Don't try and make it sound fashionable, because that isn't the way I...I've got no use for things that are current. That's why everything's in such a big state all over and decent fellows get overlooked. But that's not why I'm here. I realize that lately I've been difficult and I apologize

for that. I get uncomfortable around Alex and I know that he's she's, sorry, you're friend. Oh, but that's not why I'm here either. It's about you getting married to this Rupert fellow. I couldn't sleep last night, Lou, so I decided to ask you, um, look, will you marry me?

LOUISE   What?

BOB   It was a proposal. Of marriage.

LOUISE   Oh, Bob, not now why?

BOB   Because I don't want to lose you.

LOUISE   Look, if I thought, I mean, if getting married meant anything I wouldn't be marrying Rupert. I think more of you than that, than as a husband or...look, I don't understand this. We haven't talked about marriage for eight years. We haven't even thought about it since we lived together back home.

BOB   Will you at least think it over, please?

LOUISE   Well, I suppose I could thi — No, I don't have enough time to think it over. There's not enough time. I'm getting married on Monday.

BOB   Oh, marry me instead, please?

LOUISE   Bob, stop! There's no reason to marry you.

BOB   Oh, no? Twelve years mean nothing? Twelve years and there's all sorts of reasons to marry a perfect stranger? Oh, it's all wrong, Lou. It's too quick.

LOUISE   It has to be quick. He gets deported if he isn't out of the country by Tuesday...And it's not such a big deal. Oh, come on Bob, please? Think about it. A little more? Can you think about it a little more? It's just a legal transaction...And will you...I mean, could you do me a sort of favour? I'd appreciate it very much if you'd be my witness at the ceremony. Would you do that? I'd like that very much.

BOB   What?

LOUISE   Well, I do love you, and it is my wedding after all. I would like you to be a part of it.

BOB	That's too melodramatic for words.
LOUISE	Well, the whole thing can't be, you know, business. And if you and Chantelle play our best friends —
BOB	Me and Chantelle? A couple?
LOUISE	Yeah, wouldn't that strike an appropriate note? For the minister I mean? We didn't have enough time to book City Hall so we got a real minister from the Want Ads. A woman.
BOB	No! I'm opposed to the whole thing.
LOUISE	Okay. Fine. Okay. Yeah. Don't come to my wedding. I'll ask Alex. She'd love to.
BOB	I'll just bet she would. Go ahead! Make it a sick freak show!
LOUISE	Bob!
BOB	I'm sorry.
LOUISE	That's disgusting!
BOB	Sorry.
LOUISE	Oh, jeeze. I mean, JEEZE! *(slapping his face)*
BOB	Ow! I said I was sorry.
LOUISE	So what! Alex is a terrific person. Can't you see beyond the fact that she's a transsexual for god's sake? She's just a little bit different.
BOB	I'll say she's different. She gives me the screaming willies.
LOUISE	Get your hands off her plants! If I hadn't told you to begin with, you wouldn't know and it wouldn't bother you. That's what Alex gets for being honest and open and —
BOB	I wouldn't know. Ha ha. I wouldn't know. I just hope our families don't find out. Marrying some little foreign turd and having a maid of honour who used to be some poor woman's husband.

LOUISE   Your mind gives me the creeps sometimes; you have a
                dirty little mind.

BOB   I have a dirty mind! This marriage is immoral! Why, it's
                like spitting on your mother's grave!

LOUISE   Don't be so ridiculous. My mother is alive.

BOB   Then it's like spitting on her face.

LOUISE   Oh, come on, get lost, now who's melodramatic? And
                besides, my mother will never know.

BOB   What if the plane crashes? Huh? What happens then? They
                release the passanger list and there you are — Mrs.
                Rupert...what's the little jerk's last name anyhow?

LOUISE   He's not a jerk, and it's fairly common for married women
                to keep their maiden names. This isn't the Nineteenth
                Century.

BOB   I'll say it isn't. A hundred years ago you'd have been
                stoned to death.

LOUISE   What is this? One minute I'm dying in a plane crash and
                the next you're having me stoned to death. You're not
                usually this aggressive.

BOB   I love you! I love you and you're marrying someone else
                and moving to England as if I meant nothing. Don't we
                mean anything to you?

LOUISE   If we had meant anything to you, you wouldn't have been
                such a wimp about us! You'd get your act together and
                stop moaning about your stupid old mid-life crisis!

BOB   I have never used a topical expression like 'mid-life crisis'
                in my life!

LOUISE   I don't care what you call it, just get yourself into analysis
                or something and get rid of it! Don't you even want to
                know why you hate your father?

BOB   I'm sick of you telling me I hate my father. I do not hate
                my father!

LOUISE   That's not what your mother says.

BOB   What do you mean?

LOUISE	I mean she called me here last week to talk about why you'd forgotten his birthday again.
BOB	How did my mother get Alex's number?
LOUISE	From my mother. They bumped into each other in the K Mart. In the cat food.
BOB	And you had to tell them we weren't living together anymore. We didn't tell them we were living together until we'd been doing it for three years and now you've gone and done this and by now half of Charlottetown knows you've left, moved out on me now. Boy oh boy, that's humiliation, Lou, that's humiliation.
LOUISE	I'm supposed to lie to my mother about where I live?
BOB	Well, you're going to lie to her about getting married. What's the...darnit! I should have married you that time we thought you were pregnant.
LOUISE	Hey! Hold it! Right there! I haven't even been allowed to say the word 'pregnant' without you going off on some ten-mile walk to calm down.
BOB	Every conversation we have turns into babies lately. Why are you so obsessed with babies?
LOUISE	Because I'm not twenty-five anymore!
BOB	*(pause)* So you're getting married. Look, if we ever had a baby after Monday, legally it would belong to the jerk.
LOUISE	Oh, damn, I never thought of that. And he's not a jerk!
BOB	What do you...
LOUISE	Oh, be quiet.

* * *

Available from Playwrights Union of Canada - copyscript

Roundup

Barbara Sapergia

Verna and Paul Petrescu's cattle ranch in southern Saskatchewan is in deep trouble and so is their marriage. Things come to a boil on a blazing hot day in June — the day family and neighbours gather for the annual roundup. Paul and Verna are engaged in a skirmish, part of their larger battle, about whether their teenage daughter, Darcy, will help the women prepare the food or help the men with the branding.

> PAUL *leaves the house.* VERNA *follows him out.*

VERNA　　Paul. Wait a minute.

PAUL　　So, Verna, what is it?

VERNA　　How many calves do you have left, anyway?

PAUL　　Oh, couple of dozen.

VERNA　　What on earth do you need Darcy for?

PAUL　　We just like having her around. Tell you the truth, things seem to go that little bit better when she's there.

VERNA　　Paul, this is the last time I'm letting her work outside at the roundup. You do not need her.

PAUL　　Neither do you.

VERNA　　I certainly do. We've got a lot of work to do.

PAUL　　You got all those women in there —

VERNA　　Women! That's right. Women. Who else ever does anything in the kitchen?

PAUL　　Would you give me a break? I'm working at the corral.

> PAUL *starts to move off toward corral.* VERNA *follows him.*

VERNA	Oh sure. And you come up to the kitchen, and you plunk yourself down like...like you owned the place.

        PAUL *stops.*

PAUL	But I do.
VERNA	Like it was God's will for you to sit there like a great big lump...and have Darcy and me look after you.
PAUL	I never said you had to, did I?
VERNA	You expect it.
PAUL	For Pete's sake, I do not.
VERNA	I can see it in your body, your face —
PAUL	My face. Now even my face is wrong?
VERNA	It's your attitude. That's what I can't stand.
PAUL	I don't have any attitude.
VERNA	Like you just have to wait around and everything'll be taken care of.
PAUL	I just...try to be myself. I mean, a guy has to have confidence.
VERNA	Paul, have you ever in your life picked up a dish-rag and wiped the crumbs off a table?
PAUL	What's that got to do with anything? I do all the outside work.
VERNA	What about harvest?
PAUL	What about it?
VERNA	When harvest comes I do plenty. I drive the tractor. I haul grain to the elevator.
PAUL	Well, sure — it's our busiest time. The work's gotta get done.
VERNA	The work's gotta get done. Of course.
PAUL	All the women do it, Vern. You know they do.

VERNA	How come nobody worries about what's women's work then?
PAUL	Why should they? We're all in it together, aren't we?
VERNA	How come we're not all in it together in the house?
PAUL	But that's different.
VERNA	Is it?
PAUL	What are we talking about? You want me to wipe the table sometimes? Is that it?
VERNA	Do you have to be so bloody literal?
PAUL	Do you want me to or not?
VERNA	All right, yes! I would like it if you sometimes just picked up the dish-cloth and wiped off the goddamn table.
PAUL	Why should I?
VERNA	Out of consideration, that's why. Because they're your crumbs too. Because 'we're all in this together.'
PAUL	For Pete's sake, Verna. Is this what's eating you?
VERNA	Oh, don't be so stupid.
PAUL	Well, is it?
VERNA	It's part of it.
PAUL	Is it just wiping the table, or would there be other things?
VERNA	Wiping the table is an example.
PAUL	How often would I have to do it?
VERNA	If you have to ask, it's not going to work.
PAUL	Look, I better get back to the corral. *(starting to move off)*
VERNA	That's right, run away as soon as we start to get somewhere.
PAUL	I'm not running away. I just wanna get the job finished. Okay?

VERNA	I give up. *(turning back to the house)*
PAUL	*(moving off)* We'll talk about it later.
VERNA	Forget it. *(slamming the door into the house)*

***

Available from the Playwrights Union of Canada - copyscript

The Darling Family

Linda Griffiths

As they face the dilemma of an unplanned pregnancy, this couple's decision to search beyond their trivial self-definitions, to face every thought, every option, becomes a path to healing, courage, and growth.

HE   Hi.

SHE   Hi.

HE   Come on in. Do you want wine, or beer, or brandy, or ...

SHE   I'll take wine.

HE   I was just practicing my guitar.

SHE   It's not loud enough.

HE   I've got to have some thought for the neighbours, although I think it all evens out in the end.

SHE   Probably does.

HE   Let's sit outside.

SHE   Okay....Nice sky.

HE   Yeah.

SHE   I got home today and there were six guys with jackhammers tearing down my front steps, then this huge cement truck arrives and looks like it's going to pave both front yards. Then the city comes and digs this giant hole in the sidewalk. They're building a Portuguese Parthenon next door and they have to tear down my steps to do it.

HE   That's a drag.

SHE   I can hardly get into the house. There's just the edges of the steps left, like ruins.

HE   Do you have to pay for new steps?

SHE	No, they couldn't carve the steps in half to leave new steps so they had to replace mine anyway.
HE	That's one good thing.
SHE	Yeah.
HE	...so I've been on tenterhooks all day. What did you want to talk to me about?
SHE	Oh, I don't know.
HE	I think you do.
SHE	I just...maybe you should have a drink first.
HE	I don't want a drink. Is it that bad?
SHE	Hard to say.
HE	What is it then?

SHE *pauses.*

HE	You're pregnant.
SHE	Yeah *mon*, I am.
HE	You're kidding. How do you feel?
SHE	I feel like...I don't know...I'm just out there, really out there.
HE	It's never happened to me.
SHE	Me either. First time.
HE	It's funny, after a while you get to think you're infertile or something.
SHE	Yeah, I thought I might be.
HE	Guess not.
SHE	Guess not.
HE	Maybe I will have a drink...What do you want to do, do you want to talk about it?

SHE   I don't know. I guess not. I feel like I'm swimming, just
               swimming out there in the mid-Atlantic.

HE   Do you want to keep swimming for a while, or...

SHE   When I got the call, it was going to be a joke, I thought I
               was starting my period this morning, and I was going to
               feel like an idiot, and say, 'You wouldn't believe how
               stupid I was, I actually thought...' Then after they told
               me, I just sat there for a while, and then I realized I was
               staring at this blue book, and when I finally focussed to
               see what it was, it was your copy of the *The Silent
               Scream*, with that picture of the foetus on the cover.

HE   That's incredible. And then this morning did you see what
               I pulled out of the envelope?

SHE   I couldn't believe it. The *ProChoice News*. I thought it
               was a sign.

HE   Just goes to show this household doesn't avoid those
               issues.

SHE   I found myself imagining what you'd do. Making up a
               whole thing in my head about you, thinking for you.

HE   I'm supposed to want to run, isn't that the assumed male
               response?

SHE   Yes.

HE   It's your choice, of course, but I'm thinking that might be
               a little selfish to leave it all to you if you might be
               influenced by what I say.

SHE   It's yours too.

HE   I thought you didn't want to talk about it. If you want to
               talk about it, I'll talk about it.

SHE   No, you're right, I'd rather swim.

HE   How's the swimming?

SHE   Weird.

HE	Well, it's seven o'clock now, we could see a movie, or eat, or if we went really fast we could do both. What would you like to do?
SHE	I'm not very fast. I started getting this dizzy feeling, like the earth wasn't really under my feet, like everything just took a step sideways and I wasn't on it.
HE	We don't have to see a movie, I could just work here on my own or we could watch television or you could go off on your own and think or...
SHE	No, no, I'd like to see a movie.
HE	We could see that one where the kids find the body, that looked good, it starts at seven-forty-five.
SHE	Nooo...let's see the one about the dog.
HE	It's got subtitles.
SHE	I could take them tonight, besides it's supposed to be warm-hearted and comforting.
HE	Okay, eight-fifteen, that would give us time to eat. Do you want to eat? What have you eaten today?
SHE	Not much.
HE	Indian food?
SHE	Sure.
HE	Let's go.

SHE *sways.* HE *holds her.*

	Are you having one of these dizzy things?
SHE	Yeah.
HE	It's okay, no hurry.
SHE	I feel like I'm making it up.
HE	Making it up so that I can almost feel it too.
SHE	I'm okay now.

HE   Are you sure?

SHE   Yeah. *(nearly falling again)* Oh, Jesus, this is for real.

            The following lines are internal. How they are
            delivered is up to the actors. A slash (/) indicates
            an overlap of dialogue

HE   *The way she looked, the way I felt, I let her in, in that*
            split second, / something went in. Like some kind of
            miracle...

SHE   *The way he acted, the way he looked the way his eyes*
            shone like the warm blue sea. It went through us like a
            knife...

HE   *It's something you read about, / I thought it would never*
            happen to me ...

SHE   *I thought it would never happen to me. It could be done,*
            it could actually be done /

HE   *There's no way, I just / feel sick inside. Don't come down*
            hard, don't push her too hard, don't be too hard . . .

SHE   *It's not so crazy really, it's possible, but is it possible /*
            with him?

HE   *She's going to go through it, it's in her, / inside her...*

SHE   *He's the father now, not just some guy...*

HE   *Can' t do it, can' t do it, we should have talked / right*
            then, dangerous to wait...

SHE   *I feel real, finally something real in me. He took my hand*
            to cross the street / like there were three of us crossing the
            street. He felt it, it was in his hand, the way he touched,
            that there were three of us crossing the street.

HE   *I can' t let myself feel it. Never take her hand like that*
            again. That would be too cruel. Help her somehow. Be
            clear but not cruel. How could it have happened ?

SHE   *I know why it happened...*

HE   *There aren' t three of us crossing the street. Not now.*
        There can' t be. Not three of us crossing the street.

* * *

Published by Blizzard Publishing- trade paperback

Bat Masterson's Last Regular Job

Bill Ballantyne

Bat, an aging hero of The Old West, is offered a celebrity appearance at a second-rate boxing match. This, he naively thinks, will rocket him to fame again. With this lofty dream on the horizon he decides to rid himself of his companion, Louise.

	The hotel room. LOUISE *is dressed in a flowery, sunny frock. She is very nervous, sensing that she might have jeopardized the relationship, and determined to get* BAT *back. She dusts and cleans, meticulously sets the table and places a bottle of rye whiskey in the centre. She checks herself in the mirror.* BAT *enters, he is excited and happy; he can't wait to get to the boxing fight. In a rush, he rummages about the room.*
LOUISE	Bat, I'm so glad you're home. I went to the market today. I bought pears and peaches. I'm going to make preserves. I remember the bottle I made last winter. Did you have a walk in the park today? The clouds were beautiful.
BAT	Where are my gold spurs?
LOUISE	They're underneath the love seat. I polished them. The spokes were a little tarnished so I buffed them up a bit. I fixed the hole — it was very easy. I used a piece of velvet.
BAT	Cane! (*rummaging around, looking for it*)
LOUISE	Would you like a glass of milk? I have it fresh today.
BAT	My rattle snake sombrero!
LOUISE	That's a lovely suit, Bat. Is that your sherriff suit? I've never seen you in that before. Is that what you wore in the territories? I found your Remington long bore — it was in the kitchen, it was behind the ice box. Would you like me to open the rye?
BAT	(*without emotion*) You'll have to get out.

LOUISE	I went for a walk in the park today. I saw two chipmunks. They were so funny. They were playing with a newspaper. We're having cherry pound cake.

BAT   Pack up all your things and get out. Get out by morning.

LOUISE   I'm making Irish stew. I've got all the ingredients: lamb, potatoes, turnips, carrots, onions, celery and sage.

> LOUISE *exits.* BAT *starts to adjust his outfit.*
> LOUISE *re-enters.*

BAT   *(reciting a list, with uninvolved efficiency)* You're an idiot. You can't cook. You look stupid. I don't like your dress. You snore. You got squeeky little eyes.

LOUISE   *(frantically blocking this out)* I left the pound cake on the window. I left it there to cool. We're having cherry pound cake for dessert.

BAT   *(mechanically)* You're stupid. You got the brains of an armadillo. You can't put two words together. You're dull, you're boring.

LOUISE   Was that the suit you wore in Tuscaloosa? Was that the time you held off the Murdoch Boys? Is that when you shot Melvin King?

BAT   *(still detached)* You're a lump. You're an idiotic lump. You're sad. You're a sad case. You're a useless, dumb thing. You're good for nothin'. You're pathetic.

LOUISE   Let's go up the Hudson. You always said we could go up the Hudson. I could make a picnic. I want to see all the animals.

BAT   *(primping)* You're a waste of time. You don't have any substance. You don't make any impression. There's nothing to you. You're hollow. I don't know who you are. I don't care.

LOUISE   I can't hear you, Bat. I can't hear you. I don't know what you've said.

BAT   You're wretched in the bed. You're boring and pale and weak. You're awful to look at. You're ugly. You make me wanna gag.

LOUISE   No !

BAT	You shouldn't be takin' up air.
	LOUISE grabs the ukelele and feverishly starts bellowing "The Girl of the Golden West".
BAT	You don't know who you are. You'll never know who you are. You're a ghost rider — a wind could blow right through you. You're nobody. You're nothin'.
LOUISE	No, no, no.
BAT	You're nothing! You're nobody! You don't exist!
LOUISE	*(screaming)* No!
	LOUISE rushes out.
BAT	*(in delight)* Black sash!
	BAT puts on the sash. He studies himself intensely in the mirror. He is ready to soar. He exits vigorously.

* * *

Published by Playwrights Canda Press - trade paperback

Geometry in Venice

Michael Mackenzie

Pemberton, a young Canadian, is hired by the Moreens, a British family in Venice, as a tutor for their young son. He slowly discovers that, underneath the civilized veneer, the family is in severe financial straits. Without prospects of payment, he initially stays on for the sake of his pupil, but, when he finally tries to break away, he becomes entangled with his student's wordly and fascinating mother.

The family in this play bares a certain resemblance to one found in the novella "The Pupil" by Henry James, but herein, the famous author finally meets the characters he created in his story.

> PEMBERTON *is sitting up in bed in his small room, wearing a shirt. There is a quiet double knock at the door.*

PEMBERTON   Yes?

> MRS. MOREEN *enters in a wrap.*

PEMBERTON   *(surprised, pulling a sheet up on himself)* Oh! I thought it would be...

MRS. MOREEN   Mr. Moreen. He's left, on the overnight, for London. *(pause)* You see how obliging we are? *(looking around)* But you seem determined to be shot of us.

PEMBERTON   I simply want to be paid.

MRS. MOREEN   'I want to be paid'. Like some petty tradesman. Haven't you learned anything in this time with us — about open-heartedness and sharing?

PEMBERTON   I'm completely broke.

MRS. MOREEN   Here you are in Paris. We brought you here — the centre of the artistic, the civilized world. A well-appointed hotel. You want for nothing...

PEMBERTON   I had to have my books sold off to pay my debts.

MRS. MOREEN   Do we keep our books with us, dragging them from city to city?

PEMBERTON   My jacket has just about worn out. I can't even buy the occasional packet of cigarettes any more.

MRS. MOREEN   *(thrusting a bank note at him)* Here! Here is money.

PEMBERTON   *(recoiling slightly, brief pause)* Why are you waving a ten-franc note at me?

MRS. MOREEN   Take it.

PEMBERTON   This is 'open-heartedness'? People spontaneously shoving banknotes at each other? I have to beg, to threaten you. Has Mr. Moreen gone to beg from someone else?

MRS. MOREEN   We are not beggars!

PEMBERTON   He 'sallies forth' — to do what?

MRS. MOREEN   Always the grimy symmetry of the balance ledger. Why do you colonials always nurture the meanest aspects of the British character?

PEMBERTON   But I don't understand how you live — how I'm supposed to live. Moreen has no profession, no regular income. He disappears for a week or more and when he returns there might be a sudden spurt of extravagance, or not. Sometimes you get a check for translation.

MRS. MOREEN   Yes..?

PEMBERTON   Amy can have expensive material for frocks — fresh flowers — while Morgan's clothes are falling apart, and I am not paid.

MRS. MOREEN   My husband, through his services for various individuals and governments, is able to call on a number of informal moral obligations from various wealthy persons. We also have a number of elderly relatives. Amy has the wardrobe to match her other...attractions because we obviously wish to make a good match for her. Morgan, on the other hand — as you know — cares very little about his dress.

PEMBERTON   That tells me nothing except that you rely on the indulgence of old acquaintances and the generosity of senile relatives to keep you from poverty.

MRS. MOREEN   We're not poor!

PEMBERTON   But the chaos, the stupid expenses. Rushing here to Paris at the drop of a hat...

MRS. MOREEN   Amy must marry well! *(biting her tongue, pause)* We try to be equitable with our children, there are expenses for Morgan that we did not afford for Amy...

PEMBERTON   ...Like a tutor, you mean..?

MRS. MOREEN   Exactly.

> MRS. MOREEN *catches herself, begins to laugh.* PEMBERTON *smiles too. Pause.*

MRS. MOREEN   See! You do enjoy yourself with us. Have you any idea how dull most families are. There are rewards, there are.

PEMBERTON   Then perhaps I'm no longer sure if I can afford you.

MRS. MOREEN   You mean Morgan.

PEMBERTON   What?

MRS. MOREEN   If you can afford Morgan.

> *Pause.* MRS. MOREEN *moves closer to* PEMBERTON.

MRS. MOREEN   Can't you understand the rewards of simply being with him, the privilege of knowing and living with him? And the importance of not burdening him with...the awkward things in life.

PEMBERTON   *(pause)* You mean I shouldn't tell him I'm paid virtually nothing.

MRS. MOREEN   Not unless you want to show off.

PEMBERTON   Why me? You're well-read enough to tutor him yourself. You can read Greek, you know the classics.

MRS. MOREEN   I don't enjoy the Greeks. And I have neglected the rest of my family. Amy is almost beyond marriageable age and there are a mother's obligations, and, God knows, that can be a full-time occupation. And my husband deserves a certain amount of attention. He does his best for the family within his limitations.

PEMBERTON   Why did you...marry...

MRS. MOREEN   Moreen was a very...attractive man, and was one of the indulgences I thought I should allow myself as a passionate young woman. But then I became pregnant with Amy. I haven't always treated him well.

Silence.

PEMBERTON   Morgan is an extraordinary boy. I'm fond of him. But right now I can't even afford a haircut.

MRS. MOREEN   *(reaching out, touching his head)* I like your hair like this. And if you need, I can cut it.

PEMBERTON   ...And then call in the Philistines.

MRS. MOREEN   Why don't you write articles, even translate as I do. The family can provide the ideal environment for that.

PEMBERTON   Translating pays terribly.

MRS. MOREEN   I'm glad to make what I can.

PEMBERTON   I'm sorry. I have sent off a few pieces, but they're always refused.

MRS. MOREEN   Not such a protégé then, sacrificing your talents for us.

PEMBERTON *goes to turn away.* MRS. MOREEN *grasps his hand with both of hers.*

MRS. MOREEN   I'm sorry! You are making sacrifices, you are.

PEMBERTON   You're as strange as your son.

MRS. MOREEN   But I understand, I do. *(moving closer)* We all must make sacrifices, but I think they are sacrifices we crave to make.

PEMBERTON   And you?

MRS. MOREEN *puts* PEMBERTON's *hand to her breast and holds it there.*

MRS. MOREEN   I too can make sacrifices.

> *Long pause as* MRS. MOREEN *looks at* PEMBERTON.

PEMBERTON   *(with difficulty)* My mouth has gone quite dry.

***

Published by Playwrights Canada Press - trade paperback

Odd Jobs

Frank Moher

Tim has been laid off from his factory job and finds contentment in the employ of a retired professor. When Tim's wife is offered a job in another city, the hopes and the needs of the three come into conflict.

> MRS. PHIPPS' *yard. It has snowed; there is a dull, grey light.* TIM *is out sweeping the walk.* MRS. PHIPPS *enters, wearing her sweater. She stands watching.* TIM *spots her.*

TIM Well, I knew this was coming.

MRS. PHIPPS Did you.

TIM Well, you get so's you can predict 'er, eh? You get into October, you think maybe she's not gonna snow this year. So you wait, and just when you're sorry you put away the Bain de Soleil, wham, she snows. You gonna try still tyin' up those raspberry bushes ya think?

MRS. PHIPPS No.

TIM Nah, I'd leave 'er. Thing is they're messy. But you go and tie them up and yer just encouraging them to grow. *(pause; sweeping)* What about yer Hallowe'en costume? You goin' out for Hallowe'en this year?

MRS. PHIPPS No. You couldn't use another broom?

TIM A which?

MRS. PHIPPS Another broom. Instead of my good one.

TIM This is your good one?

MRS. PHIPPS Well it was my good one.

TIM But I found it, it was sitting right here.

MRS. PHIPPS I've a good one for indoors, and a good one for out here. And that happens to be my good one for out here!

TIM	Well that's where I'm using it.
MRS. PHIPPS	Oh go on then.
TIM	I am using it out here. Y'know, Mrs. Phipps, there's such a thing as supervising and there's such a thing as getting in the way. You haven't been working on your equation, have you?
MRS. PHIPPS	No.
TIM	No. I can tell. You always get cranky when you haven't been doing yer work. *(sweeping)*
MRS. PHIPPS	Your wife came to visit me yesterday.
TIM	Yeah I uh heard about that.
MRS. PHIPPS	She told me you're not going to Regina.
TIM	That's right.
MRS. PHIPPS	That's true?
TIM	Uh-huh. That is to say I'm not goin' yet.
MRS. PHIPPS	I told her it was the silliest thing I'd ever heard.
TIM	Well yer entitled to your opinion.
MRS. PHIPPS	She thinks so too.
TIM	Uh-huh. Well that's what makes this country great.
MRS. PHIPPS	Of course you're going to Regina. She's your wife, it's a good opportunity for her, you'll pack your tools and go.
TIM	You through dictatin' my life for me Mrs. Phipps?
MRS. PHIPPS	Well you're certainly not going to stay here!
TIM	Look, if Ginny wants to go to Regina, that's all right with me. Regina will still be there, y' know, whenever. As for me I got things to do here. Now you gonna move off the sidewalk so's I can sweep it?
MRS. PHIPPS	I might.

TIM   You might. Well I might just do it anyway. *(sweeping around* MRS. PHIPPS*)* Just leave it go, Mrs. Phipps, would you just leave it go? I got this walk to clean, I got weatherstrippin' to do. And that garage is a rat's nest, I haven't even begun to get 'er cleaned out.

                        Pause. TIM *sweeps.* MRS. PHIPPS *glances over at the bags.*

MRS. PHIPPS   You never spread those leaves like I asked, did you?

TIM   No, I didn't.

MRS. PHIPPS   Well there's no use now.

TIM   Well I'll get to it later.

MRS. PHIPPS   No there's no use now.

TIM   Mrs. Phipps, there's maybe one inch of snow here!

MRS. PHIPPS   And the painting in the basement. And the brown spots in the lawn. You haven't quite been keeping up here, have you?

TIM   Well I got all winter, don't I?

MRS. PHIPPS   Not if it's forty below out.

TIM   Well it's gonna be warm inside, isn't it?

MRS. PHIPPS   Not if you don't spread those leaves.

                        Pause.

TIM   Mrs. Phipps, I know why you're doing this.

MRS. PHIPPS   Do you?

TIM   Yes.

MRS. PHIPPS   Well then?

TIM   The answer is no.

                        Pause.

MRS. PHIPPS Well then, I'll just have to do them myself. *(starting towards the bags)*

TIM Mrs. Phipps, leave the bags.

MRS. PHIPPS Seeing as you won't.

TIM I told ya I'd do them.

MRS. PHIPPS Seeing as it's October —

TIM I'LL SPREAD THE LEAVES, ALL RIGHT MRS. PHIPPS? HERE, I'M SPREADIN' THE LEAVES. *(jumping on the pile of bags, ripping one open and swinging it about)* HOW'S THAT? HUH? I'M SPREADIN' THE LEAVES! MORE LEAVES? MORE LEAVES! WHOOPEE! LET'S SPREAD THEM LEAVES HOWZAT? HUH? YOU THINK THAT'S ENOUGH?

    Pause.

MRS. PHIPPS Yes. I think that will do.

TIM Good. I'm glad you're happy.

MRS. PHIPPS I guess this means you're fired.

TIM I'm what?

MRS. PHIPPS You're fired. Go on, get out of here.

    Pause.

TIM You don't mean that, Mrs. Phipps.

MRS. PHIPPS I certainly do.

TIM Look I'll clean up the leaves —

MRS. PHIPPS WOULD YOU PLEASE GO AWAY.

TIM MRS. PHIPPS, EVEN IF YA FIRE ME THERE'S STILL GONNA BE TRUCKS OUT THERE! *(pausing)* Look, I heard what Ginny told ya and I think that's a good idea --

MRS. PHIPPS Oh please stop.

TIM	No, no I do. You could come with us, you could sell your house here.
MRS. PHIPPS	Where would I stay?
TIM	You could get your own apartment.
MRS. PHIPPS	What would I do?
TIM	You'd do what you do here! You'd do your math, you'd do your equations. You could come over, we'd have dinner on Friday nights.
MRS. PHIPPS	Oh no, it's ridiculous —
TIM	Mrs. Phipps, it makes sense!
MRS. PHIPPS	Why? Because you say so?
TIM	Because it's the only thing to do! *(pausing)* You gotta come with us, Mrs. Phipps. I need your help with my math. *(pausing)* Okay, maybe you're firing me. But I am hiring you. *(pausing)* You're hired Mrs. Phipps. D'ya hear me? You are hired. *(pausing)* You gotta come with us, Mrs. Phipps! You gotta let someone take care of you!

Pause.

MRS. PHIPPS	Do what?
TIM	Take care of you. Listen to me. Everything's gonna be all right.
MRS. PHIPPS	Get out of my yard.
TIM	I just said —
MRS. PHIPPS	GET OUT OF MY YARD.

Pause. TIM *regards her for a moment, then starts sweeping the walk.* MRS. PHIPPS *grabs the broom and throws it down.* TIM *stoops for it, picks it up, and resumes sweeping.* MRS. PHIPPS *grabs the broom again, and throws it aside.* TIM *crosses to it, picks it up, returns to the sidewalk, and resumes sweeping.* MRS. PHIPPS *grabs the broom and throws it across the yard as far as she can. Pause.* TIM *looks at her for a moment, then turns and exits.*

MRS. PHIPPS *watches him go. She looks at
the broom, crosses and picks it up. She returns
to the sidewalk, holds the broom as if to begin
sweeping, and looks down the sidewalk at the
unswept snow. She leans the broom against the
fence. She exits.*

* * *

Published by Playwrights Canada Press - trade paperback

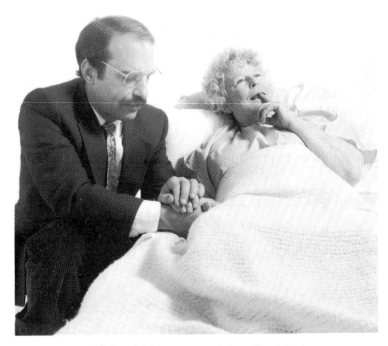

Richard Newman and Joy Coghill in
the 1990 Belfry Theatre and Touchstone Theatre
co-production of *Homework and Curtains*.
Photo by David Cooper.

Curtains for an Old Lady

John Lazarus

The second play in the matched set of theatrically quirky one acts - "Homework and Curtains" - which tell of Murray Greenspan, whose life has quietly gone into crisis. In "Homework for Men", he tries to deal with both his son and the memory of his own father, while in the moving "Curtains" he tries to deal with his dying mother who seems brave and cheerful, and, worst of all, doesn't seem to need him.

> MURRAY *sits reading.* ESTHER *speaks with her eyes closed. Her energy is lower than it has been — this scene takes effort on her part.*

ESTHER   I'm giving you my car.

MURRAY   What?

ESTHER   Decided. Separate from the estate. I told Rachel. I think you send it by rail.

MURRAY   Momma, thank you, but it's really not needed. Don't give me unless you want to.

ESTHER   Not doing anything I don't want. How often you get a car. Take it for Rachel. Off her hands.

MURRAY   Yes, Momma.

ESTHER   Snow tires in the storage room.

MURRAY   Yes, Momma. Thank you.

ESTHER   Don't thank me yet. You don't have it.

MURRAY   I'm — Jesus, Momma, I'm thanking you in advance, okay?

ESTHER   You're welcome. Now. Why did you want so much? Can't get a good trade-in on the Honda?

MURRAY   I'm not trading in the Honda.

ESTHER	Keeping the Honda. Gonna be a two-car family?
MURRAY	Momma, you're not supposed to be concerned with this.
ESTHER	Against your principles. Two cars. I thought.
MURRAY	It's got so we need them.
ESTHER	With the baby? *(beat)* Aren't your offices close by? You drive her to work, no?
MURRAY	Momma —
ESTHER	'Course — offices close by don't matter — if you go from — different homes. *(silence)* She moved out?
MURRAY	No.
ESTHER	Have you?
MURRAY	No!
ESTHER	What's going on?
MURRAY	Nothing.
ESTHER	You mention her — little as you can. Each time a different story. Stop humouring me.
MURRAY	All right. I was the one who wanted the abortion. Not because it was dangerous. Because I don't want the baby. I don't want to start over now. But she wants it. So she's having it. So we'll see. Okay? Not humouring you.
ESTHER	You still love her?
MURRAY	I think so.
ESTHER	You don't think or not think. Either you love her or —
MURRAY	Don't tell me that, all right? Please just kindly don't preach at me about love and thinking, all right? Okay so you're old but I'm middle-aged too, I've been through a few things, you ask me if I love her, my answer is 'I think so.' You don't like that answer, fine, my next answer is 'Mind your own business, keep the hell out of it,' all right, how's that?

ESTHER	I know you think it's not my business. You tell me nothing. Gonna divorce?
MURRAY	Mind your own business! Let go! I'm not asking you any more, I don't need from you any more, don't gimme money, fuck it — I'll walk!
ESTHER	Stop that filthy talk. It's a hospital, here.
MURRAY	I don't care! This is my last chance! You can't take this on. That is not your job now—
ESTHER	By you my job is to die.
MURRAY	It's not your business.
ESTHER	It's the business of — those who are going — to live.
MURRAY	Yes. This is very hard, Momma, this goes against everything. Okay, look. I don't know what's gonna happen, we may get back together, I could still change my mind about —
ESTHER	No. *Sha.* Make me no deathbed promises. But just — what you and Kate do—as long as Zalman's fine, all right? And the baby. Long as the baby's cared for.
MURRAY	They'll both be fine.
ESTHER	I know. All right. Whatever you think best. Mind you — didn't need the filthy talk. *(silence) Oy,* this label.
MURRAY	What?
ESTHER	In my robe. Scratching my neck, something, itching me.
MURRAY	Want me to take it out?
ESTHER	Please. *(as MURRAY leans over her)* No looking down my front, now.
MURRAY	Don't worry, Momma, I can't see anything.
ESTHER	Don't worry, Murray. Nothing to see.

> MURRAY *and* ESTHER *laugh.* MURRAY'*s*
> *laugh turns to weeping. He puts his arms around*
> *her and his head on her shoulder. She strokes*
> *him.*

ESTHER   All right. All right.

MURRAY   Don't go. Don't go.

ESTHER   Well. If I had a choice. All right. Surprised you stayed. Thank you. I have needed you here very much.

MURRAY   What for, Momma?

ESTHER   What?

MURRAY   What do you need me here for?

ESTHER   What a stupid question.

MURRAY   Yes I know it's a stupid question, Momma, but I'd like an answer, please.

ESTHER   You keep me from being afraid. I was afraid until you came. I hid it from all of them. But I was. But I look at you, and I see life goes on. And then I'm not afraid. That's it.

MURRAY   Ah. I didn't know that.

ESTHER   Well, I should have said.

MURRAY   It's alright. You've said. *(presenting label to her)* Here's your label.

ESTHER   Oh. Throw it out. Don't need it. I know what it's made of.

> ESTHER *closes her eyes, sleeps.* MURRAY
> *drops the label in the waste basket, returns to the*
> *chair and sits.*

          * * *

Published by Playwrights Canada Press - trade paperback

three-person scenes

Fiona Reid in the 1980 New Theatre production of *Automatic Pilot*.
Photo by Andrew Oxenham.

Automatic Pilot

By Erika Ritter

Charlie is a modern woman who writes for a soap opera by day and moonlights as a stand-up comic. She is talking to her ex-husband, who has decided he is gay, when her new romantic interest arrives.

ALAN	We've been split up almost a year. I know there've been guys...
CHARLIE	Oh dear, and I thought I was so discreet!
ALAN	Come on. You always made sure I knew.
CHARLIE	*(after a pause)* Most of those guys were clunkers.
ALAN	And Nick isn't a clunker? *(pausing)* Okay, it bothers me.
CHARLIE	*(gently)* It's just this phobia you've got. About closed doors. Most people think of the world as their oyster. In your mind, it's one big telephone exchange. With everyone on hold.
ALAN	Come here, and let me put you on hold. *(hugging her)*
	There is a knock on the door.
CHARLIE	That's Nick. I guess he forgot his credit card.
	CHARLIE *opens the door.* NICK *enters and gives her a bottle of champagne.*
NICK	Hiya, babe. Bubbly to the bubbly. In honour of your performance.
CHARLIE	I perform twice a week. Champagne is for special.
NICK	Then be specially good. Dom Perignon, kid. Don't give me no domestic-bubbly performance. *(kissing her, then seeing* ALAN*)* Oh. Hi.
CHARLIE	Nick, this is Alan. *(as the men shake hands)* My late husband.

NICK	*(dropping the hand like a hot rock)* Charlie! Jesus.
ALAN	Charlie's little joke. And it's little.
NICK	*(backing toward the door)* Look, I didn't know you were double booked here. And if you two have things to straighten out —
CHARLIE	*(quickly)* No, Alan's just dropped in from Stratford.
ALAN	*(also quickly)* Just to say hello.
CHARLIE	*(even quicker)* Not even that, practically.
ALAN	Don't mind me.
NICK	*(shrugging sheepishly)* If you'd had as many husbands sprung on you as I have...Now, whenever I hear the word, I automatically check the exits. *(to ALAN)* In from Stratford, eh?
ALAN	Couple of business things.
NICK	Ball bearings?
ALAN	I beg your pardon?
NICK	*(innocently)* That's what they do up in Stratford, isn't it?
CHARLIE	Nick's little joke. He grew up there. He knows goddamn well there's a theatre there.
NICK	She's right. Saturday nights, our idea of a hot old time was driving into town to bash a few faggot actors.
CHARLIE	*(quickly)* Have a drink, Nick. *(producing a bottle from the bag)* I got some Scotch, just for you. Alan?
ALAN	*(campy)* No thanks. I'll stick to Shirley Temples.
NICK	*(laughing)* Hey, that's good. So, you're with the Festival. Watch your ass, that's all I can say.
ALAN	*(very macho)* I'm not with the Festival yet. You think I'm watching my ass too closely?
NICK	Could be. What do you think, Charlie? You're the resident expert on the gay scene.

ALAN	*(to* CHARLIE*)* Do tell.
NICK	Babe, how does that bit go, about the faggots in the restaurant? *(to* ALAN*)* They're always sending back dirty forks, right, then they pick up some stranger and get the clap.
ALAN	That's very funny, Charlie. Not very insightful, but funny.
CHARLIE	I do a whole bunch of different stuff. You'll see.
ALAN	Some other time, maybe.
CHARLIE	I thought you wanted to come tonight.
ALAN	I've changed my mind. *(picking up his suitcase)* Have a good show. I'll call you tomorrow.
CHARLIE	Alan —
ALAN	*(more conciliatory)* Look, I've got a heavy day tomorrow. I have to be on the phone early to Grant Austin and —
NICK	Grant? You working with him?
ALAN	*(stiffly)* I'd like to.
NICK	*(to* CHARLIE*)* Grant was on that picture I told you about. Christ, I more than tripled on that one.
ALAN	*(setting down his sllitcase)* Lupercal? You have money in that?
NICK	Lucky me. You see the numbers on that fucker?
ALAN	No, but I saw the fucker. It was great.
NICK	Grant's dynamite. Camp as a row of tents but a hell of a director. You seeing him tomorrow?
ALAN	He's not sure what his time is like.
NICK	Well, he starts casting next week. You better catch him before the big rush.
ALAN	You don't happen to know what the film is?

NICK	Another blockbuster, I hope. I've got money in this one, too.
ALAN	*(avidly)* No kidding? You haven't seen a script, by any chance?
NICK	I know where to get one. Why?
ALAN	*(to* CHARLIE*)* Listen, maybe I can join you at the club. Once I dump the suitcase.
CHARLIE	I thought you had such an early day ahead.
ALAN	*(artificially sweet)* I thought you wanted me to see your act.
CHARLIE	*(the same)* A minute ago, my act rated slightly below trench-mouth.
ALAN	I haven't got any idea what you're talking about.
CHARLIE	Haven't you? I mean it's just amazing how the atmosphere in this room has warmed up since Grant Austin dropped in.
ALAN	*(to* NICK*)* You don't mind if I join you later at The Canada Goose? And maybe talk about this new script?
NICK	I don't mind. I like to talk. Charlie knows that.
ALAN	*(picking up his suitcase)* See you later, then. 'Bye, babe.
	ALAN *exits.* CHARLIE *takes a long sip of her drink.*
NICK	Nervous kind of guy. He any good?
CHARLIE	I don't know. He never gives himself a chance to find out. He's too busy making useful contacts.
NICK	You should talk. Soon as you found out I backed movies, you couldn't get your clothes off fast enough.
CHARLIE	Nick! You don't believe that.
NICK	Come on, you're entitled to your self-interest, like everybody else. It doesn't detract from the quality of the sex.

CHARLIE   I'm telling you, I'm not in it for the fringe benefits. I want to get that clear, Nick.

NICK   You people with 'pure motives.' You make me nervous.

CHARLIE   Oh, I'm not so pure...*(putting her arms around him)* Let's not talk about work. You've already got Alan prepared to lay down his life for you because you might be useful to him. Isn't that enough?

NICK   I don't get it. If I can get him in to see Austin, why shouldn't I? If I can do you a favour, why not? What is it? You've got your life in ledger columns? 'Business'. 'Romance'.

CHARLIE   That's right. Just don't mix me in with business, that's all. This town is one giant office. Casting done in bars. Contracts ratified on waterbeds. People sucking up to power because it might rub off. Those macrobiotic people had it all wrong. Around here, you are *who* you eat.

NICK   You don't know a goddamn thing about it. Work, sex, dinner, dealing — it's all the same. I don't even try keeping them apart. And I like people who do the same. No questions asked.

CHARLIE   *(pouring herself a drink)* That's a tall order.

NICK   *(indicating drink)* Hey, you're working tonight. Were you always such a little lush? Even when you were married to what's-his-name?

CHARLIE   Lush. You make me sound like a golf course. This is only my second. And anyway, what's it got to do with what's-his-name?

NICK   That's what I wonder. What broke you two up? You never told me.

CHARLIE   You never asked. I like that arrangement. *(kissing him)* I don't want to talk about it. I want to fool around.

NICK   You always want to fool around. What did you do, wear the guy out?

CHARLIE   *(sharply)* Will you forget about Alan?

NICK   No, I want to know. What was the problem?

CHARLIE	*(exasperated)* Isn't it obvious? My frigidity!
NICK	Hey. How come you always act like you'll never get laid again?
CHARLIE	Right now, I'd settle for a really decisive kiss.

> NICK *sighs, then kisses her very decisively.* CHARLIE *pulls away finally, hesitates for a moment before speaking.*

CHARLIE	Nick...Do you think I'm attractive?
NICK	You haven't figured that out?
CHARLIE	I mean — do you like being with me?
NICK	Hell, no. When you stop giving green stamps, I'm gone.
CHARLIE	*(urgently)* Nick — please?
NICK	*(pausing, then with slight distaste)* Okay. Of course I like being with you. Very much.
CHARLIE	Yeah, I figured. *(pulling him to her, kissing him)*

***

Published by Playwrights Canada Press - trade paperback.

Serpent in the Night Sky

Dianne Warren

Duff, a good-old boy, has just married and brough home Joy, a teen runaway, and this doesn't sit well with his family. They are eating super when Duff's sister, Stella, arrives.

DUFF	This is good.
JOY	Yeah?
DUFF	Yeah.
JOY	I'm glad you like it.
DUFF	*(pause)* This is nice.
JOY	What?
DUFF	This. You and me. Eating. I don't eat much at home. Usually I go to Stella's or I pick up a burger. Joy
JOY	I would've lit candles but I couldn't find any.
DUFF	Candles. Nah, I don't have anything like that in the house.
JOY	The fridge is pretty empty. *(pause)* Now that it's clean it's really empty.
DUFF	Yeah. I noticed. It looks great.
JOY	It's empty. Duff.
DUFF	Oh.
JOY	How do you want to work the groceries and things?
DUFF	What do you mean?
JOY	I mean, do you want me to give you a list, or do you want me to pick them up?

DUFF	You can pick them up if you want to. I always go to Bill's. That's the one on the hill. His food's not as good, but he'll let you run up a tab. You can go to the Safeway, but you have to have cash there.
JOY	I'll go to Bill's, if that's where you go.
DUFF	Doesn't matter to me.

STELLA *enters without knocking.*

STELLA	Well, look at this. A nice domestic scene.
DUFF	Don't start in, Stella. We're just having supper.
STELLA	I can see that.
JOY	Would you like to pull up a chair? There's plenty of food.
STELLA	No, I would not.
DUFF	Come on, Stella. It's good.
STELLA	I just came looking for Gator.
DUFF	I haven't seen him all day.
STELLA	Did you work today? Did you have any fares?
DUFF	Yeah.
STELLA	Good.
DUFF	You came over to check and see if I worked today?
STELLA	No. I came looking for Gator.
DUFF	He isn't here.
STELLA	I can see that.
JOY	Why don't you sit down. Stella. Have some coffee if you've already eaten.
STELLA	I haven't eaten.
JOY	Let me get you a plate.
STELLA	I don't need a plate. I've got supper on the stove at home.

DUFF	If you've got supper on the stove at home, what the hell are you doing here? Why aren't you at home eating it?
STELLA	I don't want to eat alone, do I? What good is a big meal if you have to eat it alone?
DUFF	What did you cook a big meal for if you knew you were going to have to eat alone?
STELLA	I didn't know that. did I? I sometimes have two people besides myself for supper, Duff. Or have you forgotten that?
DUFF	What do you mean? Me? What made you think I'd be there?
STELLA	Why wouldn't I think you'd be there?
DUFF	I'm having supper here tonight.
JOY	Please sit down. Stella.
DUFF	Joy's a good cook.
STELLA	I don't run a boarding house, you know. I don't run a restaurant. It would be nice if you could think of it as a family meal. One you're supposed to show up for.
DUFF	*(pause)* I don't have to show up at your place.
STELLA	Fine. That's good to know. Fine. I'll go home then, and throw the whole works out.
DUFF	You don't have to do that, Stella.
STELLA	Well. I'm going to do it. And whenever you need money, you just come by and pick it up. Anytime.
DUFF	Fine.
STELLA	Fine.
DUFF	Go then.
JOY	The supper you've made will keep until tomorrow.
STELLA	I don't want it tomorrow.
DUFF	Don't bother trying, Joy. It's not worth it.

JOY	This is stupid. It is. Stella, why don't you stay for supper. Look at it as an invitation out.
STELLA	I don't get invitations out.
JOY	This is your first then. Duff, get her a plate.
DUFF	Stay out of this, Joy.
JOY	Please get Stella a plate.
DUFF	If she wants to stay, she can get her own plate.
STELLA	Thanks, Duff. Thanks a lot.
DUFF	What do you mean, 'Thanks, Duff'?
STELLA	What do you think I mean?
DUFF	Do you want to stay or not?
JOY	Of course she wants to stay. I'll get her a plate.
STELLA	Don't bother. I can get my own plate, thank you very much.
	STELLA *gets a plate, pulls up a chair and sits.*
JOY	Help yourself to stew. Pass her the pot, Duff. Please excuse the pot. I'd have served it in a bowl if I'd known company was coming.
DUFF	She's hardly company.
JOY	Duff.
STELLA	Never mind. He's right.
DUFF	*(pause)* So, what are you going to do with all that money, Stella?
STELLA	I told you. I'm going to buy Marlene a trailer.
DUFF	I thought you would have changed your mind by now.
STELLA	I'm not changing my mind. What is this anyway?
JOY	Rabbit stew. I didn't have a recipe, but...

STELLA	*(interrupting)* Rabbit stew.
DUFF	What's wrong with that?
STELLA	I don't eat rabbit stew.
DUFF	There's nothing wrong with it.
STELLA	*(eating)* It's not bad.
DUFF	I told you.
STELLA	Never mind. Just shut up and eat.

* * *

Published by Playwrights Canada Press - trade paperback.

Toronto, Mississippi

Joan MacLeod

Jhanna is a passionate and humourous mentally-handicapped teenager just discovering herself in this scene with her mother and their boarder, Bill, a poet. Her father is a an Elvis impersonator. N.B. Her syntax is intentional.

BILL	Not now, Jhani. They've asked me to do a reading then a little talk on my process and that. Want to hear some?
JHANA	No. I will keep talking. See? I can sing at lunch. Not at the worktable. That worktable's for working. Everyone watches me. They love this.
BILL	What do you sing?
JHANA	*(imitating Elvis)* Good evening ladies and...ladies. It's pleasure. Elvis Presley is here!
	(singing) Love her tender, love her tender Never let her Love her tender, lover her tender Love her, love her tender
	Are you watching me?
BILL	The world is watching you.
JHANA	Good. Be Andrew. For dinner, Bill. Please?
BILL	For ten minutes. When both hands are at six then you're going to be the audience and I'm going to be the brilliant young poet behind the podium. Got that?
JHANA	Yes! Get out! Out the door, Bill.
	BILL *exits, then* JHANA *greets him at the door, role playing a dinner date.*
JHANA	Hello Andrew.
BILL	Good evening Miss Kelly.

JHANA	She's Jhana!
BILL	You look lovely.
JHANA	Please eat.
BILL	Don't you want to take my coat first, offer me a place to sit down?
JHANA	Please sit and take your coat.
BILL	How was your day?
JHANA	Funny.
BILL	Why?
JHANA	Steffie hit Peter in the wheelchair! Screws went flying!
BILL	That doesn't sound funny.
JHANA	It's funny. Eat.
BILL	What's for dinner?
JHANA	Cheerios.
BILL	Since when do you eat Cheerios for supper.
JHANA	Since I'm funny.
BILL	Aren't you though. Are you going to make a move? Casually slip an arm around *(putting his arm around JHANA)* Andrew's mammoth but trembling shoulders?
JHANA	*(beginning to act very sexually but toward herself not BILL)* I'm funny.
BILL	You going to get in there and give Andrew the business.
JHANA	The business.
BILL	You can, Jhana. If you want to, you're allowed. You do understand that, don't you?
JHANA	Kissing him on the mouth?

BILL	Absolutely. And here too. *(touching JHANA's neck)* I'm not saying you should rush in there and jump on him. Take it slow and easy. But you can reach out.
JHANA	Reach!
BILL	If you hold back everything it'll turn sour inside, or worse yet it'll turn into poetry. Then you're really sunk.
JHANA	Kiss his mouth, Bill.
BILL	Not me. That's your job.
JHANA	My job. And here. *(touching BILL's neck)* It's funny. Right? Steffie won't kiss Andrew. Only me.

MADDIE *enters.*

MADDIE	*(to JHANA)* Hi honey!
JHANA	NO!
MADDIE	Nice to see you too. How was your day?
JHANA	She's not allowed Bill!
BILL	We were just...
MADDIE	What am I not allowed to do?
JHANA	Get out!
MADDIE	My house kid.
JHANA	We're in private, me and Bill.
BILL	Jhana likes this guy at work and...
JHANA	NO! Make her get out!
MADDIE	Look. You're allowed to talk to Bill on your own but there are polite ways to explain that you're in the middle of something.
JHANA	Get out.
BILL	In fact it's more like pretend dates than just talk or...
JHANA	NO !

MADDIE	Have I interrupted you?
JHANA	NO ! *(pause)* Yes.
MADDIE	You were talking about someone and my coming in made you embarrassed?
JHANA	We're private, me and Bill.
MADDIE	That isn't what I object to. When I come in, you and Bill can move upstairs after you say hi. No one likes being yelled at the second they come in the door.
JHANA	*(pause)* Sorry, Mum.
MADDIE	It's okay. How was your day?
JHANA	Hi, Mum.
MADDIE	Hi, Jhani.
JHANA	Hi, Bill.
BILL	Hi.
JHANA	How are you, Mum?
MADDIE	Fine.
JHANA	Bill is fine.
BILL	Top notch.
MADDIE	Your reading! Was that today? Jesus, Bill I meant to...
BILL	It's tomorrow. No big deal.
MADDIE	You're not nervous?
BILL	I've done dozens of these things. Or at least a certain number.
MADDIE	You need an audience?
BILL	God yes. This is a poetry reading — no one will come. And it's in a library, in Pickering.
MADDIE	I meant do you want an audience right now. To practice.

BILL	That's stupid.
MADDIE	I don't mind. Me and Jhana will be the public at large.
JHANA	I'm cooking salad.
MADDIE	Right you are! Jhana makes salad tonight! Jhana makes dessert! How many?
JHANA	Five cup!
MADDIE	One cup of...come on Jhani...oranges
JHANA	Oranges!
MADDIE	And?
JHANA	Marshmallows. Tiny, tiny.
MADDIE	One cup...
JHANA	Coconuts...pineapple.
MADDIE	And last but not least!
JHANA	Yes !
MADDIE	What's the white stuff that holds it all together?
JHANA	Milk!
MADDIE	Sour cream!
JHANA	Sour cream!
BILL	Hallelujah!
MADDIE	Five cup salad! No recipe needed. No fuss, no muss...
JHANA	Five cup salad !
MADDIE	You know where everything is?
JHANA	The fridge. And cans.
MADDIE	And the coconut is in the cupboard above the sink in a red bag.
JHANA	Red.

MADDIE	The measuring cup is in the dishwasher. You can do all of it by yourself.
JHANA	Don't help her, Bill.
BILL	Best of luck, Jhana. And remember kid. No matter what happens in there, I loved you.
JHANA	I love you, Bill. And coconut, in a red bag, in the sink.
MADDIE	Above the sink.
JHANA	I love you, Mum.
MADDIE	Me too. Get to work.
JHANA	You're loving Bill?
MADDIE	Yup.
JHANA	She's going to work. I am working for salad and dessert.
MADDIE	And Bill and I are going to have a gigantic glass of scotch and talk poetry.
JHANA	Poetry! *(exits)*
MADDIE	So Jhana wants to sleep with someone at work?
BILL	What happened to her right to privacy?
MADDIE	I changed my mind.
BILL	Just a crush. Lots of talk about kissing.
MADDIE	*"Black Morning."*
BILL	Right. I'm going to use that quote about my being a voice for women and the responsibility that entails.
MADDIE	Your own voice, Bill. That's all we need.
BILL	It is my voice. Maybe I don't know how to make it sing or shimmy but it is mine.
MADDIE	However sleazy it may seem to you, I need him like breath right now.
BILL	It's your life.

MADDIE	And you're a big part of it. You're my best friend. It's true. Quit taking it like a slap in the face. You're just...I'm...I know he's fucked up. But at least he's out there. Trying to do something he feels about. He's always been, you know, very alive.
BILL	I find it remarkable that someone who makes his living pretending to be a dead person is living life to the fullest. Where is he anyway?
MADDIE	He's at the Elvis Museum in Niagara Falls. He might do some stuff for them for the anniversary in August.
BILL	What anniversary?
MADDIE	Elvis's death. Jesus, Bill. I can't believe you wouldn't know that.
BILL	It wasn't like Kennedy. I can't tell you what I was doing at that exact moment.
MADDIE	We were in Whitehorse. This guy called Wade, he came in with the news after the first set. The King is dead.
BILL	When Elvis Presley died I was at Carleton. We thought it was funny.
MADDIE	King hauled Jhana up on stage. Those days I put all my energy into convincing everyone she was normal. A little slow. Jesus. She had a ten-word vocabulary at five. Her first word was Mum and her second word was pig. Because of this story King had made up about this pig that was a terrific swimmer. But I used to worry about it anyway, mother then pig.
BILL	I bet you worried.
MADDIE	While she's up on stage I'm praying she won't open her mouth, won't stim out because of the lights, have a rocking fit because of the drums.
BILL	What'd she do?
MADDIE	Nothing. She loved it. Everyone loved her and were too pissed to notice she wasn't, you know, normal. *(pause)* Bill, promise me this guy at work or some old leech on the bus isn't going to hurt her. Isn't going to take advantage of all that trust.

BILL   She's okay.

MADDIE   Mother then pig.

BILL   I think you are very wonderful with her.

MADDIE   You too, Willy.

BILL   And I have been a bit of an asshole about him staying here. A little bit.

>   JHANA *enters, much slowed down, nearly dreamy.*

JHANA   It's perfect Mum. Cooking in the bowl. It's so pretty. Five cup salad. In the fridge.

MADDIE   You're all done?

JHANA   Done.

MADDIE   No problems?

JHANA   Maybe.

MADDIE   Let's not worry about it now. Come give your old Mum a hug.

JHANA   Old Mum. Old, old Mum.

MADDIE   Thanks a lot kid.

JHANA   Mine.

* * *

Published with "Jewel" by Playwrights Canada Press - trade paperback

The Queens

Normand Chaurette

*In this story of the women from Shakespeare's "Richard III", Queen Margaret,
who has long since lost the throne of England, announces her intention to leave
England, taking with her the two sons of the current queen and Edward IV, the
heirs to the throne destined to be 'the princes in the tower'.*

QUEEN MARGARET   I am leaving for China
For the peaks of fabulous Asia
These children will see the other side of the world
Where the sun shines bright.

DUCHESS OF YORK   Let me see
A few wrinkles, here and there
Make it hard to remember that you were
Scarcely more than a few days ago
Or so it seems — queen.

QUEEN MARGARET   I know by heart
How many teeth you have left
And your hair —
Wait let me count them
Try as I might
I cannot see more than eight
Provided one splits
Each hair into four
As for your wrinkles
They've frightened away our songbirds
And if I had only half
So many on my face
I would have fled ages ago
To some place on this earth
Where I could live
Far from the light of day.

DUCHESS OF YORK   If I hadn't t always
Frightened away the birds of prey
They would never cease to circle
Round your putrid lives!

QUEEN MARGARET   Putrid am I?
Today perhaps...

DUCHESS OF YORK   In those days as well.

QUEEN MARGARET   In those days in the county of Anjou
I was hale and hardy
A shameless beauty
Of boundless charm.

DUCHESS OF YORK   You should have stayed in France
Queen of the county monarchy.
Give me those children.

QUEEN MARGARET   They have no mother
I'm taking them with me.
(spreading out her baggage) I'm also taking my
slippers
My boots and my kettles
You have two or three bonnets
Which belong to me — keep them
I have however taken
My sheepskin stoles from your hutch.
There are advantages to my departure
Tucked among the ivory corsets
I found a chamois glove
Worn by Queen Eleanor
Who lived to be eighty-two
I do wish I could find the other
In France people would pay a fortune for the pair.
By the way, did you know that I was an archduchess?
I was unaware myself
On my warrant of accession to the throne
It's written black on white: archduchess.
You'll notice in my chest I've left some jewels
I'm taking only these
I've taken this vase
This lovely fabric
These fine metals
Pure bronze
Look at this aspergill
From my own christening
The Great Book of Wonders
And the *mappa mundi* of Syracuse
Which good King René
Received from Charles I of Anjou
Who received it from Pope Boniface
Who had received it in turn
From Marco Polo's mistress;
The proclamation of pardon
And the agenda of successions
I have a right to the papers of the monarchy

I am taking them with me
My powders and essences
My rags and my linens
So I can sleep on my journey
I shall abandon the rest here —
My illusions, my torments
And my sleepless nights
If I could leave my heartaches
I'd make you a present of them all.
Here, take my key
To remind you of the days
When you plotted against me.
You need only open my door
Throw back the carpet
And look carefully beneath the dust —
Just blow and see:
I have left my soul behind.

DUCHESS OF YORK   What do you expect the future queens
To do with your soul?
Erected on tombs
This house is filled to the rafters
With forgotten souls.

ISABEL WARWICK *enters.*

ISABEL WARWICK   Why Madame d'Anjou!
Does all this belong to you?
For years now I've wondered
Who collects these old stockings
These old bits and pieces, all this clutter.

QUEEN MARGARET   Clutter!

ISABEL WARWICK   Must I conclude
Oblivious to the gusts and gales
You are preparing
Your impetuous departure for France?

QUEEN MARGARET   Your countenance belies
How my departure taints your happiness.

ISABEL WARWICK   My heart is broken
To see that you are leaving.

QUEEN MARGARET   Certainly in my clutter I can find
Something to glue it together.

ISABEL WARWICK	You'd do better to clear the floor Today is Thursday. I wish I could avoid it But Thursday the laws are strict: Nothing must interfere with the Elevation of the Queens.
QUEEN MARGARET	*(devastated)* Rest assured You won't have to elevate yourself midst my clutter.

MARGARET *gathers up her clutter.*

ISABEL WARWICK	I do envy your fortune.
QUEEN MARGARET	My fortune, these old stockings?
ISABEL WARWICK	With the ambiguity of the word fortune I am only referring To your strength and your admirable courage We all dream of leaving England is so dreary... Thus in eight days time You'll have reconquered France?
QUEEN MARGARET	China.
ISABEL WARWICK	*(stoically)* China. And what will you do in China?
QUEEN MARGARET	Continue to loathe the lot of you. I want to see how far one can take contempt However distant one might be.
ISABEL WARWICK	And what about the throne? Mmmm...hard to say.
QUEEN MARGARET	The what? The throne? The throne! What throne?
ISABEL WARWICK	The throne of the...samurai why not! I assume he sits somewhere? There where you are going Isn't there always a throne to be usurped?
QUEEN MARGARET	They have real families there...
ISABEL WARWICK	...More vigilant than ours?
QUEEN MARGARET	China is in safe hands.

ISABEL WARWICK   And do the leisured queens
The fallen empresses
Have enough to eat among the mandarins?

QUEEN MARGARET   As much as sisters
Dissolute in their corruption.

ISABEL WARWICK   As much as intruders!
Farewell now, and forever
Though dare I say 'forever'
Tis no way to measure time
We shall see by the length of your absence
How far the principle extends.

QUEEN MARGARET   The principle cannot be extended
Whereas I shall go far.

ISABEL WARWICK   Then once again I say farewell
And promise I shall think of you
If and when I find the respite
Midst the throes of the reign which awaits me.
Oh — it's almost two o'clock
I must run to dress
Give me back that chamois glove —
It belongs to me.

QUEEN MARGARET   The glove of Queen Eleanor who lived to be eighty two!

ISABEL WARWICK   I've been searching for it for days now.
Come — give it back to me
It is part of the Warwick inheritance.

QUEEN MARGARET   Do you have proof?

ISABEL WARWICK   Isn't there a little *W*
Embroidered inside the cuff?
Wait...here...mmm...

QUEEN MARGARET   Only in France
Can you find these embroidered stitches.
It bears no resemblance
To your manufactured gloves.

ISABEL WARWICK   That glove is mine.

QUEEN MARGARET   Where is the *W*?
Show it to me!

ISABEL WARWICK   Mmmm...there was one on the other glove
                  Wait, I'll run and fetch it.

                  ISABEL *exits in the direction of the castle.*

QUEEN MARGARET   And why not my corsets?
                  And my warrant of accession while you're at it!
                  And why not all my baggage?
                  You've taken everything else from me
                  My joys, my dignity
                  The light heartedness of my youth
                  And now
                  You strip me of my memories...
                  (to the DUCHESS OF YORK*)* Farewell forever.
                  I am leaving and I take with me more offences
                  Than any other woman here
                  Is capable of suffering.

DUCHESS OF YORK   Leave the babes with me.
                  Think of Elizabeth's grief
                  The moment you set foot outside
                  They'll perish of the cold.

QUEEN MARGARET   I shall be the wind who carries them away
                  Or I shall stay
                  So there — consider the exchange
                  The choice is yours
                  Either I depart with them
                  And promise never to return
                  Or I leave them with you
                  And linger here till your death.

DUCHESS OF YORK   You commit yourself for little time
                  I would so like to see you
                  Far away from our isle
                  That if I didn't still have
                  A scrap of heart left in me
                  I would tell you to leave
                  With them forever.

QUEEN MARGARET   Did you never love me then?

DUCHESS OF YORK   Leave.

QUEEN MARGARET   Tell me to stay
                  And I'll stay.

DUCHESS OF YORK   This day has already begun
To see us disappear
London has buried itself
Our children are leaving for Asia
Edward is going to his grave
And the world is shrinking
Soon it shall be little more
Than a stitch of lace
Invisible in the infinite
Leave
Don't wait for me to die
Before you leave me.

QUEEN MARGARET   Farewell then.

DUCHESS OF YORK   Feed them with tender love, naught else.

QUEEN MARGARET   Did you never love me, Cecily?

Silence.

Farewell.

DUCHESS OF YORK   Farewell.

QUEEN MARGARET *exits with her
baggage and the children.*

* * *

*© Leméac Editeur and Coach House Press. Translation © 1992 Linda Gaboriau.
Reprinted from THE QUEENS.*

The Rez Sisters

Tomson Highway

This Dora Mavor Moore Award winner for Best New Play is a powerful portrayal of seven women from a reserve attempting to beat the odds by winning a bingo — and not just any bingo. It is the BIGGEST BINGO IN THE WORLD in Toronto, and a chance to win a way out of a tortured way of life.

	A beautiful late August day on the Wasaychigan Hill Indian reserve on Manitoulin Island in Northern Ontario. Pelajia Patchnose is alone on the roof of her house, in faded men's denim overalls, nailing shingles to the roof. Her sister Philomena Moosetail is offstage.
PELAJIA	Philomena. I wanna go to Toronto.
PHILOMENA	*(offstage)* Oh, go on.
PELAJIA	Sure as I'm sitting away up here on the roof of this old house. I kind of like it up here, though. From here, I can see half of Manitoulin Island on a clear day. I can see the chimneys, the tops of apple trees, the garbage heap behind Big Joey's dumpy little house. I can see the seagulls circling over Marie-Adele Starblanket's white picket fence. Boats on the North Channel I wish I was on, sailing away somewhere. The mill at Espanola, a hundred miles away ...and that's with just a bit of squinting. See? If I had binoculars, I could see the superstack in Sudbury. And if I were Superwoman, I could see the CN Tower in Toronto. Ah, but I'm just plain old Pelajia Rosella Patchnose and I'm here in plain, dusty, boring old Wasaychigan Hill...Wasy...waiting...waiting...nailing shining shingles with my trusty silver hammer on the roof of Pelajia Rosella Patchnose's little two-bedroom welfare house. Philomena. I wanna go to Toronto.
	PHILOMENA MOOSETAIL *comes up the ladder to the roof with one shingle and obviously hating it. She is very well-dressed, with a skirt, nylons, even heels, completely impractical for the roof.*

PHILOMENA	Oh, go on.
PELAJIA	I'm tired, Philomena, tired of this place. There's days I wanna leave so bad.
PHILOMENA	But you were born here. All your poop's on this reserve.
PELAJIA	Oh, go on.
PHILOMENA	You'll never leave.
PELAJIA	Yes, I will. When I'm old.
PHILOMENA	You're old right now.
PELAJIA	I got a good 30 years to go...
PHILOMENA	...and you're gonna live every one of them right here beside me...
PELAJIA	...maybe 40...
PHILOMENA	...here in Wasy. *(tickling* PELAJIA *on the breasts)* Chiga-chiga-chiga.
PELAJIA	*(yelping and slapping* PHILOMENA's *hand away)* Oh, go on. It's not like it used to be.
PHILOMENA	Oh, go on. People change, places change, time changes things. You expect to be young and gorgeous forever?
PELAJIA	See? I told you I'm not old.
PHILOMENA	Oh, go on. You.
PELAJIA	'Oh, go on. You.' You bug me like hell when you say that.
PHILOMENA	You say it, too. And don't give me none of this 'I don't like this place. I'm tired of it.' This place is too much inside your blood. You can't get rid of it. And it can't get rid of you.
PELAJIA	Four thirty this morning, I was woken by...
PHILOMENA	Here we go again.
PELAJIA	...Andrew Starblanket and his brother, Matthew. Drunk. Again. Or sounded like...

PHILOMENA   Nothing better to do.

PELAJIA   ...fighting over some girl. Heard what sounded like a
                   baseball bat landing on somebody's back. My lawn looks
                   like the shits this morning.

PHILOMENA   Well, I like it here. Myself, I'm gonna go to every bingo
                   and I'm gonna hit every jackpot between here and
                   Espanola and I'm gonna buy me that toilet I'm dreaming
                   about at night...big and wide and very white...

PELAJIA   Aw-ni-gi-naw-ee-dick. *('Oh, go on' in Ojibway)*

PHILOMENA   I'm good at bingo.

PELAJIA   So what! And the old stories, the old language. Almost all
                   gone...was a time Nanabush and Windigo and everyone
                   here could rattle away in Indian fast as Bingo Betty could
                   lay her bingo chips down on a hot night.

PHILOMENA   Pelajia Rosella Patchnose. The sun's gonna drive you
                   crazy. *(descending the ladder)*

PELAJIA   Everyone here's crazy. No jobs. Nothing to do but drink
                   and screw each other's wives and husbands and forget
                   about our Nanabush.

                         From offstage PHILOMENA *screams. She
                         fell down the ladder.*

                   Philomena! *(looking over the edge of the roof)* What are
                   you doing down there?

PHILOMENA   What do you think? I fell.

PELAJIA   Bring me some of them nails while you're down there.

PHILOMENA   *(whining from offstage, from behind the house)* You think
                   I can race up and down this ladder? You think I got wings?

PELAJIA   You gotta wear pants when you're doing a man's job. See?
                   You got your skirt ripped on a nail and now you can see
                   your thighs. People gonna think you just came from Big
                   Joey's house.

PHILOMENA   *(coming up the ladder in a state of disarray)* Let them think what they want. That old cow Gazelle Nataways...always acting like she thinks she's still a spring chicken. She's got them legs of hers wrapped around Big Joey day and night...

PELAJIA   Philomena. Park your tongue. My old man has to go the hundred miles to Espanola just to get a job. My boys. Gone to Toronto. Only place educated Indian boys can find decent jobs these days. And here I sit all broken-hearted.

PHILOMENA   Paid a dime and only farted.

PELAJIA   Look at you. You got dirt all over your backside. *(turning her attention to the road in front of her house and standing up for the first and only time)* And dirt roads! Years now that old chief's been making speeches about getting paved roads 'for my people' and still we got dirt roads all over.

PHILOMENA   Oh, go on.

PELAJIA   When I win me that jackpot next time we play bingo in Espanola...

PHILOMENA   *(examining her torn skirt, her general state of disarray, and fretting over it)* Look at this! Will you look at this! Ohhh!

PELAJIA   ...I'm gonna put that old chief to shame and build me a nice paved road right here in front of my house. Jet black. Shiny. Make my lawn look real nice.

PHILOMENA   My rib-cage!

PELAJIA   And if that old chief don't wanna make paved roads for all my sisters around here...

PHILOMENA   There's something rattling around inside me!

PELAJIA   I'm packing my bags and moving to Toronto. *(sitting down again)*

PHILOMENA   Oh, go on. *(spying ANNIE COOK's approach, a distance up the hill)* Why, I do believe that cloud of dust over there is Annie Cook racing down the hill, Pelajia.

PELAJIA   Philomena. I wanna go to Toronto.

PHILOMENA	She's walking mighty fast. Must be excited about something.
PELAJIA	Never seen Annie Cook walk slow since the day she finally lost Eugene to Marie-Adele at the church 19 years ago. And even then she was walking a little too fast for a girl who was supposed to be broken-heart...*(stopping just in time and laughing)*...heart-broken.

> ANNIE COOK, *their half-sister, pops up the top of the ladder to the roof.*

ANNIE	*(cheery, fast and perky)* Halloooo! Whatchyou doing up here?
PELAJIA	There's room for only so much weight up here before we go crashing into my kitchen, so what do you want?
ANNIE	Just popped up to say hi.
PELAJIA	And see what we're doing?
ANNIE	Well...
PELAJIA	Couldn't you see what we're doing from up where you were?
ANNIE	*(confidentially, to PHILOMENA)* Is it true Gazelle Nataways won the bingo last night?
PHILOMENA	Annie Cook, first you say you're gonna come with me and then you don't even bother showing up. If you were sitting beside me at that bingo table last night you would have seen Gazelle Nataways win that big pot again with your own two eyes.
ANNIE	Emily Dictionary and I went to Little Current to listen to Fritz the Katz.
PELAJIA	What in God's name kind of a band might that be?
ANNIE	Country rock. My favorite. Fritz the Katz is from Toronto.
PELAJIA	Fritzy...ritzy...Philomena! Say something.
PHILOMENA	My record player is in Espanola getting fixed.
ANNIE	That's nice.

PHILOMENA	Good.
ANNIE	Is it true Gazelle Nataways plans to spend her bingo money to go to Toronto with...with Big Joey?
PHILOMENA	Who wants to know? Emily Dictionary?
ANNIE	I guess so.
PELAJIA	That Gazelle Nataways gonna leave all her babies behind and let them starve to death?
ANNIE	I guess so. I don't know. I'm asking you.
PELAJIA & PHILOMENA	We don't know.
ANNIE	I'm on my way to Marie-Adele's to pick her up.
PELAJIA	Why? Where you gonna put her down?

PELAJIA *and* PHILOMENA *laugh.*

ANNIE	I mean, we're going to the store together. To the post office. We're going to pick up a parcel. They say there's a parcel for me. They say it's shaped like a record. And they say it's from Sudbury. So it must be from my daughter, Ellen...
PELAJIA & PHILOMENA	...'who lives with this white guy in Sudbury'...
ANNIE	How did you know?
PHILOMENA	Everybody knows.
ANNIE	His name is Ray*mond*. Not *Ray*mond. But Ray*mond*. Like in Bon Bon.

PHILOMENA *tries out 'bon bon' to herself.*

He's French.

PELAJIA	Oh?
ANNIE	Garage mechanic. He fixes cars. And you know, talking about Frenchmen, that old priest is holding another bingo next week and when I win...*(to* PHILOMENA*)* Are you going?

PELAJIA	Does a bear shit in the woods?
ANNIE	...when I win, I'm going to Espanola and play the bingo there. Emily Dictionary says that Fire Minklater can give us a ride in her new car. She got it through Ray*mond*'s garage. The bingo in Espanola is bigger. And it's better. And I'll win. And then I'll go to Sudbury, where the bingos are even bigger and better. And then I can visit my daughter, Ellen...
PELAJIA	...'who lives with this white guy in Sudbury'...
ANNIE	...and go shopping in the record stores and go to the hotel and drink beer quietly — not noisy and crazy like here and listen to the live bands. It will be so much fun. I hope Emily Dictionary can come with me.
PHILOMENA	It's true. I've been thinking...
PELAJIA	You don't say.
PHILOMENA	It's true. The bingos here are getting kind of boring...
ANNIE	That old priest is too slow and sometimes he gets the numbers all mixed up and the pot's not big enough.
PHILOMENA	And I don't like the way he calls the numbers. *(nasally)* B 12, O 64.
ANNIE	When Little Girl Manitowabi won last month...
PHILOMENA	She won just enough to take a taxi back to Buzwah.
ANNIE	That's all.
	Both ANNIE *and* PHILOMENA *pause to give a quick sigh of yearning.*
PHILOMENA	Annie Cook, I want that big pot.
ANNIE	We all want big pots.
PELAJIA	Start a revolution!
ANNIE & PHILOMENA	Yes!

ANNIE	All us Wasy women. We'll march up the hill, burn the church hall down, scare the priest to death, and then we'll march all the way to Espanola, where the bingos are bigger and better...
PHILOMENA	We'll hold big placards!
ANNIE	They'll say: 'Wasy women want bigger bingos!'
PELAJIA	And one will say: 'Annie Cook Wants Big Pot!'
PHILOMENA	...and the numbers at those bingos in Espanola go faster and the pots get bigger by the week. Oh, Pelajia Patchnose, I'm getting excited just thinking about it!
ANNIE	I'm going.
PELAJIA	You are, are you?
ANNIE	Yes. I'm going. I'm running out of time. I'm going to Marie-Adele's house and then we'll walk to the store together to pick up the parcel — I'm sure there'll be a letter in it, and Marie-Adele is expecting mail, too — and we'll see if Emily Dictionary is working today and we'll ask her if Fire Minklater has her new car yet so we can go to Espanola for that big pot. *(beginning to descend the ladder)*
PELAJIA	Well, you don't have much to do today, do you?
ANNIE	Well. Toodle-oo!

ANNIE *pops down the ladder and is gone.*

PELAJIA	Not bad for someone who was in such a hurry to get her parcel. She talks faster than she walks.

* * *

Published by Fifth House Publishers - trade paperback

Toronto at Dreamer's Rock

Drew Hayden Taylor

A moving portrayal of Rusty, a teenage, Native Canadian boy who is torn between the traditions of his people, which he only vaguely understands, and the lures of modern life. His magical meeting with two members of his tribe — one from 400 years ago, Keesic, and one from his future, Michael, makes him aware of how little he has thought about what it means to be an Indian. N.B. In the language of the tribe living around present day Toronto, the name of the city meant 'meeting place' or the place where people gather to trade, or even where anything important happens.

	This scene proceeds from where MICHAEL *has just appreared as* RUSTY *talks to* KEESIC *with great scepticism. The name Rusty seems to have struck a chord with* MICHAEL *who studies* RUSTY's *face.*
MICHAEL	I know your face from somewhere, and your name. Rusty! Rusty!
RUSTY	So if you're from the future, I'd have to be famous for a hundred years or something for you to know me. *(dawning on him)* Famous! Am I famous, huh, am I? What did I do? Am I a movie star or something? A rock star? *(stopping)* What am I saying? My God, it's contagious. I'm crazy too.
KEESIC	You are from this one's future?
MICHAEL	I didn't think it was possible.
KEESIC	All things are possible here.
	This is too much for RUSTY. *He starts backing up and almost falls off the rock. He looks at the others as if they are crazy.*
RUSTY	What is this? You guys travel in pairs or something? Who are you?
MICHAEL	Philosophically, psychologically, economically, culturally? Be specific.

RUSTY   *(yelling)* Who the hell are you?

MICHAEL   You look upset.

KEESIC   He yells a lot.

RUSTY   *(turning to* KEESIC*)* You shut up, I still haven't figured you out yet. Look, I don't know where you guys are coming from, but I want you to go back there now. I mean it.

> MICHAEL *turns to* KEESIC, *ignoring* RUSTY.

MICHAEL   This is interesting. Judging by the material and stitching pattern, I'd hazard a guess of approximately 500 years ago my time. I knew it was precontact.

KEESIC   Pre-contact.

> RUSTY *throws his hands up in frustration and turns away.*

RUSTY   And he still has all his teeth.

MICHAEL   It means you were here before the white man was, totally untouched, pure. I have a history teacher that would love a chance to interview subject matter like you. Both of you, actually.

> RUSTY *steps in between the two, separating them, and then turns to* MICHAEL.

RUSTY   Wait a minute, just wait a minute, Flash Gordon, I'm tired of having my leg pulled. It's probably halfway down the hill by now. And I don't buy this time thing either. For the last time, who are you? Buckskin Bill here won't give me a straight answer. You got one? Is this a regular thing with you guys, or what?

> MICHAEL *walks around* RUSTY *and looks off in the distance, taking a deep breath.* KEESIC *looks puzzled.*

KEESIC   How do you manage to hunt and feed your family when you talk so much and so loudly?

RUSTY	I think I'm getting one of my mother's headaches. I never should have come up here.
KEESIC	I've been to the Place of Dreams many times, but never like this. Michael, I am called Keesic. Welcome.
MICHAEL	*(animated)* I have this pet theory about this particular spot.

RUSTY *makes a rude noise.*

MICHAEL	Of course, I'm the only one who believes it, but I think it's true. Over those thousands of years that boys had their vision quests here, this area amassed a tremendous reservoir of power. And probably in the time between the two of you this power has gone largely unused. It's a type of emotional power, similar to the Poltergeist phenomenon common in Germany, and Rusty must have triggered it somehow! This is a pretty powerful place, Rusty, even in my time.
RUSTY	I don't care about this place, I just want to find out where you people are popping out of and why. Who's next, the ghost of Christmas present?

MICHAEL *bursts out laughing, but*
KEESIC *doesn't understand it.*

MICHAEL	Don't worry, Rusty, I'm fairly certain I'm not a ghost. How about you, Keesic?

KEESIC *has no idea what is going on.*

KEESIC	Ghost? What?
RUSTY	This is one of those days I should have gotten up, eaten my Rice Krispies, and gone right back to bed again. Look guys, I just wanted a nice quiet beer, and I didn't even get that with that damn crow bugging the hell out of me.

Suddenly RUSTY *has* KEESIC'*s complete attention.*

KEESIC	Crow?! Did you say you heard a crow? What did it say?
RUSTY	Caw. What else does a crow say? It just screeched a few times when I drank my beer, then it went away.

KEESIC *looks worried.*

	Why? What does a crow have to do with anything?
KEESIC	I don't know. But you know what a crow is.

> MICHAEL *and* RUSTY, *confused, look at each other.*

RUSTY	*(bluffing)* Yeah, of course I do, but you better explain it to Michael anyways.
KEESIC	They are the messengers of the Creator and other powerful beings. If that crow was talking to you, it must have been for a reason. You should learn to listen, Rusty, it might have been trying to tell you something important.
RUSTY	Like where the garbage dump is.
MICHAEL	Messengers of the Creator! How quaint!
RUSTY	Forget the stupid crow. If everything you two are telling me is true, then why me, why you, why here, why now? *(pause)* I don't believe this. And why am I still talking to you? My mother warned me about people like you but she said they all lived in Toronto.
KEESIC	Toronto?!
RUSTY	You know about Toronto? Then you aren't real.
KEESIC	I'm as real as you are. My people are great traders. We make trips to the south for goods. And in trade it is better to understand the language of the people you are dealing with. Those people to the south have a word for where people gather to trade, but it covers any place where important things happen. It's called 'Toronto'.
RUSTY	So we're like a little mini-Toronto right up here. That's cool.
MICHAEL	Actually in my time, the metropolis of Toronto almost reaches to the shore of Huron. Traders, eh? What nation are you, anyways?

> KEESIC *looks perplexed.*

KEESIC	We are the people.
MICHAEL	Did other nations have a name for you?

KEESIC   We are known by some tribes as Odawa.

                  RUSTY*'s ears perk up at that word.*

RUSTY   Hey, wow. I'm half Odawa. This is bizarre.

KEESIC   Half Odawa? What is your other half?

RUSTY   Ojibway, and I think there's supposed to be some
                  Pottawatami floating around in my blood somewhere, too.

MICHAEL   Genealogically, I am mostly Odawa.

KEESIC   Ojibway? They live far to the northwest. And the
                  Pottawatami don't live near here. How does their blood
                  flow in your veins?

RUSTY   It's the Three Fires.

KEESIC   I don't understand.

RUSTY   You don't understand the Three Fires? What kind of Indian
                  are you anyways?

MICHAEL   *(stepping between them)* A lot of nations were displaced
                  by the coming of the whiteman. And, as a result,
                  traditional migratory patterns were disrupted. Eventually,
                  the Ojibway, Odawa, and Pottawatami reached an
                  agreement whereby they would share Manitoulin Island.

KEESIC   That's the third time you've mentioned this white man.
                  Why is he white? Is he not well?

RUSTY   Well, that's a judgment call.

MICHAEL   I guess you could say he is another nation far to the east
                  in your time. And in time, he came to this island here.

KEESIC   I have heard stories about these people. But I thought they
                  were just stories.

                  MICHAEL *shakes his head confidently.*

MICHAEL   Well, they're coming. Taking an educated guess, I would
                  estimate you to be from approximately the 1590s. And
                  Champlain landed in this area around 1615. We're talking
                  a couple of decades at the most.

RUSTY
(laughing) Boy, do you have a surprise coming. Guess who's coming to dinner? You better put out an extra 250 million plates, but be sure and check the silverware after.

> *Even MICHAEL laughs at that one. But KEESIC remains in the dark. MICHAEL picks up RUSTY's bottle of beer and examines it as if it were an interesting museum piece.*

MICHAEL
Labatts Blue! I didn't know they made this way back then...I mean now.

KEESIC
I don't like it.

MICHAEL
Neither did I. *(an idea occurs)* That's it, maybe that's why we were brought here! *(as KEESIC and MICHAEL look at each other)* To defend Dreamer's Rock.

KEESIC
Against what?

MICHAEL
(holding up beer bottle) This!

KEESIC
That!

> *RUSTY grabs the bottle and puts it in his pack.*

RUSTY
It's an empty beer bottle. What's there to defend?

MICHAEL
This particular period of time was known in Aboriginal history as the 'Alcoholic Era.' From the mid-1800s till the late 1900s, Native people suffered due to an addiction to this liquid. Of course, the problem didn't start and stop at those times. It slowly led up to it then tapered off, much the same way the Black Plague did in medieval Europe.

KEESIC
Worse than swamp water.

RUSTY
Alcoholic Era? Black plague? I'm just having a beer, not starting an epidemic.

MICHAEL
When's the last time you consumed enough of this liquid to reach your desired effect?

RUSTY
You mean get drunk? Last weekend I guess.

MICHAEL
I thought so.

RUSTY	Don't give me that holier-than-thou attitude. You mean to tell me that there is no such thing as beer in the future?
MICHAEL	Of course there is, but people don't die from it any more. Two hundred years of suicide is enough.

> RUSTY *shakes his head as he tries to figure* MICHAEL *out.*

RUSTY	How old are you?
MICHAEL	Sixteen. Why?
RUSTY	You sure don't act or talk like you're 16.
MICHAEL	Oh trust me, I am 16, but I study history. You know what they say, 'Those who don't remember the past are condemned to relive it.'
KEESIC	But what if it is a good past?
MICHAEL	What?
KEESIC	What if the past you are remembering is a good one? Shouldn't you relive it?

> MICHAEL *is stumped.*

MICHAEL	Um...
RUSTY	Ah, this is crazy. *(to* KEESIC*)* I thought you were bad, he's worse.
KEESIC	Rusty, why is this smelly water you drink so important to you?
RUSTY	*(really losing his temper)* It's a beer, not some stupid philosophy, there's nothing to understand. Why is it so hard for you to believe that?
KEESIC	Rusty, why are you so angry all the time?
MICHAEL	All this frustration and aggression. Why?

> RUSTY *almost explodes with frustration.*

RUSTY	Ah, damn, damn, damn, damn, damn.
KEESIC	Nice. Could almost be a chant.

MICHAEL	To some people I think it is.

KEESIC *kneels down beside* RUSTY.

KEESIC   One time when I was young, I don't think I'd seen a dozen winters yet...

MICHAEL   Traditional Native Storytelling! *(sitting crosslegged, in happy anticipation)* Please, proceed.

KEESIC *eyes him narrowly before continuing.*

KEESIC   I was gathering bird eggs for my mother. I came across this duck that was splashing around in the water like it had a broken wing. I love duck, so I went after it, but every time I got close it would splash farther away. I followed that duck halfway across the lake before it miraculously healed and flew away. I told my father about this, and he laughed.

RUSTY   And the point is?

MICHAEL *has his arm up, begging to answer the question. He can't restrain himself.*

MICHAEL   Don't you see?! The duck was protecting its eggs, something very delicate and precious to it. It lured Keesic away, a long futile chase to divert his attention. People do the same thing sometimes without knowing it.

RUSTY   I'm trying to save my eggs?

MICHAEL   There is something in you that you are protecting with this anger. You are just using it to divert people's attention.

RUSTY   Quack quack.

MICHAEL   What are you afraid of ?

RUSTY   I'm not afraid of anything, you idiot.

MICHAEL   *(confused and disappointed)* Touchy. I always read that adolescence in this time was supposed to be a time of fun. Drive-in movies, hula hoop, Bay City Rollers. *(singing)* S-A-T-U-R-D-A-Y NIGHT!

RUSTY	Bay City Rollers!? Give me a break. You don't know my life, so don't start giving me suggestions on how to run it. Until you've lived my life and felt what I feel stay off my back.
KEESIC	I don't think you like your life.
RUSTY	Hey, it's the only one I got.
MICHAEL	But is it the one you want?
RUSTY	Do I got a choice? Does it really matter? Okay, I can't go to Hawaii. I'll never own a Porsche, I'll never have all those things I see on television. I'm lucky if I get a new pair of jeans for the first day of school. What's there to be happy for? I'm terrible in school, so I can't walk that side of the tracks, and as for going the traditional Indian route, that's even worse. I hate cleaning fish and I'm a terrible hunter. I don't fit in here. Last year my father took me hunting, I shot my own dog. I can't do anything right except drink. You wanted to know my problems, there they are. I hope you enjoy them.

> *Everybody is silent for a moment, letting the emotion sink in.*

MICHAEL	So that's how you deal with your problems. I must say that I'm not particularly impressed. But here. Have another beer! Everybody has problems, but they cope with them.
RUSTY	Oh yeah? Look at you. I have no idea what kind of outfit that is but it don't look like you're too bad off. And judging by the way you talk and the things you've said you're doing great in school and you know a lot of things. Keesic here only has to worry about hunting enough to eat. They didn't have complicated problems back then. At least you both have your own worlds to fit in and return to. I'm stuck smack-dab in the middle of a family war, between one uncle that's called 'Closer' because they say he's closed every bar in Ontario, and my other Uncle Stan, who is basically a powwow Indian, I never know what's going on. Sometimes I don't know if I should go into a sweatlodge or a liquor store. Sometimes they tear me apart. I don't fit in. Like tonight. It's Saturday and what am I doing? Standing on a rock, out in the middle of the woods, talking to two people who probably don't exist. How's that for a social life? Instead of looking at the two of you, I should be out with some hot babe. *(to himself)* I should have asked her out. I should have.

MICHAEL	Asked who out?
RUSTY	There's a girl I kinda like in town. For all the good it does me.
MICHAEL	What do you mean?
RUSTY	The girl doesn't know I exist. I don't know if it's because I'm Indian or because she thinks I'm a flake. I'm not sure which is worse.
KEESIC	*(puzzled)* What's an Indian?

> Both RUSTY *and* MICHAEL *look at* KEESIC.

RUSTY	Oh, that's right, you've never heard the word.
MICHAEL	It's a generic term used to describe all original inhabitants of this land. It was popular up until approximately 100 years ago, my time. In fact, right around your time. *(pointing to* RUSTY*)* The more politically correct terms in this day and age are 'Native' or 'Aboriginal'.
KEESIC	So we are all...Indian?
RUSTY	Yup.
KEESIC	Why would an Indian girl not like you for being Indian?
RUSTY	She's not.
KEESIC	She's one of these white people?
RUSTY	Uh huh.
KEESIC	Interesting. What does she look like?
RUSTY	Her name is Sherry. Doesn't that sound great? Oh, she's real pretty. She's got long blonde hair...
KEESIC	Blonde?
RUSTY	Yellow.

> RUSTY, *feeling more at ease, is exploding with energy. He does a hand spring to shake himself out of it.*

KEESIC   White people got yellow hair? Just like the sun?

RUSTY   *(smiling)* And twice as hot.

* * *

Published with "Education is Our Right"
by Fifth House Publishers - trade paperback

fourth-wall exercises

The Fourth Wall

An actor on the stage is surrounded by three physically tangible walls, or sides, to his reality, as well the imaginary wall, or side, between the actor and the audience. These few exercises are intended to help the actor create that imaginary wall, if he is inside a room, or imaginary fourth side to his reality, if he is outdoors. People constantly look at the world around them — especially when they are on the phone or writing a letter.

Before starting the exercise, the actor will spend considerable time actually placing imaginary objects on the wall and infusing them with their own history and meaning to him, determining where windows and doors are, or placing those trees and buildings so that every time he looks up they are exactly where they should be and have become second nature. These objects should be anchored to something that actually exists in the theatre and seen by the actor when he looks out. This pertains to both primary objects such as a window one has to look out of, or a clock to specifically look at, or to secondary objects that have no actual role in the play other than to make the actor feel comfortable in the scene and overcome the unease of looking into that black, gaping space. Your belief in the fourth wall is crucial to the success of the scene for you and for the audience. If you don't believe it's there, the audience won't either.

For a thorough understanding of these exercises we recommend the book, *A Challenge for the Actor*, by Uta Hagen.

Day Shift

Meredith Bain Woodward

Setting: The kitchen of a trailer on a rural backroad. There's a chair, a lamp, a kitchen counter, and an old shoe box with papers in and around it. It's dusk.

Louise, in her thirties, has been looking through the box. She wears no-one-will-see-me-so-what-does-it-matter clothes: a housecoat, long underwear, a baggy T-shirt. She stares out the window. After a few moments she turns on the light, moves to the kitchen counter, and, picking up a box of macaroni and cheese dinner, tries to read the directions. She gives up, throwing the box on the counter. She stands for a moment, staring out the window again. Finally, she picks up the phone and dials a number.

LOUISE

Shirley? Yeah, it's me. Louise. Listen, uh...Yeah....listen, I'm quittin' at the cafe...Hold on! I'm givin' ya a month's notice, eh?...I'm not just walkin' out, I'm givin' ya notice...Well that's what I'm tellin' ya. Four weeks. Okay?

You can so get along. You can hire someone else...There's Linda. What about Bonnie? There's lots of them that'll — Sure it's tourist season coming up, but there's always something, eh? Thanksgiving, Christmas — and I gotta get outta here, Shirley. I just gotta leave.

No, I'm not upset about anything. Really....It's okay. Walter explained. Said he was sorry...No, I'm not mad, I've just...I dunno, Shirley, I'm just goin' that's all...Maybe Kelowna. I hear they got some good programs at the college there. Nicky's doin' that florist thing, eh? Maybe I'll do that, or I got a cousin working in Cranbrook. Maybe I'll — No, no! I like workin' for ya, I really do...Well, I'm not so crazy about the day shift, but I told you that Shirley! I told you when you switched me. I like workin' night shift much better...There's nothin' wrong with days I just like night shift much better. What?...Oh, now you're gonna give me night shift back...Yeah...

Yeah?...Oh boy. I just can't Shirl...I've made up my mind. I mean I appreciate the offer and that, but I just can't stay here for ever.

I dunno what brought it on....It's just...*(laughing)* You wanna know what brought it on? What really brought it on? *(laughing, looking out the window)* I put seed in the bird feeder this morning. *(laughing)* Yeah. *(laughing)* No, I just got lookin' at stuff...Those dead apple trees. The empty chicken house.

Cripers!...Yeah, exactly. And then that road outta my place...I dunno, Shirl, I've been starin' at that road for what, thirteen years?

It's all I see from the kitchen window. Makes me crazy. I don't even have to look anymore. I know it off by heart. All its twists and turns. Every pot hole. Every tree. Every goddam stone.

Yeah, well, you wanna know something? Before I started workin' day shift? I'd walk out to the end of that road every morning and just wait for someone to drive by — anybody— so I could wave...Yeah. Every day...No, finally, the French couple started building their place and I figured, great! I'll practise my French. 'Bon jour!' 'Bon jour!' *(laughing)*...It was fine till they answered back...Me? No. In high school and that I was lousy in French, but I always wanted to get good at it. It's on my list, eh?...You know, the list that you have of things that you'll do someday when you get time or money or — Everybody's got one...Well I do. And speakin' French is on there. I just never got around to it...So then these people move in, and their darn dog speaks better French than I do. No kidding, they talk to the dog in French and English and it understands. They've got a goddam bilingual dog! It makes you think...Well, you make promises to yourself, you know? And then one day all they are is disappointments. Things you never did.

✳ ✳ ✳

Published in "Escape Acts"   by NuAge Editions: Montreal

Babylon and Back

M. J. Turner

Fischer, a German writer now living in Toronto, was separated from his sister Myra at the end of WWII. Until he unexpectedly meets her again, 25 years later, he has written letters to her but never sent them, creating a sister he didn't know. It is now 13 years later and he is trying to re-establish contact and determine which sister he will accept — his creation or the real Myra.

> *N.B. The actor should decide how much of the letter is already written and if he is re-reading or how much is actually written down after it is said aloud.*

FISCHER

Dear Myra: this letter comes out of the blue, I know; was your first reaction to put it aside? Did you put it on the piano with all your other junk? Did you tuck it away somewhere with the phone bill and the gas bill and the coupons? Has it sat awhile and become a little dusty, become part of the house, been accepted by the other dumb objects on the shelves and the window sills?

No harm done: it's the kind of letter you can read when you want to. Or not, as you wish. I thought of disguising my handwriting on the envelope and mailing it from another city so that nothing would give me away; so that at least you would open the envelope and begin: have you read this far, I wonder? Can you hear my voice again? Will you play the piano to drown me out for a while? After you have played, the air will swirl about the house, billowing up against the window panes and pressing the doors a little tighter into their frames. Music. How many people, Myra, use music to keep others away instead of drawing them closer?

I decided not to try the deception: let the letter lie as long as you like. Besides, I don't get out of the city much now: I'm content to go down to the market once in a while, usually very early in the morning.

Perhaps you'll read this letter very early one morning: in bed at dawn, before you are really awake, before you turn over and go back to sleep for a while. While you're reading, I'll be going down the stairs quietly, I don't use the elevator. You never know with the elevator these days. I prefer the stairs. No-one else ever seems to use the stairs. I like the light in the stairwell, the way it filters in through the dirty windows and turns into a fine white powder. It covers everything and I can always tell if another has come up or down that way. For a long time now, no-one has...Some sad news: Betty has died. She just didn't get out of her box one morning. She just waited until I got up to make some tea and then just looked up at me for a moment, just raised her head once and that was that. I buried her near the railroad tracks, where they cross the avenue. You know where I mean. Do you remember how she used to sit and watch the trains? I put her there at three o'clock in the morning and waited for the sun to come up. *(lighting a cigarette)*

I don't think she'll be dug up for a long time; I hope not. Sitting there, watching the dawn break, it reminded me of the house near Tunis. The strangest thing. The unseasonable warmth perhaps, the quality of the light...Just for a moment I was back there. The light turns into sound: the sound of a single bird, out of the dark. It happens in the coppery dark disc of that bird's eye: a dancing, flickering fringe of light on the edge of that immense, staring curve...A house bleached white like bone. Myra, I don't even know if you are still alive.

* * *

Available from Playwright Union of Canada - copyscript

I Beg Your Pardon

by Alex O'Byrne

Pierre is a young actor recently returned to Toronto from New York where he was studying. A number of serious personal and family factors forced his return and he is putting the best face forward as he generally does in all matters — he survives. Here he is talking on the telephone to an old friend.

PIERRE

No, I'd rather not...Because I don't want to...No, it's really not important...Oh, alright, alright! I'll tell you, sheesh!...I feel really stupid...No, no I'll tell you, you got me startd now...I really should call this the great Canadian mugging story. I tell it so often.

Okay, it was a coupla days after Christmas. I just got back to New York...No, it was my first year there...No, indeed, not a good way to start. Look, do you want to hear this story, or what? Alright. It was about 4:30 in the morning and I had just said goodbye to friends from Brooklyn, and I was going to the subway when I heard this voice.

'Yo! Yo!, Pierre.'

So, of course, I stopped...Well, the guy knew my name.

'It's Pierre right?'

'Uhuh,' I said. How does this guy know my name? Do I look French? Anyway, being the quintessential Canadian I said,'Can I help you?'...*(sheepishly)* Yes, I did.

Well this gave him and his friends time to cross the street and then 'click, click, click' — I've got a switch blade at my neck, one at my gut, and the third guy is dancing around waving another one in my face. Lots of drugs going on here.

'Great, just great,' I say to myself...No, no — to myself. Anyway, I always have these wonderful internal dialogues in times of stress and this was definitely a time of stress. But, but this time it was really different. My brain, uhm, bifurcated...Bifurcated...Yes it is so a word...it means, uhm, split in two, no it was more like dichotomized — two mutually exclusive parts because part of me started to freak out but the other part, somehow, was sooooo cool.

Right away the first part said, 'You can have my wallet, you can have anything you want.' and when he went to take it, the other part said, 'Oh, but don't take the credit cards: I'll just cancel them in the morning.'

...Yes I did....and he said 'Whatchew say man?'

And inside I'm saying to myself 'Yeah, what <u>did</u> you say? You may not be alive in the morning!'

Then the leader of the pack saw my school ring and said, 'Gimme that.' and I said, 'Why? You didn't go to university obviously.'...Really, I said that, then he's saying, 'You better shut up man.' Good idea.

Then while they're breaking a gold chain to get it off my wrist, I realized that these guys are only 16 or 17 but <u>really</u> stoned and those knives are pressing really hard so I'm not going to do anything even though the cool part of me wants to bang their heads together.

Then the guy says, 'Gimme your coat.'

Now, this was a beautiful, brand-new coat I just got for Christmas, you know...yeah, the blue one. So, before I had a chance to say 'Yeah, sure, take it,' — I said, 'No.'

'Whatchew say? You crazy? Gimme that coat!'

'You can't have it. It's a Christmas present'...Uhuh.

Well, by this time the scared part of me has caved in but I also realized they'd have to move the knives to get the coat, and I think the guy doing all the talking realized it too — this thing was going on a long time and a car was bound to come along soon. So, he threw my wallet in the air, scattered everything, and then punched me in the eye. When I looked around they were gone. The only thing they really hurt was my pride but, you know, I just might have talked my self out of it. Maybe I am a good actor after all. Who knows? *(taking a deep breath)*

Actually, that's just Part One of my mugging story...I got mugged again...In Toronto, yeah. I must have MUG ME on my forehead. This time I was so pissed off it happened again, I followed them for blocks, flagged a cop down and two of them actually went back to prison...No...some other time...No, I don't want to talk about it...Oh alright...

* * *

Second Thoughts

Marilyn Boyle

Helen Grant is a widow in her 60s. Her niece, Marion is offstage. HELEN enters, carrying the morning paper. She pauses and calls offstage.

HELEN

I could do those dishes myself, Marion. Oh, very well. I'll stay out of your way. I'll entertain myself with the obituaries. *(continuing to her chair, sitting, opening the paper and scanning the obituaries)* Dear Lord! How old? She was the right age. It must be she. Joanna's dead! My sister-in-law, Ken's sister. Estranged for...goodness! Forty years! Died in Vancouver.

Joanna...We were inseparable, as children. And yet, it turned out we didn't know each other at all. The family schism was a terrible shock, but I suppose it was inevitable. I was a tractable child, but the older Joanna grew, the more rebellious she became. She was expelled from more than one school. Took up with unsuitable friends. Even Ken lost patience with her, and he adored her. Oh, those episodes were minor.

She did what was, then, unforgivable. She got pregnant. In those days, people tried to pretend things like that didn't happen to 'nice girls'. I still feel guilty about the way I reacted. She refused to tell who the father was, let alone marry him. She wouldn't have an abortion, or have the baby secretly. The atmosphere in that home would have frozen fish.

By then, Ken and I were engaged to be married, so the Grants called me over, hoping I, supposedly her best and oldest friend, could talk some sense into her. But I was as hide-bound as Ken's mother. I was so shocked by her 'transgression' that I froze her as solidly as everyone else. The Grants foolishly issued the traditional ultimatum. I think they actually said, 'Never darken our door again.' She, in turn, told us all what she thought of us and left. Looking back, now, I can't say I blame her.

Yes, that's the last time we saw her. A fine friend I was! I've often wondered what Joanna would have done, if I'd given her even a little sympathy. She certainly deserved more from me than she got. Later, Ken and I tried to find her, but she'd vanished. And now, it's too late. I don't know what I could have done, but I should have done something.

* * *

Available from Playwrights Union of Canada - copyscript

Going Down for the Count

Peter Eliot Weiss

This is a fantasy based on the original vampire story, "Dracula" by Bram Stoker, that explores the hypocrisy of the post-Victorian family ideal. In this scene, Jonathan Harker, a proper Englishman, and betrothed of the lovely Mina, is approaching the castle of the mysterious Count Dracula who has hired the young man to arrange the count's voyage to England. Jonathan writes to Mina.

JONATHAN

To my dearest Mina. *(looking around)* Odd how that echoes here. Downright eerie. *(writing again)* I miss you Mina. I spend long nights in this alien land and my only comforts are thoughts of you. Last night, a dog was barking under my window, my throat was burning from the unaccustomed spices used in the preparation of my dinner. Note, must get you the recipe. Very tasty. But in bed, the only way I could calm myself as I thrashed away the hours was to picture how beautiful you will look at our wedding, dressed in the purest of white lace, a huge bouquet of wild roses pressed to your heaving bosom. *(suddenly laughing)* Odd, how stray memories pop up at the most unlikely times. I just remembered something that happened when I was a very small child. I asked my father one day whether it could be possible for little boys to grow into women and little girls into men. He laughed. So I asked him again, 'Do you think it could ever happen, Daddy, that little boys grow into women and little girls into men?' He told me to be quiet. Frustrated and enraged, I thought he was keeping some great secret from me, an ideal conception of men and women. I shouted, 'Could little boys turn into women and little girls into men?' He hit me. *(pause)*

I don't like being away from England, where life rolls along as it should, as it always has. I don't like being away at all.

* * *

Available from Playwrights Union of Canada - copyscript

Poetic Justice

Mark Leiren-Young

In this black comedy thriller, Jay struggles with writer's block until he gets a visit from his muse — the ghost of the wife he had murdered. In this scene, Jay can't start writing because he knows that another character, Alison, is watching him from another room - offstage.

JAY

I know you're there. I know you're watching. How do you expect me to get anything done if I can feel you lurking out there, staring at me, breathing down my neck. How am I supposed to concentrate? It's bad enough that I have to worry about the reviewers. I can ignore them. I can almost ignore them. Hell, I can at least pretend to ignore them. But to have you there watching every move I make. Listening to every word I say. I tell you it's bloody hard not to be self conscious — and damn near impossible to do my best work. I'll tell you what — just stop watching me for a minute, alright. Just give me one minute to get my concentration back and then, just maybe, I'll be able to ignore you and get on with it. *(pause)* Thank you. *(walking around the room, trying to loosen up, stretching, pouring a drink, massaging his temples)*

There, that's better. Now if you still want to lurk there, you can lurk there. I'm relaxed. I'm fine. I'm calm. I'm serene. I'm ready to work.

***

Available from Playwrights Union of Canada - copyscript

Index of Plays

Index of Playwrights

Publisher Information

Playwrights Canada Press would like to thank the following publishers for their kind permission to include scenes from plays published by them.

Blizzard Publishing
301-89 Princess Street
Winnipeg, Manitoba
R3B 1K6
tel: (204) 949-0511
fax: (204) 943-4129
Order from General Publishing
30 Lesmill Rd., Don Mills Ont.,
M3B 2T6 tel: (416) 445-3333
fax: (416) 445-5967

Coach House Press
401 (rear) Huron Street
Toronto, Ontario
M5S 2G5
tel: (416) 979-7374
fax: (416) 979-7006
Order from McClelland & Stewart
481 University Avenue, Ste 900
Toronto, Ontario M5G 2E9
tel: (416) 940-8855
fax: (416) 598-8864

Fifth House Publishers
620 Duchess Street
Saskatoon, Saskatchewan
S7K 0R1
tel: (306) 242-4936
fax: (306) 242-7667
Order from University of Toronto Press
5201 Dufferin Street
Downsview, Ontario M3H 5T8
tel: (416) 667-7791/2/2/4
fax: (416) 667-7832
(800) 565-9523

NuAge Editions
P.O. Box 8, Station E
Montreal, Quebec
H2T 3A5
tel: (514) 272-5226
fax: (514) 271-1218
Order from General Publishing

Williams Wallace Publishers
P.O. Box 756
Stratford, Ontario
N5A 3E8
Order from (416) 966-9646

Women's Press
233-517 College Street
Toronto, Ontario
M6G 4A2
tel: (416) 921-2425
fax: (416) 921-4428
Order from U of T Press

Samuel French, Inc.
(see page 72)

Literary Press Group
260 King Street East
Toronto, Ontario
M5A 1K3
tel: (416) 361-1408
fax: (416) 361-0643

Stop right there!

**Are you looking for the perfect
audition piece?**

**Well look no further. In this book you will
find more than 130 monologues from
Canadian plays, some reaching back 20
years, but most from recently established
masters and rising stars of the theatre.
Within these pages could be the
monologue you've been searching for, the
piece that will work for you. Break a leg!**

ISBN 0-88754-498-3
278 pp / $14.95

The Perfect Piece
Monologues from Canadian Plays

Printed in Canada